The Fundraising Series

Corporate Fundraising

Editor: Valerie Morton

FOURTH EDITION

dsc
directory of social change

The fundraising series
For all titles available in this series see:
www.dsc.org.uk/fundraisingseries

Published by the Directory of Social Change (Registered Charity no. 800517 in England and Wales)

Head office: Resource for London, 352 Holloway Rd, London N7 6PA

Northern office: Suite 103, 1 Old Hall Street, Liverpool L3 9HG

Tel: 08450 77 77 07

Visit www.dsc.org.uk to find out more about our books, subscription funding websites and training events. You can also sign up for e-newsletters so that you're always the first to hear about what's new.

The publisher welcomes suggestions and comments that will help to inform and improve future versions of this and all of our titles. Please give us your feedback by emailing publications@dsc.org.uk.

It should be understood that this publication is intended for guidance only and is not a substitute for professional or legal advice. No responsibility for loss occasioned as a result of any person acting or refraining from acting can be accepted by the authors or publisher.

First published 1999 by the Charities Aid Foundation
Second edition published 2002 by the Directory of Social Change
Reprinted 2006, 2007
Third edition 2007
Reprinted 2010
Fourth edition 2012
Reprinted 2015

ISBN 978 1 906294 58 8

British Library Cataloguing in Publication Data
A catalogue record for this book is available from the British Library

Cover design by Kate Bass
Original text design Eugenie Dodd Typographics
Typeset by Keystroke, Wolverhampton
Printed and bound by Page Bros, Norwich

Contents

The Fundraising Series

The trouble with change is that it never stands still! And that is no less true for fundraising than any other professional discipline. The economy, political landscape and the ways people exchange information and communicate with each other all impact on the way in which charities ask for and raise money. That is what makes fundraising such a challenging and dynamic profession. I am not sure I will be popular for comparing fundraising to dabbling in stock market futures, but successful fundraisers are often those who can predict and be responsive to social change and be able to adapt their fundraising strategies accordingly – to be effective it is vital to stay ahead of the game.

The Directory of Social Change's Fundraising Series seeks to address the full range of fundraising activity and techniques in one series. Each successive volume aims to address one key element in the spectrum of fundraising techniques. As fundraising techniques evolve and develop, new titles in the series are added to and old ones revised.

The titles are intended as texts that encourage and debate fundraising within a professional framework: written and used by academics and practitioners alike. Each title seeks to explore a fundraising activity within its historical, ethical and theoretical context, relate it to current fundraising practice as well as guide future strategy.

We thank all those who have contributed and continue to contribute to the most comprehensive fundraising series available today.

Debra Allcock Tyler, Chief Executive
Directory of Social Change

About the authors

Chris Ashworth

Chris Ashworth is the Head of Corporate Partnerships at Oxfam. Chris joined Oxfam in 2006, leading on donor acquisition and advertising. Having previously held a career in marketing management in retail, a period of volunteering for HIV and AIDS programmes in southern Africa precipitated a switch to the charity sector. Whilst managing Oxfam's relationships with the private sector Chris also mentors and supports social enterprise start-ups and is a Director and co-founder of Be More – a charity which runs short-term volunteering placements across Africa.

Alison Braybrooks

Alison Braybrooks is Managing Director of Impact abc, a consultancy that helps companies to manage their social impact. She has worked in sustainability for over 20 years, with 10 years in the voluntary sector, followed by heading up EDF Energy's community programme, then as Director of LBG (London Benchmarking Group), where she led the group to focus on impact measurement.

Rachel Billsberry-Grass

Rachel Billsberry-Grass works as a fundraising and management consultant. Her consultancy, Causeworks, offers strategic and practical advice and training to a wide range of voluntary organisations as well as corporate responsibility advice for companies.

Rachel began her charity sector career in 1991 and quickly pursued her interest in marketing by specialising in corporate fundraising, managing award-winning partnerships with companies such as Tesco and Transco. She has held senior management roles with Muscular Dystrophy Campaign, the Royal Opera House, Mencap and Age Concern England.

Rachel is also a trustee of the children's cancer charity, CLIC Sargent.

Beth Courtier

Beth Courtier has worked at BT for some 20 years, undertaking a variety of work including HR, training, work with the further education and higher education sectors and sponsorship. For the last 15 years Beth has managed different Community Investment programmes, including, most recently, BT's charity and employee engagement activities.

Beth is committed to embedding BT's charity activities across the business. She is committed to delivering business benefits and developing innovative, replicable and sustainable initiatives for charities. She leverages in-kind support in addition to the company's financial investment; she has also leveraged additional funds working with suppliers, other partners and through lobbying government.

Beth has contributed to numerous publications and spoken at events across the world. She has won corporate responsibility, cause-related marketing, marketing, public relations, brand and reputation and innovation awards as well as charity sector awards. Beth is a Clarion Awards industry champion, has received a ChildLine Patron Award and is an Honorary Member of Council for the NSPCC.

Martin Croft

Martin Croft is Head of Communications for the Institute of Promotional Marketing and also writes for various publications on marketing and branding. He spent 20 years associated with *Marketing Week* magazine, and has written for a range of business titles and national newspapers, including *The Times, The Telegraph, The Guardian, The Scotsman* and *The Observer*. He has also worked for the Institute of Chartered Accountancy and the Institute of Direct Marketing.

Michael Fairclough

Michael Fairclough took up the post of Head of Community and Co-operative Investment at The Co-operative in October 2007, following an amalgamation with United Co-operatives where he previously worked. The newly combined business has a turnover of over £14 billion and employs 110,000 staff. His responsibilities include developing and maintaining a community investment framework, overseeing the strategic development and delivery of the Group's community programmes and co-ordinating support for the co-operative sector.

Prior to this, Michael worked for the international development agency, Christian Aid, in a campaigning and adult education role. Most of his early career was spent working in and with communities across North West England.

Amy Franklin

Amy Franklin developed a keen interest in fundraising whilst studying at the University of Warwick. Graduating with an honours degree in law, Amy began her career at Tommy's, the baby charity. At this small but ambitious charity she worked on a diverse range of accounts and special events. Amy has managed the corporate accounts team at Alzheimer's Society since 2008. Leading on high-profile Charity of the Year accounts with companies such as KPMG, Credit Suisse and Tesco, Amy has successfully steered her team through a time of intense change and growth.

After university Amy worked in an orphanage in Ghana, which she has continued to support and visit every year since.

Ruth Freeman

Ruth Freeman started her fundraising career in 1984 as a House to House Coordinator for Barnardo's and has remained in the charity sector ever since. Ruth developed experience across a wide range of fundraising disciplines, including workplace giving, which is where her interest in payroll giving began.

After four years and with over 200 successful payroll campaigns under her belt, Ruth was promoted to National Marketing Manager for Workplace Giving where her work on payroll giving resulted in a new workplace payroll giving strategy for the charity. In 2005 in a combined role as Head of Partnerships at Barnardo's, Ruth shared her passion for creativity in payroll giving by jointly presenting Creative Campaigns at the Institute of Fundraising conference.

From 2006 Ruth has been Director of Income Generation and Marketing for the Myton Hospices working across Coventry and Warwickshire . . . needless to say, they now do payroll giving.

Rebecca Fry

Rebecca is a solicitor in the Charities Group at the law firm Farrer & Co. She advises a broad range of charities and not-for-profit organisations on governance and other operational and regulatory issues, including grant making, fundraising and the establishment and use of trading subsidiaries. Educated at Oxford University, Rebecca trained at Farrer & Co and qualified in 2011.

Richard Gillis

Richard Gillis is an award-winning journalist, working for *The Wall Street Journal*, *The Irish Times* and *The Independent*. He was founding editor of *Platform* magazine and created Unofficial Partner (www.unofficialpartner. co.uk), which reports on the role of the brand in the sport, arts, music, charity and public sectors. Richard serves on the advisory board for the Future Sponsorship conference and is a judge of the prestigious Sport Industry Awards. Previously, his series, 21st Century Sport in *The Observer*, was nominated for the Foreign Press Association Award and was highly commended by the Sports Journalist Association Awards.

Mathew Iredale

Mathew Iredale is a freelance prospect researcher and founder of The Prospect Research Toolkit, the first website specifically designed to provide in-depth information and support to prospect researchers in the UK. For six years he was Fundraising Research Manager at the Stroke Association and prior to this he was Prospect Research Manager at Great Ormond Street Hospital Children's Charity and a high value donor fundraiser at Imperial Cancer Research Fund. He has been on the committee of Researchers in Fundraising since 2006 and was chairman from December 2007 to December 2009. He has twice spoken at the Institute of Fundraising's National Convention and co-presented the CASE Prospect Research Seminar in 2008.

Alice Jackson

Alice Jackson started her career in the private sector and spent five years working for a young consultancy. She progressed through the sales team and worked with a number of blue chip organisations, selling in and managing large-scale learning solutions. Alice joined the Alzheimer's Society in 2009 as head of their new business corporate fundraising team. She successfully created winning pitches and negotiated major corporate partners, helping to double corporate income in one year. Currently, Alice is Head of Corporate Fundraising at Sue Ryder.

Ian MacQuillin

Ian MacQuillin is head of communications at the Public Fundraising Regulatory Association (PFRA). Prior to joining the PFRA in June 2009, he had been an account director at fundraising public relations specialist TurnerPR, working with leading fundraising suppliers and charities. A journalist for most of his career, Ian was editor of *Professional Fundraising* (PF) between 2001 and 2005.

Ian blogs on UK Fundraising and has presented regularly at fundraising conferences on subjects including charity/media relations, fundraising ethics and F2F fundraising. He is a guest lecturer for the on MSc in Management in Civil Society (Marketing and Fundraising) at London South Bank University.

Valerie Morton

Valerie Morton is a lifelong fundraiser, in both her professional life and her personal life. She has held senior management roles in charities including Help the Aged, NSPCC and RNIB and is also a trustee of Central YMCA and her local almshouse charity. Her charity sector involvement is complemented by her role as a Non-Executive Director in the NHS. Valerie's passion for corporate fundraising was ignited at the NSPCC in the days when the Charity of the Year concept was in its infancy and the payroll giving scheme was about to be launched. Now a fundraising and management consultant, Valerie's work includes advising and supporting charities and companies on how to maximise the benefits of partnerships and on developing and running training courses to fulfil her commitment to best practice in the sector.

Edwin Mutton

From 1965 until 1980, Edwin Mutton ran his own wholesale distribution business. In 1980, he joined Kimberly Clark Ltd, the manufacturers of Andrex and Kleenex products, and was Trade Promotions Manager, Sales Promotions Manager and finally Sponsorship Manager.

In 2000, he joined the Institute of Sales Promotion (now the Institute of Promotional Marketing) and from 2001 to 2007 was its Director General. Now semi-retired, he heads the IPM's compliance function and runs its Awards programme. He is a member of the Committee of Advertising Practice (CAP), which draws up the CAP Code, the rules which UK advertising and marketing must follow.

Andrew Peel

Andrew Peel is a freelance fundraiser and consultant with 19 years' experience in the charity sector. He has led corporate fundraising teams at Sightsavers, the British Red Cross and Help the Aged and as a consultant has worked with a wide range of organisations including Guide Dogs for the Blind, Diabetes UK, the RNLI, the British Heart Foundation and Maggie's Cancer Caring Centres.

He specialises in interim management, strategic planning, mentoring and in delivering impactful corporate fundraising proposals, pitches, campaigns and strategies for clients.

A member of the Institute of Fundraising, Andrew won its Professional Fundraiser of the Year Award in 1997.

Anne-Marie Piper

Anne-Marie is a partner at the law firm Farrer & Co, where she heads the Charities Group. Her job involves acting for sponsors of new charities, directors, trustees and officers of existing charities and other not-for-profit bodies, as well as individuals and companies wishing to make charitable gifts or do business with charities. She is also well known for her expertise in charity fundraising law and also for her handling of Charity Commission investigations and complex mergers and reorganisations of charities and their subsidiary and related entities. Founder, former secretary and chairman of the Charity Law Association, Anne-Marie also lectures and writes regularly on charity law subjects.

Simon Sheehan

Simon Sheehan joined as Director of the Hilton in the Community Foundation in 2004. Since then the Foundation has almost tripled its grant-giving, quadrupled its fundraising and expanded its work from two to 26 countries across Europe.

Prior to joining, Simon was the Communications and Fundraising Manager for the Aga Khan Foundation (UK). His work included community fundraising, inter-government and government communications, and filming in Afghanistan, Tajikistan and Pakistan. Simon's previous roles included working for the International Crisis Group, an independent research and advocacy body working in Bosnia, Sierra Leone and the Great Lakes region of Africa. Simon has a BA in Zoology and Botany from Reading University.

Anne Shinkwin

Anne Shinkwin is a fundraising consultant with many years of experience working in fundraising and the private sector. Most recently Anne was Head of Corporate Partnerships at UNICEF UK for five years (2005–10) building the team and doubling income in four years. Prior to this, Anne worked at the British Red Cross for two and a half years managing key corporate partners such as Tesco, Barclays and GlaxoSmithKline and securing new business opportunities such as Blue Peter and Deutsche Bank Charity of the Year. Anne started her career working in the private sector for Kimberly-Clark as European Research & Development Project Manager.

Claire Wilson

Claire Wilson worked in the charity sector for 20 years, starting her career as Sponsorship Manager at the Prince's Trust.

As a Director of strategic fundraising consultancy Cooper Wilson, Claire worked with a broad range of clients from business and not-for-profit, advising on corporate cause partnerships and implementing fundraising strategies.

Claire was a strong advocate of sharing and driving forward best practice. Her vision was for charities to be able to take their rightful place on the world's stage and to achieve lasting social impact.

Alix Wooding

Alix Wooding has been working with corporate supporters and sponsors for the past decade. Since 2005 she has been growing the corporate fundraising team and income at Alzheimer's Society, where Alix has been involved in delivering new business and in overseeing the growth and development of the corporate partnerships strategy. During this time the team has won and delivered significant partnerships with KPMG, Bupa and Tesco.

Prior to this she worked at public relations agency Lexis PR, engaging companies in sponsorship of public sector projects, including international ministerial conferences. Before this she worked to engage companies in education initiatives on behalf of the Department for Education and Skills.

About the Directory of Social Change

The Directory of Social Change (DSC) has a vision of an independent voluntary sector at the heart of social change. The activities of independent charities, voluntary organisations and community groups are fundamental to achieve social change. We exist to help these organisations and the people who support them to achieve their goals.

We do this by:

• providing practical tools that organisations and activists need, including online and printed publications, training courses, and conferences on a huge range of topics;

• acting as a 'concerned citizen' in public policy debates, often on behalf of smaller charities, voluntary organisations and community groups;

• leading campaigns and stimulating debate on key policy issues that affect those groups;

• carrying out research and providing information to influence policymakers.

DSC is the leading provider of information and training for the voluntary sector and publishes an extensive range of guides and handbooks covering subjects such as fundraising, management, communication, finance and law. We have a range of subscription-based websites containing a wealth of information on funding from trusts, companies and government sources. We run more than 300 training courses each year, including bespoke in-house training provided at the client's location. DSC conferences, many of which run on an annual basis, include the Charity Management Conference, the Charity Accountants' Conference and the Charity Law Conference. DSC's major annual event is Charityfair, which provides low-cost training on a wide variety of subjects.

For details of all our activities, and to order publications and book courses, go to www.dsc.org.uk, call 08450 777707 or email publications@dsc.org.uk

Acknowledgements

We are grateful to the following people and organisations for their permission to use case studies featuring their organisation and/or for reproducing their material(s).

Chapter 2: The British Heart Foundation for the case study, and Sarah Hoare, Competence and Quality Analyst at Simplyhealth, for the use of her quote.

Sarah Arnold, Corporate Fundraising Manager at Chestnut Tree House Hospice, and Southern Water for the Chapter 3 case study.

Rachel Williams of CLIC Sargent, for the Chapter 4 case study.

Lorna Clarke of Above & Beyond, for the Chapter 5 case study.

Business in the Community for the reproduction of its Community Footprint image in Chapter 7.

Simplyhealth and Peter Newman, Chief Executive of Dreams Come True, for the Chapter 8 case study.

Heart UK and Kellogg's, for Chapter 9 case study.

Ben Treadaway of Sponsorium, for his help and the use of his quote in Chapter 11.

Belinda Briones, Corporate Fundraising Manager, The Place2Be and Joanna Keefe, Program Officer, EMEA Corporate Citizenship, Credit Suisse UK, for Chapter 13 case studies.

Marks and Spencer, for Chapter 15 case study.

Manny Amadi for reproduction of some findings from the *C&E Corporate–NGO Partnerships Barometer*.

Further, we are grateful to the following people for their various contributions to this title: Romana Abdin, Andrew Ball, Beth Breeze, Kate Duggan, Celine Gomez, Jamie Grier, Sarah Klueter, Mark Line, Linda Main, Paul Morrish, Ben Savage and Adrian Sargeant.

Foreword

Corporate fundraising has really come of age in the past ten years and now presents charities with fantastic opportunities to build and develop mutually beneficial long-term partnerships within the corporate sector.

Undoubtedly the most exciting relationships change in shape, style and structure throughout their term and, to support their development, it is vital to fully understand your partner's motivations and objectives, ensuring the best result is achieved through your partnership. When managed successfully, great partnerships should deliver huge benefits not only to both parties but also, and most importantly, to your beneficiaries.

Many charities are starting to focus more time and resources on building strong and ambitious teams within this area of fundraising, so it is very timely to launch the revised and updated edition of *Corporate Fundraising*. There have been some really innovative achievements and developments within corporate fundraising over the past few years and, by sharing experience and best practice across the sector, we can help each other to continue to grow this exciting area of fundraising.

Tanya Steele, Director of Fundraising
Save the Children (April 2012)

Introduction

Thirteen years have elapsed since the first edition of *Corporate Fundraising* was published in 1999, so now would seem to be a good time to look back over the previous editions, compare them with this latest fourth edition and see what has changed in the world of corporate fundraising.

Firstly, let's look at the statistics. In the year 1996/1997 Charities Aid Foundation stated the value of corporate donations from the top 500 companies at £305.6 million (Pharoah 1998). Similar research in 2009/10 shows the top 574 companies giving £512 million with a further £250 million of in-kind support (Lillya 2011, p. xvii). Taking the donations alone and without even allowing for the difference in company numbers the increase is only marginally above 3% a year compounded.

Instinctively this figure seems very odd. Whereas some years ago it would be difficult to find examples of product promotions, research at the time of writing came up with a range of examples including, interestingly, a building society canvassing views of customers about a potential savings account which would donate a percentage of the interest to charities. Charity of the Year partnerships, whilst admittedly common in 1997, are now considered the norm for well-known companies and regularly found in small and medium enterprises too. Local papers are full of companies – architects, solicitors, estate agents and the like – proudly showing off their latest golf day or charity ball for their adopted charity.

The *C&E Corporate–NGO Partnerships Barometer 2011* indicates that there is a growing trend towards strategic partnerships between companies and charities – a theme reflected in the case studies from the Co-operative in Chapter 17 – and also that businesses (88%) and NGOs (93%) expect the role of cross-sector partnerships to become much more important to their organisations over the next three years (C&E 2011, p. 5). It will be interesting to follow up on this prediction in future editions of this book.

A theme which I anticipate will be subject to much discussion during the life of this book is that of the pitching process which accompanies many charity–corporate partnerships. Although there have been moves to ensure such processes are open, transparent and equitable, there is still concern about whether companies appreciate the true impact their processes have on charities.

One thing that remains a constant is the need for corporate fundraisers to have a commitment to following best practice. At the time the third edition of this book was being published in 2007, the Fundraising Standards Board (FRSB) was being launched to the public. Not only has this reinforced amongst fundraisers the need to follow the Institute of Fundraising Codes of Practice but, as corporate fundraising so often has a very public face, the efforts of the FRSB to encourage public trust and confidence in charities will benefit this area of fundraising.

The structure of this edition has been refreshed. In addition to four case study chapters, most individual chapters include case studies to illustrate that chapter topic. I am delighted that some of the most respected and talented people involved in the world of corporate fundraisers have given freely of their time to contribute to this book and I also appreciate the contributions from authors who have provided examples from the corporate perspective and those whose professional experience offers valuable guidance to readers.

Valerie Morton

References

C&E (2011), *C&E Corporate–NGO Partnerships Barometer 2011*, London, C&E Advisory Services Limited

Lillya (2011), *The Guide to UK Company Giving*, London, Directory of Social Change

Pharoah (1998), 'CAF's top 500 corporate donors' in C. Pharoah and M. Smerdon (eds) *Dimensions of the Voluntary Sector*, West Malling, Charities Aid Foundation

Changes in the Institute of Fundraising's Codes

Please note that a new Code of Fundraising Practice will be launched during 2012, in which the standards and legal compliance aspects of the various codes are pulled into one document. The best practice elements of the codes will remain in separate guidance documents. The new Code will be in HTML format and easily accessible from the Institute's website. Current codes which are referred to in this book, such as *Charities Working with Business*, will be still identifiable within the new merged Code and also within the separate best practice guidance documents.

Dedication

This book is in memory of
Claire Wilson
1961–2012
A dedicated corporate fundraising professional
Inspiring and full of joy

CHAPTER ONE

Corporate community partnerships: history, evolution and future

Claire Wilson

Introduction

In 1887, Lever Brothers ran what is believed to be one of the earliest recorded cause-related marketing campaigns in the UK. Archives from the Royal National Lifeboat Institution show an engraving of Sunlight No. 1 lifeboat (featured in *The Illustrated London News*, 10 October 1889: see fig. 1.1), which was donated by Lever Brothers in 1887. Llandudno Lifeboat station reports that Lever Brothers 'ran a special competition to fund the new lifeboats' (Llandudno Lifeboat n.d.).

Fast forward to 2011, and the most admired corporate cause partnership as voted by companies and non-governmental organisations in the *C&E Corporate–NGO Partnerships Barometer 2011* report was for a cause-related marketing programme run by Oxfam and Marks and Spencer. This programme included the simple concept of revitalising Oxfam's falling shop donations by giving an M&S money-off voucher in exchange for donating second-hand M&S clothes.

This was a highly effective idea which was rewarding for all. It has empowered consumers, shop staff and management from both organisations and has been a success in terms of heightened reputation for the company and new income generation for the charity. The partnership involves both organisations 'sharing knowledge and working together to drive sustainable production and consumption', not forgetting the obvious bottom line of shared financial gain. Pampers' (Procter &Gamble) work with UNICEF to provide maternal and infant tetanus shots in less-developed countries was the second most admired partnership and Sainsbury's partnership with Comic Relief won third place. The report states:

> Partnership professionals rate these as the most admired partnerships because of their ambition, scale, ability to innovate, and to communicate. They are also highly rated because of their success in blending corporate, brand and commercial objectives with a clear focus on social impact.
>
> C&E 2011, p. 24

1

FIGURE 1.1 SUNLIGHT NO. 1 LIFEBOAT AS FEATURED IN *THE ILLUSTRATED LONDON NEWS*

All these factors could quite possibly have been applied to the Sunlight lifeboat campaign over 120 years ago.

Plus ça change? So what's changed for charities doing business with companies over those 120 years? How effective is the sector being in driving growth and innovation? Corporate partnerships are viewed as the linchpin in many fundraising strategies, but what is the reality behind the assumption?

The reality is simply that a lot in corporate–charity partnerships has changed and yet much has stayed the same. There has been a major evolution in the past ten years both in the way that companies have embraced the concept of working with charities and in the increased number of businesses that are proactively engaged in corporate responsibility. This has come about through the activation of business interest which has been driven by both businesses and charities. However, the beating corporate heart has clearly always been there. From Cadbury and the chocolate company's creation of cocoa as the healthy alternative to alcohol to the Joseph Rowntree Foundation and social housing, many businesses have established themselves with sound principles which aim to help the local people and their communities. The good old corporate fundraising maxim – people give to people – lies at the centre of all corporate cause partnerships.

Furthermore, personal engagement of the individual, whether the managing director of a small business or the personal assistant to the social committee, is the starting point to finding the people who will really influence and champion the development of mutually rewarding partnerships. And the good news is that, according to the C&E report, while there are some challenges (such as some large differences in how charities and companies view the benefits of non-financial support), the survey reports a buoyant market and the general opinion is very positive and looking towards growth on both sides (C&E 2011, p. 5). The question now, therefore, is how to maximise the opportunity?

What do businesses want from charities, and why do charities want to work with them?

For those new to the world of corporate–charity partnerships, understanding the basic concepts of why businesses want to partner with causes and, from a charity's point of view, understanding what is available from the business world, are essential to pursuing successful partnerships.

It is possible to track the change in corporate–charity partners decade by decade; each has had its own particular flavour and tone. Charities' relationships with companies have developed significantly from the 1980s when, to a large extent, the chair or chief executive sat on the board of trustees and dictated the company's charitable support: the great-and-the-good approach with often little involvement or feedback from the staff or connection to the business. In the 1980s it was common to give sponsorship in return for the company's logo on the charity's headed paper or in the pages of the high-profile event programme. During the 1990s the emphasis moved to corporate cause involvement, which reflected a significant shift from the previous decade towards a more considered, business-like approach and set a new corporate cause agenda. It was at this time that the corporate social entrepreneur emerged and companies looked more closely at what they were donating to and started to want greater involvement in the cause.

One of the first breakthroughs of this sort was the Prince's Trust's £1 million Mercury Communications sponsorship, which was an initiative led from the marketing departments of Mercury and the Trust's fundraising team (Drew 1993). Because of Mercury's major financial commitment, the partnership travelled throughout the company top-down. This was a multi-stranded, multi-functional relationship that involved national and regional events, senior management, employees, marketing, suppliers and customers and resulted in what is now the well-established Mercury Music Awards.

Moving to the new millennium, there has been an increase in focus on what the charity agenda could bring to business. Companies began creating what was called corporate social responsibility (increasingly called just 'corporate responsibility'): strategies with three- and five-year cause-led partnerships which, while great for the charities chosen, tie up the company and its giving. One of the first examples was the Vodafone Foundation and its three-year, three-tier corporate responsibility programme with Shelter, Youthnet and Samaritans, which reflected a major breakthrough in genuine social investment over donation (Vodafone 2007, p. 6).

In 2010, new driving factors for the corporate–charity partnership emerged and, crucially, companies and charities entered the corporate responsibility stakes from very different angles. The first edition of the C&E report, which came out in 2010, served to corroborate what was already accepted sector wisdom: businesses and charities want different things from the partnership. An overwhelming 94% of companies questioned said that it was corporate reputation first and an opportunity to find new ways of addressing challenges second that drove the corporate responsibility agenda. For charities, it was unreservedly financial support first: 95% put this as the primary driver, with the second being access to people and contacts (C&E 2010, p. 8). The second edition of the report reiterates these findings with 92% of companies stating that their main motivation for partnering was for reputation and credibility, while the same percentage of charities – 95% – cited access to funds (C&E 2011, p. 12).

The desire for corporate responsibility programmes to support companies' corporate reputations is not to be underestimated. The number of award schemes for businesses and their corporate responsibility programmes is increasing all the time. The Third Sector Business Charity Awards ran their inaugural event in 2010, with 60 companies entering. In 2011 the number had doubled to more than 130 and included household names like Virgin and Tesco, and smaller businesses such as Simplyhealth and Coventry Building Society all keen to make their mark (Cook 2011). Charities can be active in helping their company's corporate reputation by proactively demonstrating the strength of the partnership and its impact.

The fact that charities see financial support as their main priority in a partnership is unsurprising. However, the opportunities for charities to work with the business sector are wide and need to be viewed beyond just providing funding. For many companies this means that the relationship is increasingly a part of a growing collaborative approach which opens new doors for the charity partner. Most partnerships are the result of fundraising and a good fundraiser will look at what the partnership as a whole can offer.

One of the most striking aspects of corporate responsibility these days is that it is essential to demonstrate the impact that the partnership is having on specific issues. Another striking aspect, as noted, is the increasing levels of company involvement in causes. Companies are willing to put serious resources into the partnership; for example, by hosting events for the cause, using senior management, supporting the marketing and opening up the supplier network – areas that they can easily access which can be of major benefit to the charity. A second is the involvement of employees. This has developed a life of its own and witnesses a shift from painting the homeless shelter to a more strategic role. Businesses are using the skills and expertise of their people to maximise the effectiveness of the partnerships. Some of the current favourites are mentoring young people in schools and peer mentoring: chief executive to chief executive, for example. In doing this they are applying business techniques to charitable endeavours and creating new opportunities for charities to connect.

This difference in goals and vision creates an interesting dilemma for charities. In particular the company, with its financial muscle, can tend to take the dictating role when negotiating the partnership. Money is a major influencer and cash is king, but businesses cannot do it by themselves. The company's business within the partnership is neither delivering pro-grammes nor demonstrating the impact that the campaign or programme has had on the cause: it does not have the knowledge or expertise to do so. So what companies 'buy' from the charity sector is priceless. What charities have to be clear about are the cards they hold; the sector often fails to understand the power it wields and becomes the weaker partner because of this. Negotiation is peer to peer. It is then up to the charity to be vigilant in its focus and delivery.

Corporate responsibility innovation in business

There are many examples that could be chosen to demonstrate best prac-tice; the ones below each reflect new innovations which are driving forward the next stage of corporate responsibility.

GlaxoSmithKline IMPACT Awards

The GlaxoSmithKline (GSK) IMPACT Awards[1] have been running for the past 14 years in partnership with the King's Fund to recognise and promote excellence in community healthcare. Over 400 community healthcare charities have received grants totalling £3 million. The 2011 Awards were won by Step Forward: a lean, grass-roots charity based in Tower Hamlets that works with young people and is making an amazing difference (GSK 2011).

What is interesting about the Awards is the way that GSK has devel-oped them to go beyond the grants. Senior management from GSK and the King's Fund work with the category winners to help each charity achieve a fresh perspective and to draw up a new agenda for best healthcare practices across the country. What is new and exciting about this is the level of support from the business in creating real change, impact and extended learning opportunities. The change felt by the charities as a result of this effort has been tangible, and is compelling evidence of true business corporate responsibility investment.

Starbucks and corporate responsibility

Starbucks incorporates corporate responsibility into most of its activities, from its coffee suppliers and its Starbucks Shared Planet commitment to its work with the Prince's Trust, its baristas and its new Starbucks Youth Action programme. Corporate responsibility runs throughout the company and this is evidenced in the attitude of its staff and its commitment to driving an all-embracing culture of corporate responsibility.[2]

Starbucks Youth Action encourages young people to get involved in their communities. The brightest ideas are rewarded with a £10,000 grant to turn the ideas into reality. It is a great example of a grass-roots initiative that has created a platform for anyone to have the chance to impact positively on society.

Aviva and Street to School

Aviva has done what many businesses would like to do if they were starting again. It has chosen a single-focus, one-brand corporate responsibility campaign: Street to School.[3] This campaign champions the needs of street children around the world through country partners; in the UK it is Railway Children.

The most interesting aspect of this programme is that Aviva has taken a raw issue, one that does not have a natural conclusion or directly tangible results, and is working it through every aspect of its business. Employees are encouraged to fundraise and volunteer, and senior management, business networks, customers and suppliers are all becoming involved. The general public too is being invited to join the project by signing a petition about street children. It is a brave move but one that is paying dividends as the corporate responsibility programme builds pace and presence in a crowded market.

Trends and future opportunities

Into the second decade of the new millennium, what does the future hold for charities and their corporate fundraising? Are we witnessing a fully matured market? What are the strengths and weaknesses that we need to understand in order to exploit the opportunities fully?

There is room to increase opportunities, including encouraging those companies which are still hiding behind their tick-box corporate responsibility programmes, and helping to develop the small and medium-sized enterprises sector. The aim will be for charities to work more effectively with medium-sized to small businesses to help steer their corporate responsibility strategy and agenda and to help them get employee engagement, a business edge through enhancing their corporate reputation and access to new networks.

It is worth noting that when small and medium-sized enterprises put their corporate responsibility alliances alongside the multinational brand charities – owing to the size and scale of these charities – they risk getting lost within the myriad corporate–charity partnerships and may not achieve the impact for which they were hoping. £10,000 means a great deal more to a smaller charity, and a partnership between a small or medium-sized enterprise and a smaller charity can prove to be much more dynamic.

The necessity for a company to demonstrate its connection to the charity's cause continues to grow in importance. Businesses must be completely transparent about their return on investment, and so they are often drawn to issues that are high in the public's consciousness. The current key social issues for business are care of:

• war veterans as troops pull out of Afghanistan;

• young people and their future driven by university fees;

• the lost generation through high unemployment.

In relation to high unemployment, there is growth in business involvement in apprenticeship schemes and this will likely be the major focus of partnerships now and in the next few years. Furthermore, pushed by the collective guilt of such campaigns as *The Evening Standard*'s Dispossessed Fund, businesses are becoming involved in education and early intervention to challenge poverty and disadvantage.

Companies like being associated with innovation, with charities with a track record and with projects that can be replicated. A great example of recent innovation in the charity sector is Help for Heroes, which has inspired a whole new generation to give to the armed forces where other charities had failed to capture the spirit of support, not to mention the £100 million raised (Knox 2010). Replicating this may seem a tall order, but innovation is what the charity sector is about. That is to say, it is about changing the way society operates, and only organisations with access to social programmes can deliver it.

In times of enforced austerity, increased collaboration through multi-stranded partnerships will be the sensible trend to follow. Namely, charities, the government, businesses and individuals will collaboratively support a cause or issue to achieve maximum impact and will thereby multiply their effectiveness.

In cause-related marketing, there have been some highly successful cause–brand promotions, but it remains an area that has not been fully exploited. Now could be the perfect time for charities to explore this further as an answer for businesses looking for bottom-line returns on their social investment.

In summary, the three top pointers for charities to drive successful corporate partnerships are:

- **issue authority:** taking control on what the charity can deliver;

- **targeted impact:** clarity and focus on key end results;

- **innovation:** what it is that is making the difference, that no one else is doing.

What are the projections for the next few years? Companies are committed to continuing and growing charity partnerships and investment is forecast to increase (C&E 2011, p. 5). Most practitioners are confident that strategic partnerships will meet their objectives and deliver value (C&E 2011, p. 22). The clear goal is to focus on the assets that each partner brings to the table, and make these work to everyone's advantage. This can be done by demonstrating growth in corporate reputation and projects which impact on particular issues, which should result in increased financial and resource investment for the charity.

Conclusion

The reason why companies want to work with charities and why charities want to partner with companies is simple: mutual benefit. This is made easier by each side recognising the part the other plays.

Cross-sector partnerships are essential for meeting society's development needs and always have been, which is why there have been corporate cause partnerships dating back to the late 1800s. Companies cannot claim to be the experts on matters that are outside their core business, and charities cannot operate in isolation from private-sector influences. Companies need the support of charities to tackle issues; charities need businesses to provide resources and capabilities.

Given that corporate responsibility is unlikely to go away, it is encouraging to know that both companies and charities need each other in the pursuit of their various objectives and overall in driving social impact: a powerful partnership.

Notes

1   For more information go to www.kingsfund.org.uk/projects/gsk-impact-awards, accessed 18 November 2015
2   For more information see starbucks.co.uk/responsibility, accessed 18 November 2015
3   For more information on Aviva and Street to School go to www.aviva.co.uk/street-to-school, accessed 18 November 2015

References

C&E (2010), *C&E Corporate–NGO Partnerships Barometer*, London, C&E Advisory Services
C&E (2011), *C&E Corporate–NGO Partnerships Barometer*, London, C&E Advisory Services
Cook, Stephen (2011), 'Shortlist published for Business Charity Awards 2011', *Third Sector Online*, 21 March
Drew, William (1993), 'Prince's Trust gets the buzz with Mercury', *Marketing*, October 14, Haymarket Media, retrieved 12 December 2011 from accessmylibrary
GSK (2011), 'The GlaxoSmithKline IMPACT Awards' [web page], Brentford, www.gsk.com, accessed 12 December 2011
Knox, Julie (2010), '£100 million milestone smashed for Help for Heroes' [web article], *British Forces News*, BFBS, June
Llandudno Lifeboat (n.d.), 'Sunlight No. 1 1887 to 1902' [web page], www.llandudno lifeboat.org.uk, Llandudno, Royal National Lifeboat Institution, accessed 12 December 2011
Vodafone (2007), *Collaboration: Working together for a better future*, Newbury, The Vodafone UK Foundation

CHAPTER TWO

The role and remit of corporate fundraising

Andrew Peel

Introduction

Against a backdrop of shrinking corporate donations budgets and a heightened awareness of corporate responsibility, this chapter examines the form and direction that corporate fundraising now needs to take. It outlines the strategic role that it can play for a charity in terms of promoting its wider messages and services, and strategies that fundraisers should develop in order to build strong, sustainable corporate relationships in what is, for most, a challenging and uncertain climate.

The chapter underlines that corporate fundraising is not a fast track to easy money, and that the path to what funding there is can be a difficult one to negotiate. If a charity urgently needs funding but has limited resources to devote to one income stream for several months without realising a net gain, then this is probably not the right income stream in which to invest. Corporate fundraising can be a slow process, often involving periods of lengthy research and analysis, relationship building with key individuals, both inside and outside the organisation, and plenty of dead ends. Despite some charity chief executives' and trustees' views to the contrary, corporate fundraising was never about one or two 'salesy' fundraisers securing quick wins and effortless cash injections over boozy lunches, and it never will be.

Finally, the chapter also outlines some of the other components which need to be in place before corporate fundraising can begin to reach its full potential.

From philanthropic support to strategic partnerships

The overarching purpose of a charity's corporate fundraising function might be said to be: *to initiate, develop and retain relationships with businesses that maximise net income for the charity and, where feasible and desirable, to generate additional opportunities and benefits for both parties.*

There is far more to corporate fundraising than simply attempting to secure a financial contribution. In fact, although some charities do manage to regularly land significant corporate donations, large no-strings cash gifts are rare. Companies are seldom the vast financial reservoirs that many perceive them to be, and those that are tend to feel more beholden to their shareholders than to their community stakeholders. The level of corporate giving is still startlingly low in the UK, accounting for around 5% of charities' income. Despite more intense scrutiny and pressure from customers, charities, the media, staff, government and more enlightened shareholders, latest figures from the Directory of Social Change reveal that the most generous 600 companies gave away an average of only 0.43% of their pre-tax profits in 2009/10, and that includes contributions of gifts in kind (Lillya 2011, pp. v and xviii).

Furthermore, many companies that have traditionally provided financial support to charities have shifted their focus in recent years from philanthropy towards relationships of a more *strategic* nature: a move, in other words, from donations towards investment of resources, expertise and assets. Such a change of emphasis has been driven, in the main, by the need for companies to be regarded as socially responsible and for more tangible business benefits to come out of such associations. This is not only because of stakeholder pressure but also because it now appears to make sound business sense, with evidence of a demonstrable link between business success and a corporate commitment to social responsibility (Roman, 1999).

There is little doubt that this shift in emphasis has significantly increased the scale of the task facing those charities targeting the corporate sector. It presents such organisations with a considerable set of challenges and yet, for the creative, astute and commercially-minded fundraiser, this new climate means that there really is no limit to ways in which a charity can engage with a company.

This assertion is borne out by a quick trawl through the annual Business Charity Awards. The winning partnerships reveal the unprecedented depth and scope of many of today's best charity–corporate partnerships. The 2011 winners, for example, range from the global five-year link between the International Red Cross and Red Crescent Societies and Land Rover (incorporating financial donations, gifts of vehicles, off-road driving instruction for Red Cross drivers and first-aid classes for Land Rover employees) to an impactful six-month relationship between the charity VoiceAbility and healthcare provider, Simplyhealth.[1]

This project saw the company's staff leading on the process of renaming and rebranding the charity following a merger: in-kind support which not only saved the charity as much as £50,000 but also served to develop individuals in the company and took its charitable activities into a new area. Sarah Hoare, Competence and Quality Analyst at Simplyhealth, observed: 'I've got to know my colleagues better, as well as the challenges faced by a charity'. And Amanda McLean, one of the judges, said that

Simplyhealth 'identified something it had been through – merger and rebranding – that it could pass on. They did so, very effectively, and it made a real difference to the way the charity worked' (Third Sector 2011).

A focus on *value*, not cash

Clearly, corporate–charity partnerships should no longer be viewed simply from a financial perspective, but in terms of the wider value that can be gained by both parties. It is also evident that the corporate fundraiser who thinks of him or herself only as a 'raiser of corporate funds', with the simple job of extricating as much cash from businesses as possible, is going to be destined for disappointment and failure. Some might also argue that the very label 'corporate fundraiser', while remaining a useful generic term, has become something of a misnomer because of the need to think about the role in a broader, more strategic way.

The time has come to regard a corporate partner not as the proverbial cash cow to be milked as rapidly as possible, but as a multi-dimensional resource that, if managed skilfully, can present a plethora of opportunities for colleagues across both organisations. For the charity, the corporate partner might represent a source of invaluable pro bono support or gifts in kind, a new audience for its challenge events or perhaps a new market for its consultancy service or earned-income initiatives. For the company, the charitable link might provide benefits such as staff development opportunities, access to policy makers, improved sales from cause-related marketing promotions and perhaps positive public relations and publicity.

Adopting a broader, more marketing- and customer-orientated approach, with the charity seeking to open up the relationship on a number of mutually beneficial fronts (and encouraging the company to think in the same way), is far more likely to keep a business engaged over the longer term. Not only will it lead to a more equal and sustainable partnership but it may, in due course, help to generate at least some of the funding the charity's chief executive and trustees had hoped for in the first place!

The customer comes first

The key implication of this more externally focused approach is that a big shift in mindset is usually required on the part of the fundraiser and the charity. The charity or cause should no longer be the fundraiser's focal point, regardless of how deserving they regard their cause. It should, rather, be the *company's* (i.e. the *customer's*) objectives that become the primary focus. Of course, that is not to say that fundraisers should lose sight of their charity's own priorities. On the contrary, they need to possess a heightened awareness of their charity's brand, values and offer,[3] so that they are in a stronger position to negotiate and blend their needs with those of the company.

Of course, a proposal will occasionally hit the mark if a fundraiser has done a good job of crowbarring their cause or project to fit a company's criteria, and if their proposal lands on the right desk at the right time. But more often than not, this half-hearted, generic approach to corporate fundraising fails because, having avoided direct contact with the prospect, the proposal is likely to fall wide of the mark. More often than not, it will lack that crucial element of strategic insight into the company's priorities, plans, budgets, commitments and partnerships, or any number of other factors which could have a major bearing on the company's ability or propensity to work with the cause in question.

If, however, the fundraiser's starting point when seeking support (and particularly when developing a new project or product) is to examine the target company's needs carefully, to engage them in dialogue, and then to create something tailored and customer-led, the chances of success are significantly increased.

This is an important principle. Look at any successful modern company, be it Tesco, Google, Specsavers or Amazon, and it is clear that they are where they are today because they have put the customer at the core of their planning. Amazon's chief executive, Jeff Bezos, is widely quoted as saying 'We start with the customer and we work backwards'. Corporate fundraisers could do well to take a leaf out of their book.

Adopting an organisational approach

Another key principle is that corporate fundraising is unlikely to succeed in a vacuum. It requires a coordinated organisational approach and, in particular, the support and buy-in of the senior management team and trustees. They have a pivotal role to play in the development of a charity's corporate fundraising, whether that be by fronting approaches or pitches, or by using their networks to open doors (though they may well need some gentle coaxing to do this). In addition, they are likely to be the key to future investment, in terms of sign-off whether for additional staff, training, a new database, or perhaps the use of external agencies. At the very least, it is vital that the challenges faced by corporate fundraisers are widely understood at a senior level and that a pragmatic, medium- to long-term view is taken of this area of fundraising.

Corporate fundraisers will also find that, if they are to deliver on their promises and fulfil their obligations to companies, they will be dependent upon the support of a wide range of individuals across the charity. It is therefore important to get key colleagues onside as early as possible: encourage them to think about how the partnership might work for them and how, together, the best offer can be presented to companies. In particular, corporate fundraisers may find themselves working closely with colleagues in the communications/public relations/press team, the major giving fundraiser(s), the events team, the finance function, community or regional fundraisers and, of course, those who are responsible for delivering the charity's programmes and services.

With productive relationships in place across the organisation, a corporate fundraising team will find it is able to present a broader, more compelling proposition to companies that, in turn, delivers far greater impact for the charity.

Corporate partnerships as a *platform*

If they are well managed internally, corporate partnerships can not only act as an income generator in their own right, but also represent a *marketing platform* or *hub* upon which the charity can promote its wider products, messages, services and brand. This is particularly the case when working with blue-chip companies with large workforces and customer bases, though it is just as feasible on a smaller scale, as long as the charity has the skills to deliver and the company in question represents the right partner for that charity. What is certain is that one well-chosen partnership, whether local, regional or national in nature, can open up a wide range of opportunities for collaboration, often leading to a step change in a charity's profile and income.

The British Heart Foundation (BHF) is one such charity that regards corporate fundraising as a key marketing and promotional platform. Their pan-organisational approach is outlined further in the following short case study.

Case study: The British Heart Foundation

The British Heart Foundation (BHF) regards corporate fundraising as a key marketing and promotional platform and actively targets companies with propositions developed pan-organisationally. Its corporate partnerships strategy is built, in the main, around the targeting of customer-facing businesses such as banks, large retailers and membership organisations, all of which can provide millions of opportunities to see[3] the BHF brand, and a raft of additional fundraising, marketing and communication angles.

The British Heart Foundation and Lloyds Banking Group

The BHF has recently completed a major Charity of the Year relationship with Lloyds Banking Group that far exceeded both parties' expectations. The original fundraising target was £2 million over a two-year period, but the partnership, extended by six months, generated an impressive £3.63 million in total. This will fund 15 BHF Heart Nurses, 12 Heart Health Professionals and 500 BHF Heart Nurses' specialist training programmes.

The partnership involved traditional staff fundraising and matched funding, but also a cause-related marketing promotion (with the Scottish Widows brand) and several other customer-facing initiatives. These included an HBOS Give a Little Extra Christmas promotion; the Change from the Heart foreign coin appeal; and brand promotion to millions via the Group's website, Lloyds TSB ATM receipts and Halifax ATM screens.

The relationship enabled BHF to achieve a number of organisational objectives, including:

• increased income and the recruitment of new donors/customers (15,000 were recruited);

• enhanced public awareness of the charity and brand;

• the communication of key heart health messages to a wide audience;

• the promotion of BHF's established flagship campaigns such as National Heart Month and the BIG Donation (a shop stock campaign).

The main benefits to Lloyds Banking Group related to staff motivation and engagement (during what was a particularly challenging time for the industry), heart health education and public relations. The partnership:

• united staff, improved teamwork and raised morale during the Lloyds TSB/HBOS merger;

• enabled healthy lifestyle messages to be communicated to over 122,000 employees;

• resulted in significant numbers of staff signing up to BHF events and policy campaigns;

• saw Heart Health Assessments delivered at key sites to over 1000 employees;

• enabled BHF Heart Health Awareness campaigns to be widely promoted;

• saw 87,000 copies of *Heart Matters* (BHF's free magazine) distributed;

• involved 85 staff in Emergency Life Support skills training.

Finally, significant public relations coverage was generated during the partnership for both parties. Two hundred and fifty-six pieces of coverage were achieved in broadcast, national, regional, trade and online media. In terms of print coverage, this equated to an Advertising Value Equivalent of £482,959, with a total of 26.3 million opportunities to see the BHF and the Lloyds Banking Group brands.

The customer comes first

BHF fundraisers put their 'customers' first by providing them with the tools and information to help them live with a healthy heart. This helps to embed the charity's core aims within the companies that they work with, increasing overall support for the charity. In a corporate fundraising context, this leads to a focus on developing real value for both partners outside traditional staff fundraising models. The Charity of the Year partnership with Lloyds Banking Group is a clear demonstration of this strategy playing out.

Building networks, opening doors

As well as building bridges internally, corporate fundraising success depends to a large extent upon a charity's external relationships and profile. Though it can be a time-consuming activity, building solid, reliable networks can provide a catalyst for corporate fundraising and marketing and access to hitherto unreachable budgets, and help to open up a wide range of new and often unexpected partnership opportunities. Corporate fundraisers must therefore master the art of strategic networking and aim to build significant senior-level relationships within a variety of businesses. It is no exaggeration to say that by developing expertise in this area, a charity's corporate fundraising can suddenly shift into a higher gear.

One tactic can be to pursue a policy of constructive engagement with target companies or sectors and other influential, senior-level prospects. By developing a range of suitable engagement devices, such as business breakfasts, networking dinners and thank-you events for donors, and targeting the most appropriate individuals within each business, the charity should gradually begin to raise its profile, build credibility and strengthen its brand awareness.

Additionally, corporate fundraisers might consider forming an advisory group or a corporate development board, perhaps comprising a small number of well-connected business people who are prepared to share their knowledge and experience with the charity.

Other key factors for success

One of the most frustrating aspects of managing corporate fundraising is that, even if the team is made up of the most talented, creative, well-connected and business-minded of individuals, all of whom are working to a sound strategy, success is by no means guaranteed. This is because it is generally dependent upon a complex blend of additional components being in place and, unfortunately, these are often outside the corporate fundraiser's direct control or remit. This can include the following factors.

A clear case for support

This is a key strategic tool which formally articulates the role of the charity, its vision and mission, what makes its approach unique and why it needs support. For a company audience, a sound case for support is needed that can be adapted into a bespoke proposition that articulates what support is needed and what benefits the charity can offer. A weak organisational case makes the corporate fundraiser's job that much harder as it will inevitably dilute the passion, urgency and impact of a pitch or proposal.

A strong, foot-in-the-door product or project

Few charities are lucky enough to have a product as simple or as compelling as Macmillan's World's Biggest Coffee Morning, or BHF's Heart Nurses, or Guide Dogs' corporate Sponsor a Puppy offer. However, it is well worth taking the time to develop workable equivalents to these; for example, one or two engaging products or devices that capture the essence of the charity and will engage both new supporters and existing business partners.

A striking, modern, relevant brand

We operate in an extremely competitive environment in which companies prefer to direct their support towards emotive causes, tangible, high-profile projects or services and a strong brand. Thus, the stronger and more contemporary the brand, the more likely a charity will be to secure corporate partnerships. This is particularly the case when it comes to negotiating marketing-led tie-ups as these depend to a great extent upon leveraging perceived brand strength.

Investment in press, public relations and other promotional activity

Similarly, companies will always be more drawn to charities with a pro-active approach to public relations and publicity, whether local, national or regional. This means that corporate fundraisers are usually in the position of having to push for more organisational investment in press and public relations activity in order to catch the eye of prospective partners and to deliver publicity and exposure for existing supporters.

Availability of more opportunities for company staff involvement

Companies are seeking ever greater opportunities for non-fundraising employee involvement, particularly in the form of hands-on volunteering and pro bono support. Unfortunately, the absence of such initiatives can be a deal-breaker, particularly in the context of Charity of the Year negotiations. Charities need to be aware of this trend and, frustrating and time-consuming as it can be, do what they can to identify suitable activities. That said, it is important not to be sidetracked by trying to devise bespoke new corporate volunteering projects which are not needed and that will be a struggle to deliver.

Infrastructure and business systems

Whether they work for a national charity or a small local organisation, corporate fundraisers will always require certain back-office systems and structures to be in place and to be functioning smoothly. These might include, for example, effective financial systems, including the provision of monthly management accounts to inform decision-making; a smooth-running 'thanking and banking' process to ensure good donor relations; or a decent database to help manage supporter relationships, targeting and marketing.

The absence of any of these components can severely compromise efficiency and have a profound effect on a corporate fundraising team's performance and bottom line.

Conclusion

Corporate partnerships can certainly present charities with a unique set of challenges and pitfalls. However, as this chapter highlights, if there is a readiness on the part of a charity to invest in this area of fundraising *organisationally* for the medium to longer term; a willingness to take the rough with the smooth; and an ability to navigate carefully through sometimes choppy, shark-infested waters, then corporate fundraising may offer considerable potential to the organisation in question. Even for smaller charities and niche or so-called 'challenging' causes, corporate alliances can be – if planned well and managed skilfully – extraordinarily rewarding on many different levels.

Notes

1   For more information on the Business Charity Awards go to www.business charityawards.com
2   The term 'offer' is used frequently in both business and fundraising. It describes the full package that you are offering a customer and inviting them to 'buy'. It includes the physical product, if there is one, and other factors which together make the sum total of what is on offer. In fundraising direct marketing 'the offer' refers to not only how much is being asked for but also the rationale for giving, such as what the money will be used for and how the person will feel as a result of giving. In corporate sponsorship the offer might be made up of tangible benefits along with the expectation of good customer service from the charity and the intangible warm glow from being involved with a charity.
3   A measure in advertising meaning the number of times that someone is likely to see a particular advertisement.

References

Lillya, Denise (2011), *The Guide to UK Company Giving*, 8th edn, London, Directory of Social Change
Roman, R. M. (1999), 'The Relationship Between Social and Financial Performance', *Business and Society*, vol. 38:1, pp. 109–126
Third Sector (2011), 'Business Charity Awards: Charity Partnership: Short-term – Winner: Simplyhealth and VoiceAbility', *Third Sector*, 17 May

CHAPTER THREE

Corporate fundraising mechanisms

Rachel Billsberry-Grass

Introduction

We are a long way from the early days of corporate fundraising, when corporate support frequently meant a cash donation or a gift in kind. These days, the choices for how a company might choose to support a charity are much more varied, and many companies will take a strategic view of how and why they should engage with a certain cause.

The charity will have many factors to consider when deciding which corporate fundraising mechanisms will be included in its strategy. They will include how much time and money it is willing and able to invest in this area, whether the income need is short- or long-term, the need for unrestricted income versus restricted and the cost income ratio or return on investment that is considered acceptable. In addition the charity needs to decide to what degree it is prepared to develop new out-of-budget projects to meet a company's needs and expectations. While it is accepted that charities should avoid being donor-led, some corporate support may only be available to certain types of projects. These may be consistent with the charity's objectives even if not included in its budget.

Charity of the Year

Many companies will adopt a charity for a defined period, most often a year, putting all their effort into raising money for that charity. Traditionally, Charity of the Year opportunities are about staff fundraising, but some companies will also provide other support for the charity during the period, such as sponsorship or cause-related marketing. In some cases the company will match the funds raised by the staff, which can help to motivate them to raise more and demonstrates the company's commitment to the partnership.

Charities should be clear about whether Charity of the Year partnerships are appropriate given the nature of their cause. Given the potentially large sums raised, fundraisers often feel under pressure to pitch for every partnership available. The cost-effectiveness of the time put into pitches should be considered, alongside factors such as whether the process includes a staff vote, which often favours particular causes. Deciding which partnerships not to pitch for requires careful thought.

In choosing a Charity of the Year, a number of companies will look for volunteering opportunities for their staff. Because of the short-term nature of the relationship, the companies are commonly interested in one-off, team-building volunteering days, but in some cases may take a more long-term view and encourage their staff to volunteer regularly. Even for charities which have a huge property portfolio, it can be difficult to find and coordinate the type of one-off volunteering placements that are popular, such as refurbishing a room in a day. In addition, owing to the legislative environment being as it is, many charities must go through rigorous time-consuming checks before recruiting a new volunteer. Some charities accept that they cannot offer the volunteering opportunities that are required, and so avoid partnerships that demand them. Others have identified that this will continue to be an important aspect of staff-involvement partnerships and are investing time and resources into identifying suitable volunteering opportunities that will appeal to a variety of companies and their different strategic needs.

The Charity of the Year partnership can require significant expenditure for both parties if it is to be managed effectively. Companies often have very high expectations of charities when it comes to delivering a partnership. The charity might find that in being chosen as Charity of the Year for a company, it needs to provide large quantities of support materials such as leaflets, t-shirts, collecting boxes, sponsorship forms and jointly branded promotional material. The staff resource may also be substantial. The charity will need a member of staff to be the account manager for the partnership and is likely to be expected to provide public relations and marketing support, regional staff and some time from the most senior people in the organisation.

Much of this investment will be upfront before the fundraising activity has begun; this being the case, there is an inherent risk, as amounts raised can vary dramatically from year to year and from charity to charity. This risk can be mitigated by negotiating a minimum guarantee and asking the company to underwrite initial investment costs.

By their very nature, Charity of the Year partnerships have a definite timescale but often, as a result of good management, it is possible to build lasting relationships. This may involve an extended partnership, sponsorship or cause-related marketing opportunities or being adopted again sooner than expected. However, as the number and size of adoptions rarely follow a regular pattern, there can be major budgetary implications of partnerships. Charities need to consider how they will manage peaks in income as a result of adoptions and also how to manage trustees' expectations in this area.

Cause-related marketing

Cause-related marketing (CRM) is where a company uses a good cause to help market a product or service, for example by donating a sum of money to charity for each unit sold. Companies that utilise this method commonly do so as one part of their marketing mix.

There is an increased expectation for companies to behave in a socially responsible way and CRM publicly demonstrates a company's credentials in this area. In addition, a research study indicates that consumers are more likely to purchase a product which supports a charity than one which does not, providing other factors, such as price and perceived quality, are the same (BITC 2004, p.6).

The implication of this is that a company wanting to undertake a CRM partnership will choose a charity that has a particular resonance with its target market, or one that can offer some other clear benefit such as defined routes to market or leverage with a major retailer. The type of charity, therefore, is likely to be one that has clear mass-market appeal. Charities such as Comic Relief and Children in Need which have guaranteed television coverage attract several major CRM deals, as do the breast cancer charities during Breast Cancer Awareness Month, a particularly high point of their year for the charities' profiles. However, there are examples of promotions on niche products and ones where the match is not obvious but there is a personal motivation from someone within the company.

Given the high public profile of promotions, charities should carefully consider which company or product they are willing to work with and be sure that an appropriate price is negotiated.

While the investment of staff time may be dramatically lower than for Charity of the Year partnerships, this is balanced by the need for specific knowledge on promotions to be able to manage complex contract negotiations. Without this, risks can be high; for example, reputation damage and undervalued contracts such as one which limits potential for working with other brands without the appropriate financial consideration.

CRM arrangements involve commercial benefit and are therefore viewed as trading. Charities will need to examine the financial arrangements for VAT and the likelihood of the contract needing to be with a charity subsidiary trading company. As the overriding factor in most CRM partnerships is the business benefit rather than the purpose for which any resulting donation will be used, income is unrestricted funding, which simplifies the relationship with that trading company.

Licensing

Licensing is defined as a contractual agreement between two entities (in this case usually a charity and a company) in which the licensor permits the licensee to use a brand name, patent, image or other proprietary right in exchange for a fee or royalty.

There are a number of ways in which licensing agreements can be relevant to charities:

• The charity is given a licence free of charge to use an image to raise money for the charity; for example, an image to use on a pin badge or on fundraising materials.

• The charity sells a licence to a company to use its logo on a product or as part of a partnership such as Charity of the Year.

• The charity creates an image with the specific intention of generating income from its sale (such as BBC Children in Need's Pudsey Bear).

Licensing agreements can be very complex and there is a need to protect the charity's reputation and also to ensure fair and enforceable financial arrangements. The example of creating a new image can be a very exciting prospect but it needs to be recognised that, in doing so, a charity will be in direct competition with commercial organisations which invest significant sums developing and promoting their images, so charities need to be sure they have a solid business case for such investment. Where a charity does have specialist knowledge, intellectual property or a strong brand identity, licensing may be an appropriate income-generating/business development activity even if it does not fit within the scope of a fundraising operation.

Sponsorship

Sponsorship is a well-recognised commercial marketing technique in the sports and arts fields and increasingly in the charity sector. Sponsorship of a charity might be of an event, activity, publication or a capital project. The key feature of sponsorship is that the value is based on the benefits offered to the sponsor, rather than the actual cost of the activity.

Charities may include sponsorship as part of their corporate fundraising mix for reasons such as opening up access to a wider range of corporate partners, the benefits of being associated with a well-known brand, the potential of benefiting from the company's existing marketing activity and access to a brand's customers.

A robust contract will be needed to define the terms of any sponsorship agreement and the exact benefits the charity is committing to offer. Once the contract is signed, the income is relatively risk-free, but there is a reputational and potential legal risk to the charity if it does not deliver the contracted benefits. Unlike CRM, the emphasis is on the charity to deliver the results and demonstrate the value of the sponsorship.

Sponsorship is a trading activity, so the charity will need to charge VAT and, as the company is 'buying' benefits, the income will be treated as unrestricted.

There are costs associated with this type of corporate fundraising. As well as the management of the partnership, there may be some additional costs incurred in delivering the benefits, such as the costs of supplying tickets to an event. Sponsorship packages are often enhanced by including additional benefits which ultimately will be paid for from the sponsorship fee. While getting approval for these costs is not easy, by having processes in place and recognising the potential return on investment, charities can enable the expenditure to be made. However, some benefits, such as including the sponsor's logo on all materials, can be delivered within the budgeted costs for the activity.

Sponsorship deals have the potential to last several years: marketeers will look for a sponsorship opportunity that they can continue to work with, building a brand association with the activity, to the extent that people inextricably link the two partners.

Project funding and donations

Although recent years have seen a growth in mutually beneficial partnerships, some companies still take the traditional route of making a donation to support a particular aspect of a charity's work. Although in many cases this donation will be made through the company itself (and making use of Gift Aid so that the donation is tax-effective when received by the charity), a significant number of companies channel their charitable support through a grant-making trust.

This area of corporate fundraising presents a more level playing field for all types of charities as there will be many reasons why a company might choose a particular cause. It could be the charity's relevance to its staff, a decision by the chair, geography or a perceived compatibility of the two organisations.

Whatever the company's decision, it will be looking for specific information about the charity's work such as details of the project including costs and outcomes. Many companies want to support brand-new projects and may try to influence the development of those projects. If charities are able to plan the development of new services alongside a corporate fundraising strategy they will have a strong platform from which to build corporate donations. The alternative is less attractive: agreeing to develop out-of-budget projects, just because the funding is offered, at the expense of in-budget priority projects.

Any income from donations is more likely to be restricted and although not all companies will demand that it is, there will be an expectation that the donation will be spent in the way the charity has suggested.

Relatively little investment is needed in this type of corporate fundraising, other than a member of staff to identify opportunities, make approaches and build relationships. Like a trust or major donor fundraiser, much of their role will be in gathering the information needed to present a project to a potential funder, or provide feedback to a current donor.

Once a company has agreed to a donation, provided it is creditworthy, there is a relatively low risk that it will not pay. If it has agreed to several interim donations, it is useful to have a letter of agreement or contract to secure the funds. This is particularly important if the donation is to fund a new project over forthcoming years, as the charity's auditors will be keen to see evidence of the agreed funding.

Some companies will support different charities each year; but often, once a donation has been made, it is a chance for a charity to engage the company, build on the relationship and secure ongoing donations in the future.

An internal decision to think about is the respective role of trust fundraisers and corporate fundraisers in the management of corporate trusts. As discussed, many of the skills required in this area are more akin to those of a trust fundraiser (for example, a detailed focus on the project and outcomes). However, a corporate fundraiser's involvement may help to maximise cross-selling to other forms of corporate support such as sponsorship.

Payroll giving

Payroll giving is a hybrid fundraising product in that the route to market is through companies and therefore can be a useful product for charities in their corporate fundraising portfolios. However, the management of payroll donors is usually carried out alongside that of donors recruited through any other means such as direct mail. Many charities choose to invest in payroll giving because it is an excellent source of unrestricted income, and attrition (drop-off) rates are generally low compared with cash donors.

General fundraising and employee-led support

Alongside specific corporate fundraising mechanisms there is also a wide range of general fundraising activities which are appropriate for companies and which can be marketed through companies to staff or initiated by staff themselves. These include participation in events (particularly team or challenge events), social events, sale of pin badges, sales of Christmas cards, adoption of charity collection boxes, raffles and lotteries and raising money at corporate hospitality events. Although the emphasis is often on Charity of the Year partnerships and CRM (because of the high profile they receive), these classic fundraising tools can be very lucrative for charities too.

Strategic partnerships

There are some corporate–charity partnerships that focus on delivery of the charity's objectives. This is often the case where a charity has a strong campaigning message which aims to effect change in corporate behaviour; for example, an environmental charity which questions the way food is produced. By engaging with companies, the charity can influence their behaviour and work towards the achievement of its charitable objectives. Such partnerships may have the potential to be income-generating (for example a health-related charity running health checks on employees of a corporate partner), but recognition should be given to the fact that there are often commercial competitors offering similar services. These companies may have access to greater levels of investment than a charity, and purchasers will choose the most cost-effective provider regardless of whether it is a charity or not. Indeed, the charity may be at a disadvantage, as companies will sometimes feel that a charity should provide a service free or at a very low price because they are supporting its mission.

Case study: Chestnut Tree House children's hospice and Southern Water – when relationship-building leads to greater things

Chestnut Tree House is the only children's hospice in Sussex. It cares for children and young adults with progressive life-limiting and life-threatening illnesses from all over the county.

Southern Water first approached the hospice in 2009, inviting the charity to be one of the seven chosen charities for its annual race day. Many of the charities were local and nominated by staff, and each benefited to the tune of £10,000.

Before the race day even took place, the hospice saw an opportunity to build a longer-term partnership and invited Southern Water's chief executive for a tour of its building. During the visit the chief executive met one of the families using the hospice and was moved to want to do more to support the organisation.

An idea was presented by the Lottery Manager who at the time was trying to get promotional leaflets more widely distributed across the region. The chief executive agreed that Southern Water would print over 750,000 lottery leaflets and distribute them with water bills. The saving for the hospice on printing alone totalled £13,000, and the initiative resulted in over 500 additional lottery members, signed up by direct debit to a total value of around £26,000 per year.

The hospice was well aware that future support relied on continued commitment by the Southern Water staff, so it worked hard to build a good working relationship. The hospice tried to be flexible and accommodating and prompt in responding to requests.

The approach has paid dividends and Southern Water is now supporting Chestnut Tree House through its race day for the third year. In addition, during the past three years, as well as benefiting from the lottery promotion, Southern Water has provided support for the hospice through:

- payroll giving;

- bag it and give: a promotion to generate donations for the hospice's shops;

- sponsorship of the hospice's annual ball;

- donation of Christmas hampers to the hospice;

- sponsorship of a promotional film;

- an introduction to their suppliers, Morrison Utility Services, which undertook a major groundwork project saving the hospice £9,000.

Conclusion

There are many different ways for a company and charity to work together, and what will work well for one organisation will definitely not for another. To develop a robust and convincing sales pitch, a charity should assess what it has to offer a corporate partner and which types of corporate fundraising will be most appropriate. Taking a realistic view of its strengths will ensure that the charity has a much greater chance of success.

References

BITC (2004), *Brand Benefits: How Cause Related Marketing impacts on brand equity, consumer behaviour and the bottom line*, London, Business in the Community

CHAPTER FOUR

Corporate team structures and recruitment

Anne Shinkwin

Introduction

This chapter explores the different ways to structure your corporate fundraising team, how to recruit the best fundraisers and then how to retain them.

Different structures for corporate teams

Firstly, there is no right or wrong way to structure a team. The key is to structure to deliver the corporate fundraising strategy, ensuring that team members are clear about their individual roles and responsibilities so that they may achieve the overall objectives and targets. The structure of a corporate team will depend on factors such as fundraising and corporate team strategy, the size of the organisation, the number of current partnerships and the investment strategy for growth.

Evaluating current team structure and roles

Team structures and responsibilities generally evolve over time due to preferences, partnerships and specific needs at the time. Therefore, it is important to step back and evaluate current team structure and roles. Look at both immediate needs and long-term needs for the next three to five years.

Here are some of the questions to consider:

• Are the current team structure and roles enabling the team to achieve its strategy and fulfil the needs of the organisation?

• Are team members clear about their specific roles and responsibilities and how these all fit together? Are donors clear about who to contact?

• How does the team spend its time on a day-to-day basis? How much time are team members spending facing externally (for example, meeting current partners or new prospects)?

• Is the split right between time spent on current partnerships versus new business to ensure that income can grow over time?

- How much time are team members spending doing work which could be done by someone else such as a volunteer or intern (for example research or sending out materials)? Is there enough support within the team?

- Are there opportunities for team members to progress their career within the team or organisation or will they need to leave for the next step up?

- What are the barriers to successful fundraising and achieving more income?

It can be beneficial to develop a checklist of areas for the team structure such as capacity for new business growth, supporting and expanding current partnerships, and career progression for team members or a structure to allow future growth and expansion. With any change in structure, it is essential to communicate clearly with the team throughout the process and involve them in discussing possible options where they are available.

Short-term contracts are always an option and may be an easier way to gain approval for the expenditure budget or to test a new position. However, good fundraisers may be unwilling to give up a permanent position for short-term contracts.

Corporate team structure options

From experience of working in different organisations, these are options for structures for corporate fundraising teams:

- **A sole corporate fundraiser:** within a fundraising team, common in small to medium-sized organisations and when starting to test corporate fundraising opportunities.

- **'All hands on deck' approach:** a few corporate fundraisers with responsibility for both managing partnerships and generating new business. Often used for small corporate teams.

- **Separate partnerships and new business teams:** the trick with this structure is to have clear processes when any new partnerships gained are handed over to a partnership team, or to involve them early on in discussions so that corporate partners do not get too accustomed to one person. In larger corporate teams there may be a few layers, with team leaders of sub-teams and account managers to manage larger partnerships (see the UNICEF UK case study).

- **Sector-focused approach:** account manager and new business teams structured around certain key sectors such as finance, retail and technology. This allows recruitment of fundraisers with specific sector knowledge, often from the corporate sector, who can seek new opportunities.

- **Product-focused teams:** with responsibility for different areas of corporate fundraising such as commercial activities – sponsorship, affinity marketing, licences, trading activities and non-commercial activities – employee fundraising, payroll giving and corporate foundations. It is important to have a coordination process and to provide clear points of contact if corporate partners want to have multiple funding streams.

- **National and regional corporate teams:** many organisations have regional or community teams which are responsible for securing income from local companies and/or supporting a national partnership at a local level. There are many opportunities for both as long as roles and responsibilities and ownership of income are clear. Good coordination between the two teams is essential as part of one overall corporate fundraising strategy.

- **Managing a major partnership:** if the team is successful in being chosen for a major partnership, additional resources will need to be recruited to maximise the opportunity (see 'Increasing resources to manage a specific partnership').

Larger teams may also have a research-function, product-development or programme person to source suitable projects for funding, either within the corporate team or within fundraising.

The key with any team structure is for the manager to be very clear about roles and responsibilities. These will need to be constantly reviewed and changed as partnerships are gained or expanded, or as they end. Remember that when a team structure is developed it is like a new car model which still needs a test drive and potential modifications.

Provide a support resource

As part of the team structure, it is important to provide a support resource through an assistant role, a personal assistant, volunteers or interns to complete research or send out materials to partners. This will enable the team to focus its time on working externally with companies.

An intern programme can be a valuable way of gaining resources and allows the intern to gain experience in the charity sector. In addition, it can provide management experience for team members and the opportunity for them to learn new skills.

Intern positions can be for between two and six months, part or full time. Think through what is required and develop a role description with specific tasks for recruitment. For example, is someone needed to provide additional support to the whole team or to support a few key partnerships, or do they need specific skills in a particular area such as social media? It can be beneficial to give an intern a specific project to lead on during their internship in addition to day-to-day duties.

Case study: UNICEF UK

In 2005, UNICEF UK had nine people in the corporate team as detailed in the diagram below. There were challenges with this structure, including limited capacity for new business, only a temporary support role and everyone reported to the head of department so there were no career progression opportunities.

FIGURE 4.1 UNICEF UK'S CORPORATE TEAM STRUCTURE IN 2005

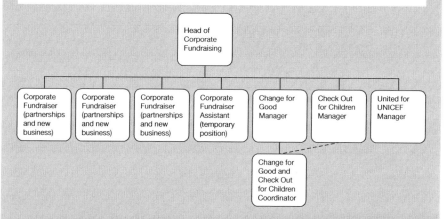

The organisation saw potential within the corporate team and expenditure was assigned in the five-year plan to allow further recruitment to support the target of doubling income in five years.

A review of the current structure was conducted and this took account of short- and long-term needs. Discussions with other charities helped the organisation to understand other potential structures. With the involvement of the team, different options were developed and the following structure was agreed. This structure met all of the organisation's criteria: to increase the capacity for new business, to provide internal support for the team and corporate partners and to allow future growth within the team and career progression.

The new structure included creating two new team manager positions for partnerships development and new business and two corporate executive positions to provide internal and external support.

Through the yearly planning process a case for support and a budget were developed, which were approved. A corporate intern programme was started, recruiting one intern initially; this later

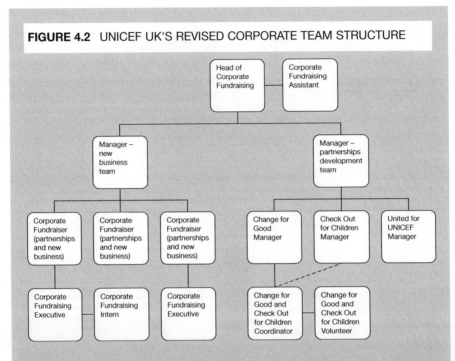

FIGURE 4.2 UNICEF UK'S REVISED CORPORATE TEAM STRUCTURE

increased to three across the team. In addition, the media team also needed to increase its resources over time to support the increasing number of partnerships.

The new structure enabled the team to be expanded as new partnerships were gained, and to increase support to existing partnerships as required. This enabled the goal of doubling income to be reached within four years.

Increasing resources to manage a specific partnership

For some partnerships, it may be necessary to recruit a specific account manager on a fixed-term contract. To maximise the opportunities to deliver Tesco Charity of the Year, for example, all charities big and small would need to increase their resources in the short term.

Before applying for major partnerships, it is worthwhile discussing internally how such a partnership would be resourced and developing a rough budget so that senior management and the trustees have an understanding of the potential expenditure if you are successful. Recruiting additional resources may be required before any income is received. The partnership, therefore, could potentially run at a deficit for a period or cross two financial years, which could cause issues for return on investment or financial accounts.

It is beneficial to talk to the charities that were previously partnered with the company. This will help you to find out how the partnership was resourced on both a national and a regional level, and to understand the different roles and responsibilities, any pressure points for managing the relationship and what they would have done differently. The objectives of the partnership may be different year on year but it is a good starting point. Talking to the company to understand their needs and expectations from fundraising, communications and volunteering perspectives is essential.

A partnership team structure and resource plan can then be developed to suit your particular organisation and calculate the associated budget. It is useful to build in flexibility in the budget to respond to opportunities as they arise during the year. The challenge in winning some major partnerships is that the planning stage starts immediately, and the difficulty can be trying to manage a partnership before the additional resources are recruited. Prioritisation across the team will be vital at this stage.

A major partnership will involve departments across the organisation – such as design, finance, purchasing and human resources – so ensure that the heads of departments are aware of the resource implications.

Case study: CLIC Sargent and Tesco

CLIC Sargent won the Tesco Charity of the Year in 2010. Initially, following advice from Tesco and past charities, it recruited five additional positions to manage the partnership centrally: a campaign manager, an account manager to support the stores, an account manager to support the headquarters, the distribution centre and cause-related marketing activities, an executive to manage the hotline and a public relations manager.

It quickly became apparent at the start of the partnership that extra resources were required to maximise the potential income. A strong business case was developed detailing the additional £2 million income that could be achieved with further resources. Approval was gained and an additional account manager, two more executive positions to support the hotline and a marketing manager to support the internal design team on materials were recruited.

The result was outstanding and £7.45 million was raised, £2.45 million higher than the original target. The partnership with Tesco revolutionised the way they worked together across the organisation.

Recruitment and getting the best people

Fundraising is the lifeblood of most charities; however, recruiting and retaining good fundraisers is a perennial problem. Good corporate fundraisers will always be in high demand, so how do you find them?

What are the skills needed for a good corporate fundraiser?

Communication and the ability to build strong relationships are vital skills for a corporate fundraiser. With fundraising, personal relationships are critical. Often a company contact is choosing to work on a day-to-day basis with the account manager for a year or longer. Good verbal and written communication is needed both externally and internally, as corporate teams work very closely with other departments to deliver successful partnerships.

Commercial awareness and an understanding of how companies operate are vital. Good judgement and the ability to spot opportunities and potential challenges are also important qualities alongside a logical, problem-solving approach (see the sample job descriptions in Appendix 4).

Team members specialising in new business will have slightly different skills from account managers, such as negotiating and influencing skills. Experience in sales may be beneficial. However, it is worth noting that account managers also need new business skills to spot opportunities and expand existing relationships to other parts of the business.

Some of these skills can be developed over time or through training, and some are inherent and will need to be tested during the interview process.

Ensuring the application process delivers the goods

With any role, the more specific the job description, the more likely it is to attract, find and keep the right candidate. A relevant job title that details the correct level is important to encourage potential candidates to investigate further; for example, 'New business team leader, Account Executive'. Be really clear about which skills are essential and which are desirable.

It is important to be clear on whether candidates from the corporate sector will be considered for the role. Often skills are transferable; however, this is dependent on the specific role and experience needed. Allow the candidates to decide if they will accept a drop in salary as opposed to thinking that it is not worthwhile interviewing them.

Searching for good fundraisers should be conducted in the same way as the approach to attracting new corporate partners. The application materials will give potential candidates a feel for the organisation, so it is essential that they are appealing and clear to encourage good fundraisers to apply, in addition to a professional recruitment process.

Where to advertise? It is worth spreading the net wide during the process, through posting adverts on free charity websites, via the Institute of Fundraising corporate special interest groups, using personal networks and briefing recruitment agencies on specific needs for the position. It is important to attract candidates who are seeking a new position and also those who are not actively looking but might move for the right organisation or role. Headhunters can be used if the role is very specialised or if it has been difficult to find anyone suitable. LinkedIn is being used more and more as a valuable tool for recruitment and finding suitable candidates.

To help with the decision process and gain their support, it is beneficial to include a colleague on the interview panel who is from another team and who will work closely with the new employee. If the candidate is to be the sole account manager, involve the corporate partner in the decision process for the same reasons. This can be in the second round of interviews, in a separate discussion or over a coffee. However, do not put any candidates in front of your corporate partner unless you are prepared to appoint them.

It is essential to use the interview process to ensure that you have the information you require to make an informed decision. Here are some suggestions to help with this process:

• **Probing questions:** in addition to prepared interview questions, probe any areas of ambiguity on the application form such as time without work and short periods in jobs; understand what their specific role was in gaining new partnerships.

• **Role plays:** to test the key skills required as a corporate fundraiser, use a ten-minute role play at the start of an interview to test how candidates would build relationships with corporate contacts either at a mock initial new business meeting or sitting next to a potential partner at an event. This exercise will reflect how a corporate partner will feel with the potential new team member.

• **Presentations:** being able to deliver compelling presentations is a key skill for a corporate fundraiser, so ask the candidate to either prepare a presentation or deliver one they have given recently.

• **Judgement through scenarios:** good judgement is vital for corporate fundraising, so give the candidates some scenarios that have happened to team members to see how they would deal with the situation, and understand their thought process. For example, ask how they would deal with a situation where a corporate partner is demanding more than the organisation can deliver, or an internal issue with another department, or ask who they would involve or consult with regard to a specific ethical dilemma. Candidates can prepare for the usual questions in an interview but their responses to scenarios, role plays or presentations can provide useful insights into their true skills.

The key thing to remember is that, if in doubt, don't appoint. It is better to advertise again, as it can save you time in the long run.

An induction process can help new team members to get up to speed quickly, including meetings organised to meet relevant team members and colleagues from other departments, relevant documents to read and clear objectives and initial tasks.

Retaining good corporate fundraisers

Fundraising is a small enough sector for talented corporate fundraisers to get noticed quickly or want to move on to the next level after 18 months to 2 years. Therefore, in order to retain good fundraisers, it is important to think through a strategy to retain them and support their professional development, be it formal training or less formal opportunities such as mentoring.

Given that every person is different, it is important to find out the factors that motivate and demotivate individual team members through regular staff meetings and appraisals. Increases in salary are not always feasible in the sector; however, there are many more ways to retain a good corporate fundraiser at whichever level they are.

Firstly, ensure that the team member knows that they are valued. It may sound obvious, but how many times is this only communicated when someone is about to leave? Let the team member know what the options are regarding their career progression within the organisation, if that is an option.

Is there a structure which allows good fundraisers to grow and develop within the team as opposed to leaving for a step up? Having a structure such as this will be more beneficial for the team and the organisation. Can a short-term position be created until an opportunity becomes available? If opportunities are not available within the team to move up a level, look for ways to stretch them within the existing role by setting challenging objectives or giving additional responsibility such as managing a larger partnership, becoming the lead for a project within the team or planning a section of the team away day.

It is important to discuss and develop together a clear plan for their professional development such as training courses, attending external conferences and having an internal or external mentor. Most fundraisers are motivated first and foremost by the cause, so a visit to a project to see the organisation's work in practice can be inspiring.

Increased flexibility such as flexible working hours, working from home or other benefits can be motivating for staff. This is also becoming increasingly important as more organisations are offering it.

Retaining good fundraisers is a challenge across an organisation. Does a formal policy or talent management programme need to be developed with human resources to aid retention in your organisation? It is worth doing everything possible to retain good fundraisers: they are worth their weight in gold.

Conclusion

Getting the right corporate team structure for your organisation is vital for successful corporate fundraising. Through judging whether the team structure and roles will allow the team to achieve its strategy and fulfil the needs of the organisation, you can decide which team structure will best suit the team. This arrangement, with the right support, can gain new partnerships for an existing team and therefore enable it to expand. Along with having the right structure, taking the right steps to recruit and then retain good corporate fundraisers (rather than taking them for granted in a competitive environment) will ensure the longevity of the team's success.

CHAPTER FIVE

Developing a corporate fundraising strategy

Andrew Peel

Introduction

The shift from philanthropy towards what is generally a more sophisticated and strategic form of corporate engagement – and the need for tangible business benefits to come out of such support – has clearly changed the nature of corporate fundraising. Although the financial and non-financial benefits for charities working in this arena can now be substantial, the same is true of the associated challenges. As such, this is an area of fundraising that requires considerable thought and planning and is certainly not something to be entered into lightly.

As has been explored in earlier chapters, a charity will only reap the rewards from corporate fundraising if the organisation is fully committed, and if there is a willingness (and an ability) to take a long view of this income stream and a strategic approach. A charity must also have confidence in its positioning and clarity over its niche or angle in relation to the business sector. If it is unclear about what it stands for and what it can offer to companies, a charity will always struggle to make a compelling case for itself in a competitive and tough marketplace.

There are a number of key stages a charity should go through before embarking upon, or seeking to grow, corporate fundraising. What follows is a step-by-step guide to developing a well-measured and coherent approach to corporate engagement that can be tailored to your own organisation, and revisited and adapted as necessary.

Step 1: Analysing your situation

The first step in scoping out your strategy is to take stock of where you are now, understand your strengths and your weaknesses – as a charity, a corporate partnership proposition and a fundraising team – and start thinking about how to develop your business. There are numerous tools available for helping you define your strategic approach, but experience has shown that the following ones can help you answer most of the key questions and identify your priorities.

(i) 'SWOT' analysis

The dependable 'SWOT' (Strengths, Weaknesses, Opportunities and Threats) analysis has yet to be beaten as a tool for helping you quickly unpick your organisation's and your team's core competencies (or lack of them). It can help you to: identify opportunities that you may be in a position to take advantage of; consider your organisation's and/or your team's weaknesses; and highlight any threats you are facing. It can also be a useful tool for identifying and grouping any recurring themes (such as 'our poor internal communications' or 'the need for more training') that are affecting your work. With this information to hand, and agreed by your closest colleagues, you will be in a strong position to plan for a range of scenarios and start scoping out a clear strategic direction.

(ii) 'PESTLE' analysis

A 'PESTLE' helps you consider a wide range of external factors – Political, Economic, Social, Technological, Legal and Environmental (or Ethical) issues, influences, trends, likely future events or outside forces – that may have an impact upon your fundraising. Although you may not be in a position to control any of them (for example a general election or an economic downturn), it is important to be aware of them and think through their possible impact on your strategy.

(iii) Competitor analysis

There are, of course, thousands of charities and voluntary organisations operating across the UK, a percentage of which will represent direct competition. It is helpful to catalogue the activities of those you regard as the key players – whether local hospices or the local or regional offices of national charities – and to map out their sphere of influence in terms of service delivery and/or fundraising and marketing. But most important of all, you must be clear about what it is that differentiates you from them and what you can offer a company that they cannot. You won't be able to do anything about their presence but, by noting their existence and their modus operandi, you are giving yourself the best opportunity to make your corporate approaches stand out from the competition.

(iv) The Boston Matrix

The Boston Matrix is another simple analytical tool, devised by the Boston Consulting Group, which helps you visualise the probable life-cycle of your projects, products, clients, donors (plus colleagues and trustees if necessary). It will help you identify your Cash Cows, Rising Stars, Sick Children and Dead Dogs, thereby highlighting not only which aspects of your current corporate strategy/portfolio yield the best return on investment, but also those which are likely to require more attention and investment in the future (and of course those initiatives probably best left alone to quietly wither and die). It will also help you appreciate which corporate fundraising techniques or products your team are likely to get the best return on in the future, be that Charity of the Year, payroll giving, sponsorship, challenge events and so on.

(v) Ansoff Matrix

The Ansoff Matrix, a tool that was devised in the 1950s by H. Igor Ansoff, helps you to decide how and where to expand your activities. Although a rather commercial-looking tool, it can be very useful in terms of helping you think through your markets, products or offers,[1] and the growth strategies which are open to you; i.e. whether you should be targeting new or existing markets with new or existing products.

Broadly-speaking, the four choices defined by Ansoff are:

A: 'Market Penetration' strategy

This strand of the matrix (see figure 5.1) helps you consider whether you should be promoting existing products, projects or services to existing markets perhaps in greater numbers than you are at present. Could you develop your existing products and heighten your marketing or promotional activity? Or could you look at ways of ensuring greater loyalty among your customers or supporters?

The key implication of this approach is that you will probably need to focus more on sales, marketing and promotional activity. Although this route is generally low-risk and low-investment, it is also less ambitious with lower returns, since you tend to be operating inside your comfort zone.

B: 'Market Development' strategy

Could you look to introduce existing products or services into a new market? This option might involve expansion into another town, region or country; different 'packaging' and pricing of your work for companies; or perhaps the targeting of a particular sector which you have recently identified as resonating with your cause. Again, this is a fairly low-risk strategy since the focus is primarily going to be on your current products and sales, and marketing strategies with which you are familiar.

An example of the Market Development approach would be for an established charity, based in London, to take the decision to set up a new corporate fundraising function in Scotland. The organisation would need to invest in a new fundraiser and office, and almost certainly package its work slightly differently in that new market.

C: 'Product Development' strategy

Should you consider creating new products, projects or offers for existing markets or customers? There is a level of risk attached to this approach, since the success of a new product can never be guaranteed. This is, of course, countered by the fact that you know your markets better than your competitors, you have established marketing channels in place and your customers know and trust you.

D: 'Diversification' strategy

Should you think about introducing new products or offers into new markets? This is, of course, the riskiest strategy since it involves the organisation moving some of its focus away from the products, markets and customers it knows best. Unless continuous expansion is one of your core objectives, you would normally go down this road only when forced to do so, for example because your market or market share is diminishing. Of course, the returns from successfully penetrating a new market with a fresh offer ahead of the competition can be considerable.

The post-2008 economic downturn has forced many charities to do just this: to evaluate their assets and their offer and assess whether untapped markets exist, or could be created, to generate sustainable income. This may range from paid-for services such as training and consultancy, to other more innovative trading initiatives such as the venture philanthropy-funded expansion programme recently pioneered by Scope, which used a mixture of loans, donations and commercial finance to fund a major housing project in Essex.

(vi) Fundraiser's instinct

Finally, don't forget to take an objective look at where you are. Having been through a period of analysis and tried some of these analytical tools, take a few steps back at the end of the process and review the bigger picture. If your various workshops, grids and matrices are telling you one thing, but your instinct is telling you another, take a closer look at the outputs. Remember that you know far more about your organisation than Messrs Boston and Ansoff and other business gurus, so the chances are that you will have the greatest insight.

FIGURE 5.1 ANSOFF'S FOUR STRATEGIES

	Existing products or offers	New products or offers
Existing markets	**A** 'Market Penetration' strategy	**C** 'Product Development' strategy
New markets	**B** 'Market Development' strategy	**D** 'Diversification' strategy

Lower risk/ lower return

Higher risk/ higher return

Step 2: Articulating your vision

By this stage, you should have a good appreciation of the internal and external environments for corporate fundraising, as well as a range of options for your marketing and positioning.

It can now be helpful to paint a picture of what the future will look like for your corporate fundraising. This vision needs to be something that encapsulates the opportunity and the goal; inspires and appeals to your team and the wider charity; is feasible, flexible and focused; and, ideally, can be easily explained in a few minutes and summarised in a few seconds.

It must also, of course, be informed by the charity's overall funding requirements (and the way in which those break down by income stream) and it should be both ambitious and realistic. There is little point, for example, in setting your team the goal of generating £5 million net in three years if all you have achieved to date is a £5,000 partnership with a local law firm.

See Appendix 2 for an example of how a corporate fundraising vision can feed into the strategy.

Step 3: Developing your strategy

It now makes sense to start plotting your general strategic direction. The hooks upon which to hang your strategy could look something like this:

(i) 'Maximise the potential of existing relationships and fulfil all contractual obligations'

The fact that you are developing a new strategic plan should not impact negatively upon the corporate relationships already on your books. If you are only half-way through a three-year partnership, for example, you must be careful not to lose sight of your commitments to that client. Your existing partners are your most important ones. And remember, it's far more resource-intensive to bring on board a new supporter than to retain or develop an old one.

(ii) 'Develop new fundraising or marketing activities with current corporate supporters'

For the reason given above, it's likely to be more effective to develop new income from your supporters than to rely heavily upon researching and securing new business relationships from scratch. A key objective for your team, therefore, should be to look at ways of developing existing supporter relationships, bringing them closer to your cause by using some of your established fundraising products or engagement tools.

(iii) 'Develop new relationships through existing networks'

There may well be informal opportunities for doing this – by talking to your trustees or existing corporate supporters and by endeavouring to gain access to their contacts or networks; or formal ones – such as by establishing a fundraising appeal board or corporate panel.

(iv) 'Attract new corporate supporters'

Whether your corporate fundraising function is new or has a successful track record, you will always need to consider how to attract new supporters to your cause. If you have exhausted your contacts and networks, this will inevitably involve researching businesses and sectors which have clear links with your work, beneficiaries, brand and location (and ideally all four).

Let us take the example of an international eye care charity. The corporate fundraising manager might map out a number of sectors with a relevance to, or resonance with, the charity's work (see figure 5.2 overleaf).

FIGURE 5.2 TARGET INDUSTRIES RELEVANT TO THE WORK OF AN EYECARE CHARITY

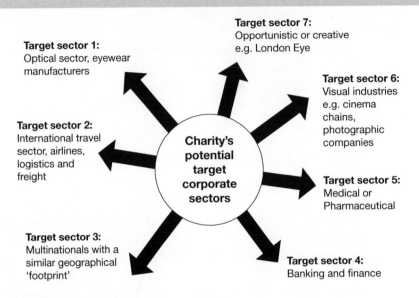

Target sector 1:
Optical sector, eyewear manufacturers

Target sector 2:
International travel sector, airlines, logistics and freight

Target sector 3:
Multinationals with a similar geographical 'footprint'

Charity's potential target corporate sectors

Target sector 7:
Opportunistic or creative e.g. London Eye

Target sector 6:
Visual industries e.g. cinema chains, photographic companies

Target sector 5:
Medical or Pharmaceutical

Target sector 4:
Banking and finance

Get to know your target

Once you have identified a range of relevant industries or sectors in this way and narrowed down your targets to individual prospects, you must thoroughly familiarise yourself with them. You will need to research each company's activities, their businesses, their brands and sub-brands; stay attuned to any pronouncements by the chief executive on charities or corporate social responsibility; and note personal factors (such as family circumstances germane to your cause) which could pave the way for a successful approach.

It also helps to have a clear understanding of how the company is structured and the key personnel. Sometimes, such information can be gleaned from the company's website, Companies' House, companygiving. org.uk[2] or a friendly receptionist. Alternatively, you might be lucky enough to have one of your payroll givers working for the company who you can talk to, or an ex-employee on your staff or board who can shed light on the company's culture and operations.

While some may regard it as rather Machiavellian, this kind of ongoing, strategic research can mean the difference between a well-targeted approach and one that falls on stony ground. Not only will it help you appreciate your target's business better and thus improve your positioning, but also it could reveal potential warm entry points and inspire imaginative angles to build into your approach.

Step 4: Developing your corporate offer

You will need a strong, bespoke corporate proposition that conveys your partnership vision; clarifies the support you need and why you need it; and clearly sets out your unique selling points and the benefits you can bestow on the company. You will also need a compelling 'ask' – the right product, project or device pitched at the right price which will serve to engage your target.

Most companies these days are not prepared simply to provide 'free' money to good causes, preferring instead to tie their support into a charity's brand or a particular project, service or product. This being the case, how do you position your charity appropriately and decide what to pitch to the company?

What to put in the shop window?

A simple analogy is to think of the corporate fundraiser as a shopkeeper who must work hard to tempt people onto their premises. In the shop-keeper's shoes, you need to think carefully about a wide range of issues such as your pricing (and profit margins), packaging, branding, customer care and so forth. But by far your biggest challenge relates to your *products* and particularly, what to put in your shop window. What is most likely to catch the eye of a busy passing crowd and entice them in off the street to sample your wares?

As a charity fundraiser, this might take the form of your charity's 'bestsellers' (i.e. the project(s) for which you are best known), or it might be an attention-grabbing new project or service. You need to give careful thought to your products and what makes them special. Learn all about them, polish them and perfect them, and then proudly display them in your window.

Create a product matrix

The main downside to the shopkeeper analogy, of course, is that corporate fundraisers can rarely afford to behave so passively. With thousands of charity competitors out there, it is a risky strategy to sit back and wait for customers to come to you. The charities that are going to succeed in the current climate are those which are prepared to get out into the market-place and actively seek out corporate partners with high-quality and tailored applications and approaches. This will be a particularly important strand of activity if you are not fortunate enough to have access to good senior-level networks and other door-openers.

To help clarify your corporate offer, one approach is to take a blank sheet of paper and write down, in a column on the left-hand side, a list of anything that you do, or own, in which a company might have an interest. This should not only include those activities which are fundable in a traditional sense, but also those which could provide more innovative ways to engage companies, perhaps by involving their staff, tapping into marketing budgets or focusing on donations of products.

Your list of products might encompass, for example, the names of your main programmes, projects or services, or your publications, flagship events, shops or training and consultancy services. You might also want to include other embryonic ideas here. Perhaps you are planning a new challenge event or a business advisory group which could, in itself, provide reasons to enter into dialogue with a particular company.

Along the top of the page, write in headings describing the different ways in which companies may support you – the *mechanisms*. Then put a mark in the matrix where you feel there is a likelihood of support, as in figure 5.3.

The 'back door' approach strategy

If corporate fundraising is about creating unique business propositions that set you apart from the competition, it can help your cause even more to consider using a less conventional route into your target company. For example, if you have developed a strong employee engagement proposal, you may find that it receives a warmer response channelled through the 'back door', for example via the human resources team, than if directed to the corporate social responsibility or community affairs department. You may also discover that, because you are dealing with people who are less used to working directly with charities, you experience fewer of the usual blockers and standard rejections.

When the author was working for Sightsavers, the corporate fundraising team developed a successful cause-related training partnership with Sony, involving all its European marketing managers, using this very tactic. Sony's UK human resources director bought into the project fully (and helped sell it internally too) as she could see real benefits to their business in involving senior staff in an innovative outward-facing training project, the objective of which was to generate fresh fundraising and marketing ideas for the charity.

In short, by taking time to identify and thoroughly research your sectors, prospects and products, you will find it easier to decide which part of a business to target – whether it be the corporate social responsibility, marketing, sponsorship or human resources team – in order to stand the best possible chance of success.

The art of creating successful new business approaches is explored in greater detail in Chapter 9.

FIGURE 5.3 CHARITY X'S 'PRODUCTS' AND CORPORATE ENGAGEMENT ANGLES

⇩ Charity X's products ⇨	Philanthropic corporate support	Marketing-led support (e.g. sponsorship and cause-related marketing)	Charity of the Year or staff fundraising	Volunteering or skills exchange	Networking or profile raising	Trading or earned income	In-kind support
The cause	■	■	■				
Programmes, projects or services							
Older people's day centre	■		■	■			
Home Truths campaign	■	■	■	■			■
Youth outreach			■				
Playgroup							
Mentoring service				■			■
Other activities or properties							
Charity shop		■				■	
Meeting rooms							
Consultancy (training etc.)						■	■
Publications		■					
Brighton Marathon							■
Future activities or products							
Quarterly business breakfast		■			■		
Churches' Information Pack		■	■				■
Schools' Fundraising Pack		■	■		■		
Paris Bike Ride		■	■				
Three Peaks Challenge		■	■				■
Mobile phone and inkjet recycling		■					

Case study: Above & Beyond

Above & Beyond is the charity for Bristol's nine central hospitals, which include the Royal Infirmary, the Bristol Heart Institute, Bristol Haematology and Oncology Centre and Bristol Dental Hospital. Its aim is to invest in projects that provide high-quality care to the half a million or so people who receive treatment at the hospitals every year. In 2010 the charity generated £3 million to fund research, improvements to the hospitals' environment, training and support of hospital staff, and the provision of state-of-the-art equipment.

Until 2010, Above & Beyond's fundraising focus had been mainly on community fundraising and legacies. However, the decision was taken to widen the charity's funding base, with greater emphasis being placed on corporate fundraising as well as on trusts and major donors. Following this shift in emphasis, the charity has witnessed a significant increase in funding.

Developing the corporate fundraising strategy

While the charity already had a few well-established relationships with local businesses that had been generated by the community team, a new head of corporate partnerships, Lorna Clarke, was recruited to develop a more strategic approach to this fundraising stream and, in particular, to develop existing corporate relationships, secure new partnerships and grow net income over the short, medium and long term.

This work involved the use of a range of planning tools to understand the internal and external environments for corporate fundraising, including SWOT and PESTLE analyses. Then, in order to clarify Above & Beyond's position in the market, a competitor analysis was conducted that looked at the charity's immediate competitors, best practice among other National Health Service charities and the activity of successful corporate fundraising teams across the wider charity sector. This stage of the planning phase also included an audit of past corporate support in order to understand giving patterns and to establish whether any previous relationships had the potential to be reignited.

Given the low level of awareness of the charity in Bristol, its limited resources and the number of sizeable companies across the South West, Lorna placed her short-term focus on trying to strengthen and leverage Above & Beyond's existing relationships. These were seen as the key to increasing income in the short term and to generating profile and new partnerships over the longer term. Furthermore, with no corporate marketing material to work with,

Lorna ensured that existing and past relationships were captured in the form of case studies and testimonials to help 'sell' the charity in proposals, pitches and presentations.

The charity's corporate offer focused initially on staff fundraising and events – both the charity's own community-led events and company-driven activities. Using these as an initial relationship builder and engagement tool, the aim has been to build firmer Charity of the Year partnerships and then move the focus in subsequent years onto a more commercial footing (for example with a greater emphasis on sponsorship and other marketing-led activity). In the knowledge that more strategic relationships such as these generally require greater levels of management, it is now recognised that the team will require further investment and support in the future.

Lorna also invested time in building relationships with colleagues internally – especially the community team – the objective being to create a more open and collaborative pan-organisational culture for contact cultivation and corporate engagement. A more focused approach to external communications was also a key part of the plan as it was recognised that this would help to raise awareness of the charity and drive new business activity.

The situation now is that the charity has much stronger relationships with its existing client base, is working with a number of new companies (including a key Charity of the Year partnership) and is developing a strong pipeline of prospects. In addition, a more focused communications strategy means that the charity's profile is increasing and this is impacting positively upon the work of the corporate fundraising team. Lorna observes:

> When I mention Above & Beyond now, people don't look at me blankly as they once did. There's much more to do, but I certainly believe that we're moving in the right direction.

Conclusion

Despite the fact that charities are arguably in a better position than ever before to broker new alliances with the corporate sector (and on the whole, companies are more prepared to consider them, as long as there are clear benefits for them), there is always more that corporate fundraisers can do to hone their approach to such relationships.

By formulating a clear vision and strategy for your corporate fundraising, giving careful thought to how you package your cause and products, and investing the necessary time and resources in researching your target companies, you will find that your hit-rate improves, your portfolio of partnerships grows and your net income from this source increases in a sustainable way.

Notes

1   See Note 2, Chapter 2.
2   The Directory of Social Change's searchable subscription website of companies and businesses which provide support to voluntary organisations in the UK.

CHAPTER SIX

Take it or leave it: corporate fundraising ethics

Ian MacQuillin

Introduction

In March 2005, a cancer charity tied itself in philosophical knots when it became embroiled over a decision to reject a donation from a man whose professional life involved the killing of animals for sport.

Although this incident was not in relation to a corporate gift, the ethical questions are exactly the same as those that would be faced by any corporate fundraiser. The charity's wavering between different types of ethical decision-making perfectly illustrates the main thesis of this chapter.

The charity in question was offered a substantial sum from someone involved in recreational shooting who had raised the money through sponsorship of his activities. What exactly happened is disputed. In a nutshell, however, the charity accepted and then rejected the donation. Its justification of the rejection was that it was necessary to minimise the suffering and pain caused to animals.

However, the donor claimed that he was told his donation would be accepted if it were handed over quietly to avoid opposition from animal rights groups (the charity had already been the subject of such targeting because of the experiments it funds on live animals). The donor claimed that it was only when he went public to the media that the charity handed the first instalment of his donation back.

Here are the two reasons this is such a mess. First, the justification for returning the donation was that pain and suffering to animals should be minimised. Yet the charity funded research that involved animal testing. This opened the charity to charges of moral inconsistency. Second, according to the donor, it was only after the donation became public that the charity justified the rejection by implying it was the morally right thing to do. This is the ethical knot this charity tied itself into: it got bound up in, and slipped between, two different ethical standpoints.

This example illustrates that ethics is one of the most poorly understood concepts in fundraising. And not only is ethics poorly understood; many, if not most, fundraisers believe they have a grasp on corporate fundraising ethics that is not reflected in their actual understanding of the issues.

Let's start by stating what corporate fundraising ethics is not. Corporate fundraising ethics is not:

- necessarily the same as your own personal morality;
- dependent on the majority view of fundraisers;
- non-evidence-based risk avoidance or minimisation;
- non-evidence-based reputation management;
- public relations;
- human resources best practice;
- necessarily fundraising best practice.

But corporate fundraising ethics is:

- a system or code by which you can determine whether you should or should not accept an offer of corporate support that is independent of the factors listed above.

In practice, however, many so-called ethical decisions made by corporate fundraisers are actually based on a guesswork approach to risk avoidance or reputation management or even human resources best practice and are not ethical decisions at all. In the worst cases, so-called ethical decisions are based on the personal prejudices of individual fundraisers.

So, the starting point for a discussion of corporate fundraising has to be with a discussion of ethical theory itself.

What is ethics?

A broad two-fold definition of ethics is as follows:

1. The philosophical study of the moral value of human conduct and of the rules and principles that ought to govern it.

2. A code of conduct considered to be correct, especially for a professional group.

Ethics in corporate fundraising can therefore be based on whether it is the right thing to do according to the industry's code of practice or the right thing to do according to a set of higher moral values. But the two may not always conform, and they may conflict.

As a minimum you, as a corporate fundraiser, have an ethical duty to conform to the Institute of Fundraising's code of practice on charities working with business, and other relevant codes, especially the code of practice on the acceptance and refusal of donations.

For example, *Charities Working with Business* stipulates that a charity should not work with two companies from the same sector if this produces a conflict of interest (IoF 2006, p. 5). That would be unethical. But perhaps this is not what a lot of fundraisers have in mind when they consider the ethics of corporate fundraising. Rather, they are thinking of ethics according to the first definition; in other words, is it the right thing to do?

According to this way of thinking, when a donation from a defence firm is turned down, for example, it is because it is the right thing to do (i.e. it is ethically correct to refuse donations from companies engaged in the defence industry), not because it conflicts with the Institute of Fundraising code of practice.

Ethical theory

So how do you decide the 'right' course of action? There are two broad categories of ethical theory:

Consequentialist (for example, utilitarian): Decide on the right course of action based on what consequences carrying out (or not) that action would have.

Deontological (for example, rights-based): At least partly independent of the consequences of the action. It is the right thing to do according to sets of circumscribed moral rules.

Corporate fundraisers often conflate the two categories and switch between them when making – or more often, retrospectively justifying – their ethical decisions.

A decision to reject a donation from an arms company is often taken on deontological grounds (i.e. it is the right thing do to). But when asked to justify that decision, the argument switches to a consequentialist position (for example, it would have a negative effect on public opinion and the charity's reputation and so would have damaged the charity's fundraising in the future).

But consequentialism of this type is actually testable. If you say your donors won't give if you accept this or that corporate partnership, you have a big database that you can segment and ask. If they say they will continue to give, the consequences you fear will not happen, so the consequentialist ethical argument for refusing the donation is undermined.

The consequentialist position is of paramount importance in fundraising because both Charity Commission guidance on the duties of charity trustees and the Institute of Fundraising code of practice on the acceptance and refusal of donations are consequentialist ethical codes.

Charity trustees – and by extension their delegates working for the charity – 'must only act in the interests of the charity and its beneficiaries' (Charity Commission 2009, p. 30). The Institute of Fundraising code of practice says:

> Trustees (or their delegates) have a duty to consider carefully, on the basis of the *evidence* [my italics] available to them, whether the charity's interests will be better serviced by accepting or refusing the donation and to act accordingly.
>
> IoF 2006, p. 4

The code goes on to say:

> In making these judgements, trustees and their authorised decision-makers MUST NOT allow individual or collective personal, political or commercial interests, nor personal views on political or ethical issues, which are not directly related to the interests of the charity, to affect their judgement.
>
> Ibid.

This means that all charities that raise money from companies must:

- have a clear policy on the acceptance and refusal of donations;
- act in the best interest of the charity.

This in turn means basing what is in the charity's best interest on evidence. Corporate fundraisers therefore also have an ethical duty to establish this evidence base through a risk assessment. This could include the following tasks:

- A public relations risk analysis to assess the likelihood of negative media coverage.
- Surveying a sample of donors to assess their likely giving behaviour were you to accept the donation.
- Asking your beneficiaries.
- An examination of the company's previous charity partnerships.

It is not enough to say that you think that partnering such-and-such company would damage your reputation. That is not evidence; that is a gut feeling, which will not suffice to fulfil your responsibilities in establishing evidence.

That is why it is absolutely vital that all corporate fundraising departments have in place robust risk assessment and reputation management procedures (a risk assessment is required under the Institute of Fundraising code of practice (IoF 2002, p. 6). These procedures would allow you to conclude, for instance: 'Our research has shown that, were we to accept this donation, XX per cent of our current major donors would be likely or very likely to withdraw their support, costing us £XXX,000 a year.'

It is important to clarify that a risk assessment and reputation management are not the same thing as taking advice from someone with expertise in a particular field. Very early in 2011, a disability charity signed a corporate partnership with a major tobacco company, with all the ensuing criticism that it must have been expecting. The following month at a charity law seminar, a practitioner from a specialist charity public relations company said that this charity's communications team should have advised the charity not to accept the partnership, because it was inevitable that there would be bad publicity and a potential for reputational damage. Not only is this not a risk assessment; bad publicity (even if it is inevitable) is not a sound ethical reason for rejecting a donation.

The consequentialist nature of the Charity Commission guidance and the Institute of Fundraising codes of practice all but eliminate the need for a judgement based on deontological grounds.

Even if you were to accept that there is a deontological case for refusing a donation from a company, this position still needs to be justified. If you say it is wrong to accept money from a defence company then you must say why it is wrong; it is not necessarily self-evident. To say it is wrong 'because they make weapons and sell them to governments' merely begs the question, because this is just another way to describe what an arms company does. A proper deontological justification could be: 'It is wrong for us as a charity to accept a donation from this company because it sells weapons to a regime that uses them to enforce ethnic cleansing.'

Therefore, anyone who made a deontological rejection of a corporate donation would then be required to return to the consequentialist position and show why rejecting a donation from a company that was a party to ethnic cleansing was not in the best interest of the charity. In this case, it is not in the best interest of the charity to partner such a company because on deontological grounds genocide is wrong, and on consequentialist grounds it would be straightforward to show evidence (using the methods outlined earlier) that your reputation and levels of support would suffer.

The original argument of 'because they make weapons' is nearly impossible to justify on consequentialist grounds (unless, of course, there is a specific connection to the charity and its cause). So, in the absence of other reasons, a charity that rejected a donation from an arms company just because it is an arms company would be acting unethically.

To return to the example that began this chapter, it can now be seen that any decision to have accepted the donation was in fact made on consequentialist grounds. It is wrong not to minimise suffering to animals, but the suffering of animals shot during the fundraising venture is outweighed by the good consequences this donation will bring. However, the ultimate decision to reject the donation then appears to shift to a deontological framework: it was the right thing to do because suffering to animals should be minimised, irrespective of the good consequences that might result. However, on closer inspection, the deontological decision to reject the donation was actually made on consequentialist grounds: the charity was saying that rejecting the donation was the right thing to do so that it could avoid the consequences of attacks by animal rights activists.

What, then, should the charity have done to avoid this muddle? Those in charge of making the decision should have established the charity's evidence base for either accepting or rejecting the donation and taken the decision using the weight of that evidence in accordance with any relevant codes of practice. They would then be in a strong position to defend their charity and the decision, were there to be any bad publicity as a result of it.

Other deontological considerations

Is that it then? Is all corporate fundraising ethics based on a consequentialist ethical code that leaves no room for what the morally correct choice is, as you might see it?

After all, charities are about changing the world, so surely there has to be some element of doing the right thing, irrespective of the consequences. Isn't it wrong that you are legally and ethically obliged to accept a donation from a company that you consider to be morally bankrupt? What about that first definition of ethics, about judging according to a higher set of human moral values?

These are valid questions, but nevertheless the law and the codes of practice are quite clear on this. Decisions must be taken in the best interest of the charity, based on evidence, and not swayed by personal political, commercial or moral preconceptions.

So if you are faced with a corporate partnership that you personally want to refuse on deontological grounds but your professional consequentialist ethical code requires you to accept, how do you resolve this dilemma?

Take some of the following considerations in turn.

Knowledge

How much do you know about a company's business practice, ethics or corporate social responsibility programme – or lack of it? The example of the defence industry has been used throughout this chapter, but most companies or industry sectors will have some ethical skeletons in the closet (such as supplier practices, fat-cat salaries, their environmental footprint, or exploitation of less-developed countries).

Suppose you as a corporate fundraiser reject a donation from a company on deontological grounds (or because of your own personal moral position), because, say, you object to the way it treats its workers in less-developed countries? Then you would also be compelled to reject support from a company that refused to recognise its staff's right to belong to a trade union in the UK, or refused to give them a cost-of-living pay rise. If you didn't, you would leave yourself open to difficult questions about why you are prepared to reject donations from one charity that doesn't treat its workers fairly but accept them from another company that doesn't treat its workers fairly either.

It would be relatively simple to respond to accusations of moral inconsistency if the decisions were taken on consequentialist grounds; it would be less so if the decision were a deontological one.

Your professional ethical code of practice requires you to act based on evidence. So it is your responsibility to find out as much as you possibly can about the company under consideration. It may be ethical to decline a corporate partnership once you have thoroughly researched the issues at hand; it is most definitely not ethical to do so because you heard political comedian Mark Thomas bad-mouthing the company on his television programme. (I once heard a fundraiser cite the Mark Thomas Comedy Product as the source for her information on one controversial company.)

Are you an ethicist (and would it matter if you were)?

To put it bluntly, what makes you think you are qualified to pronounce on ethical issues? Have you studied philosophy at university? Do you have a layman's grasp of ethical theory?

Let's say, for argument's sake, that you are an expert in ethics and can show in your considered opinion that accepting a donation would be wrong on deontological grounds. The point would be that just because you are a corporate fundraiser (and are knowledgeable about ethical theory) doesn't mean that you *should* make personal ethical decisions about corporate fundraising.

Take a comparison with the medical profession. A surgeon may be qualified to perform an operation to separate conjoined twins, during which one is certain to die. But this practical ability doesn't qualify him to decide whether or not he *should* carry out this operation. And as we have seen with the disability/tobacco company example, just because someone is professionally qualified to advise on the risks of taking a particular decision does not mean they should unduly influence the making of that decision.

If you feel you are in a personal or professional moral dichotomy, then begin to resolve it by understanding a little more about the theory and practice of ethics, especially the distinction between consequentialist and deontological codes.

It's not about you: 1

Moral values are not determined by public vote. If there are deontological moral values, they are not arrived at by majority decision. If they were, it would be ethically correct to execute murderers and shoot burglars in this country. All ethical theory recognises this and attempts to separate ethical decision-making from personal opinion.

As we have already seen, the Institute of Fundraising's code on acceptance and refusal of donations makes this perfectly clear. Yet there has been talk in the charity sector of canvassing staff opinions on whether or not to accept corporate support. A few years ago, after a staff vote, a face-to-face fundraising agency rejected an offer to work for a charity that held a share portfolio with a defence company. All that decision shows is the personal moral preferences of its staff: it contributes nothing to whether it is morally acceptable for charities to hold shares in companies that make weapons.

It should be clear, after the preceding discussion, that in no way could a decision to reject a donation arrived at by staff vote be seen as ethical. It might be based on the sum of the personal moral values of its staff, but the final decision would be unethical because:

• there would be no *evidence* that the decision would be in the best interest of the charity;

• staff would be unlikely to have had sufficient knowledge of the company or of ethical theory to have made an informed choice;

• the act would contravene the Institute of Fundraising code of practice (*The Acceptance and Refusal of Donations*) in that it was swayed by personal opinion.

How do you resolve this quandary? You have three choices:

1. Resign out of moral principle.

2. Subordinate your personal moral values to your consequentialist code of practice and carry on with your job.

3. Lobby for the charity to change its position or lobby for a change in the codes of practice. We will return to this third option in a moment.

Best interest of the charity

What does 'best interest' actually mean? And what constitutes the 'charity' in this regard? Is it the staff, the corporate entity, the cause, the assets, the beneficiaries, or the services it provides?

The law is extremely unsatisfying in this respect. Investigations launched under section 8 of the 1993 Charities Act have intended to safeguard a charity's 'property' (i.e. its tangible assets) rather than have regard to its human capital (its beneficiaries, services and staff) (Legislation.gov.uk 1993). The 2006 Charities Act left this unchanged (Legislation.gov.uk 2006).

This notwithstanding, the 'best interest of the charity' is vague enough to allow sophisticated argument (or maybe rhetoric?) to justify any course of action – even rejecting a million pounds – as 'in the best interest of the charity'.

But consider this . . .

It's not about you: 2

As a fundraiser, your overriding ethical duty is to your beneficiaries. Faced with a difficult ethical choice over an offer of corporate support, what would your beneficiaries want you to do? Would they thank you for refusing £1 million from a defence company?

If you are able, ask them, as this will contribute to your evidence base. Beneficiaries are the most important yet most disenfranchised stakeholders in charities. No one speaks for the beneficiary group in matters such as this: only they can tell you how it would affect them. In other words, it is your responsibility to respect the dignity of your beneficiaries.

If then you know or you believe that your beneficiary group would want you to accept an offer of support, and if you reject it (without there being extremely good reason from your risk analyses, research, etc.), you are putting your own personal morality before your duty to your beneficiaries. Should your beneficiaries bear the consequences of your satisfying your own conscience?

But, you might ask: why, if moral values are not determined by public vote, can I not use my beneficiaries' views as a vote? The answer is that it is not a vote; it's evidence gathering. These are the people for whom your charity exists, and so if you are going to alienate these people by either accepting or rejecting a donation from any given company, then you can demonstrate a strong case that accepting (or rejecting) that support is in the best interest of the charity's core stakeholder group. In this way, your charity is not being purely governed by its beneficiaries' views, but it is taking into account an important viewpoint that matters in a way that your views, and the views of your charity's donors and staff, do not.

The third option we touched on above to resolve a personal moral quandary is to lobby for the charity to change its position or lobby for a change in the codes of practice. Of course, unethical practices can be enshrined in law (slavery, for instance), which are then every ethical person's duty to change. But there are always extremely strong deontological reasons for effecting a change and usually very good consequentialist ones too.

However, as there is no clear evidence to suggest that either Charity Commission guidance or the Institute of Fundraising code of practice on the acceptance and refusal of donations is ethically unsatisfactory, there are no ethical grounds to lobby for change.

This third option is therefore an ethical non-starter. A corporate fundraiser facing this choice should either resign or subordinate their personal morality, but should not try to adapt the corporate fundraising environment to accommodate that personal morality.

Marilyn Fischer, American author of *Ethical Decision Making in Fund Raising*, says that an ethical decision-making process in fundraising must contain three 'basic value commitments' (Fischer 2000, p. 21):

1. The organizational mission that directs the work.

2. Relationships with people with whom fundraisers interact.

3. A sense of *personal integrity* [my italics].

The last of these three value commitments needs to be considered very seriously. 'Personal integrity' in the context in which Fischer uses it relates to how a fundraiser should act in their role, in the context of their charity's fundraising activities. It is not a green light to impose your values on the charity you work for. If your personal integrity is irrevocably compromised by working for a charity, you should resign.

Professor Hugh La Follette, an ethicist at East Tennessee State University, says:

> We must scrutinise our beliefs, our choices, and our actions to ensure that we a) are sufficiently informed, b) are not unduly swayed by personal interest and c) are not governed by the views of others. Otherwise we may perpetrate evils we could avoid, evils for which future generations will rightly condemn us.
>
> La Follette 1997, pp. 4–5

Conclusion

The adaptation of La Follette's words provides an appropriate way to conclude this chapter:

Otherwise we may reject donations we should have accepted, actions for which our beneficiaries will rightly condemn us.

References

Charity Commission (2009), *The Essential Trustee*, CC3, Liverpool, Crown copyright

Fischer, Marilyn (2000), *Ethical Decision Making in Fund Raising*, New York, John Wiley and Sons

IoF (2006), *The Acceptance and Refusal of Donations Code of Fundraising Practice*, London, Institute of Fundraising

IoF (2002), *Charities Working with Business*, London, Institute of Fundraising

La Follette, Hugh (1997), *Ethics in Practice*, London, Blackwell

Legislation.gov.uk (1993), Charities Act 1993, London, HMSO

Legislation.gov.uk (2006), Charities Act 2006, London, HMSO

Further reading

Anderson, Albert (1996), *Ethics for Fundraisers*, Bloomington, Indiana University Press

Charity Commission (2010), *Charities and Fundraising*, CC20, London, HMSO

Hare, RM (1986), 'What is Wrong with Slavery', in Peter Singer, *Applied Ethics*, Oxford, Oxford University Press

Markkula Center for Applied Ethics (2009), 'A Framework for Thinking Ethically' [web page], www.scu.edu, Santa Clara University, accessed 4 November 2011

CHAPTER SEVEN

Measuring social impact

Alison Braybrooks

Introduction

This chapter gives an overview of measuring social impact. The landscape is changing rapidly, with companies increasingly managing their own impacts alongside their more traditional community investment activity. Voluntary sector organisations need to be aware of this, and the reporting requirements on companies, so that they can work strategically with their corporate partners to maximise the impact of their partnership.

Measuring social impact: a new landscape

Companies have developed increasingly sophisticated approaches to managing and measuring their impact on the environment. For example, if you gave a leading chief executive two minutes to tell you about their company's record on the environment, they would probably give you some insightful statistics on water, carbon and waste management that would let you know that the company is making progress and is focused on the issues that matter.

Now ask them about their company's impact on society and you will probably still get its donations budget and the number of employees who volunteer, not the interesting and relevant information on the difference it has made to its local communities, or how it has been part of solving a big social problem.

Research by the Global Reporting Initiative (GRI) supports this view. It found that companies very rarely report negative social impacts, and don't set and track progress against social impact targets (GRI 2008, p. 4).

But all this is set to change, led by the United Nations and sparked by the actions of some global businesses. There is an emerging trend for companies to identify their key impacts on society and report regularly on how they are tackling them using a multi-stakeholder approach.

Here is an example to illustrate this development:

SABMiller's contribution to tackling HIV/AIDS

SABMiller plc Sustainable Development Report 2010 names tackling HIV/AIDS as one of the company's ten sustainability priorities:

> The joint United Nations Programme on HIV/Aids estimates that 33.4 million people are living with HIV across the world, based on latest published figures. Of these, 22 million live and work in sub-Saharan Africa. Aside from the social and moral imperative to take action, our extensive presence in affected countries makes it commercially important that we take steps to address the issue.
>
> HIV/Aids has the potential to affect our workforce, erode the disposable income of our consumers, damage the supply of raw materials as farmers become unable to tend their crops and ultimately weaken the economic development and stability of communities in which we operate. The extent and consequences of the HIV/Aids pandemic make managing the issue an operational priority.
>
> Our goal is to reduce the impact of HIV/Aids through our spheres of influence, namely our employees and their families, our supply chain and the communities in which we operate.
>
> SABMiller 2010, p. 28

The company identifies its sphere of influence on this issue as its supply chain and local communities, and its employees and their families. The programme started with the company's employees, but as it has grown and developed, it also now operates in the wider community.

The programme includes education programmes, access to treatment and care and testing for all those within this sphere. These are all proven techniques for helping to reduce the incidences of HIV/AIDS in the population.

SABMiller and its partners also set targets for the take-up and effectiveness of their programmes and regularly track the impact.

The company is expanding its approach to include more aspects of human rights and, to kick off this process, has produced a study in partnership with Oxfam and the Coca-Cola Company on potential human rights issues in the companies' value chains (Oxfam et al. 2011).[1]

Which new global standards for tracking social impact are influencing this change?

One of the key issues facing companies as they try to track the social impact of their programmes is the lack of global frameworks to put their activity into context (as opposed to the focus of older models on the tracking of inputs, outputs and impacts). However, this is changing as various global initiatives have emerged in the last couple of years.

Guiding Principles for Business and Human Rights

The first and most important of these is the endorsement of the United Nations Human Rights Council in June 2011 of a new set of Guiding Principles for Business and Human Rights. These guiding principles are designed to provide for the first time a global standard for preventing and addressing the risk of adverse impacts on human rights linked to business.

The principles provide a blueprint for companies on how to understand and demonstrate that they are respecting human rights in their local communities, through their value chains, with their employees and with their customers. The Organisation for Economic Co-operation and Development has also endorsed these guidelines, thereby strengthening and supporting the work of the United Nations.

While companies do not report to the United Nations using these guidelines, they are used by other organisations such as the Global Reporting Initiative to set their own guideline standards to which companies do report.

Global Reporting Initiative guidance

At the same time, there has been new guidance from the GRI – the G3.1 Guidelines, launched in March 2011 – on reporting social impacts including human rights. The GRI is a network-based organisation that produces a comprehensive sustainability reporting framework that is widely used by companies around the world. The number and variety of stakeholders from across the world involved in agreeing the GRI reporting standard, including companies, non-governmental organisations and labour organisations, makes it very important to most companies that they describe their community and social impact activity to meet GRI guideline standards.

It was GRI's research that found that the social impact reports of the leading companies differed from their environmental reporting. Rather than having clear sections and specific goals, the reports they researched often:

• grouped community activities together rather than outlining specific areas of focus;

• used lots of case studies, but had no common method of what to include;

• made very little reference to policies and goals;

• showed that companies were not able to define their community impacts.

GRI 2008, p. 4

In response to this, GRI developed the G3.1 Guidelines to lay out what it expects companies to report on and to give them detailed support on what indicators to use.

The guidance recommends that companies report on their organisation-wide local community engagement, impact assessment and community development programmes based on local need. It defines community development programmes as plans that detail actions to minimise, mitigate and compensate for adverse social and economic impacts, and to identify opportunities and actions to enhance positive impacts of the project on the community. The guidance asks for evidence such as baseline studies to support the reporting. In addition, GRI asks for traditional community investment data based on the LBG model.[2]

GRI also has a Sustainability Disclosure Database (database.global reporting.org) where users can see all the sustainability information that organisations have disclosed and compare how transparent companies have been in their reporting.

Corporate responsibility ratings agencies

Where the GRI leads others often follow; hence there is a renewed focus on reporting social impact from the major corporate responsibility ratings agencies such as the Dow Jones Sustainability Index and FTSE4Good.

The Dow Jones Sustainability Index website states:

Launched in 1999, the Dow Jones Sustainability Indexes are the first global indexes tracking the financial performance of the leading sustainability-driven companies worldwide. [They are] based on the cooperation of Dow Jones Indexes and SAM.

DJSI 2011

With both these ratings agencies, if companies fall foul of any of the standards in the criteria, they are taken off the rankings list. The FTSE website states:

Criteria are developed using an extensive market consultation process and are approved by an independent committee of experts. A broad range of stakeholders help shape the criteria, including NGOs, governmental bodies, consultants, academics, the investment community and the corporate sector.

To remain consistent with market expectations and developments in CSR practice, the inclusion criteria are revised regularly. Since launch this has included tougher environmental and human rights criteria as well as new supply chain labour standards and countering bribery requirements. FTSE then engages with companies to ensure that they understand the new requirements. Companies that do not meet the standards are deleted from the index series.

FTSE 2008

This increased pressure from global raters, GRI and the United Nations means that companies have to start to report the impact of their activities and their community programmes if they want to maintain their place in these key rankings, or report to the influential GRI standards.

Standards for measuring community impact

The LBG model

LBG remains the global standard for measuring traditional voluntary charitable giving. This model of inputs, outputs and impacts enables companies to assess their contributions to the community and aggregate the impact of their programmes using a clear and tested framework.

With the new focus on impact, why is tracking inputs – the what, where, why and who – still so important?

• Understanding where a company is investing in the community is a key part of the information it needs in order to set its broader strategy.

• Understanding how a company's giving is balanced between cash, volunteering time and in-kind giving can give a pretty clear understanding of how embedded the programme is in its business. The proportion of in-kind and time contributions, compared to simple donations, indicates whether the programme is aligned with the core activities of the business, and utilises the skills of the employees.

• Understanding where a company's programme operates enables managers to see if its community programme is reflected in its global footprint, and not just active in the company's traditional heartlands.

• Knowing why the company is giving helps it to understand the proportion given in simple philanthropic donations and which donations are given as part of a business strategy. And, similarly, the causes it supports give a clear understanding of whether the programme is aligned with the business.

The LBG model also allows companies to track leverage – the amount that their support has enabled their community partners to secure from other sources (employee fundraising being the classic source) – and it has now developed a comprehensive approach to tracking impact. Rather than taking a project-by-project approach it enables companies to aggregate the impacts of all their programmes to enable them to see the total impact.

It is important to emphasise that LBG is not a standard or ranking tool; it is there simply to enable companies to improve the quality of their data reporting. It does not help companies to judge the standard of their community programmes or whether they have chosen the right objectives or strategy.

However, other tools have emerged over the last couple of years that go beyond straightforward measurement and have started to rate companies according to their investment in the community.

CommunityMark

The first of these to emerge was CommunityMark, launched in the UK by Business in the Community in 2007. In order to take part, companies are required to complete the CommunityMark survey, which assesses how a company develops, integrates and manages its community investment across the business.

The survey also assesses the positive difference made in the community and in the business as a result of community projects, partnerships and employee engagement.

The assessment is based on five principles:

1. Identify the social issues that are most relevant to your business and most pressing to the communities you work with.

2. Work in partnership with your communities, leveraging your combined expertise for mutual benefit.

3. Inspire and engage your employees, customers and suppliers to support your community programmes.

4. Plan and manage your community investment using the most appropriate resources to deliver against your targets.

67

5.   Measure and evaluate the difference that your investment has made in the community and on your business. Strive for continual improvement.

Here is a case study of a partnership between Macmillan Cancer Support and Boots, which enabled Boots to achieve CommunityMark status. It demonstrates the depth of the partnership and the strategic fit.

Case study: Macmillan Cancer Support and Boots

Boots UK is working with Macmillan Cancer Support to help provide the two million people living with cancer, and their families and friends, with increased access to the information and support they need – when they need it, where they need it.

As well as the partnership's aim to develop and provide a number of services for people wanting to know more about cancer, Boots UK aims to increase access to and awareness of the services and support Macmillan Cancer Support provides. Boots UK offers invaluable access to a huge number of people through its stores and the millions of customers who visit them each week.

Boots UK and Macmillan Cancer Support will deliver more ways to access information about living with cancer to the high street, in local communities and online. Macmillan Cancer Support has developed training for the 15,000 Boots UK pharmacists, dispensers and healthcare assistants on the issues surrounding cancer. This builds on the specialist training that Boots UK's healthcare colleagues already receive to enable them to offer even more.

Boots UK's No7 consultants use their time and expertise to support Look Good . . . Feel Better beauty workshops for women with cancer, an initiative sponsored by the cosmetic industry. The free sessions take place in hospitals across the UK. Many Boots UK No7 consultants regularly volunteer at these sessions, providing morale-boosting make-overs and advice on skin care and make-up. By the end of 2009/10, workshops were taking place in 59 hospitals, with over 110 Boots UK No7 consultants volunteering. Boots UK also donated over 40,000 No7 products during 2009/10 to support these workshops.

Business in the Community 2011

We can see that although this example is based on simple community investment, CommunityMark does go further in assessing whether companies are tackling the issues that are most relevant to their business and how involved their stakeholders are in this.

The next development reflects better the recent trend of looking at the impact of a company's entire operations on the community.

Community Footprint

Again developed by Business in the Community (with sponsorship from Santander and supported by a working group of eight member companies), Community Footprint enables companies to understand their impact on the communities around them. It defines a company's community footprint and both the positive and negative impacts it makes on the world around it. These impacts result from both what businesses do and the choices they make.

The tool explores the impact of a local business operation from the point of view of employment, products and services, location, supply chain, and community investment. A business's Community Footprint is the sum of all these activities and how it affects the local people, economies and places it works in. The framework that the Community Footprint provides mirrors the GRI guidance (on managing a relationship with local communities) by assessing what difference companies make (both positive and negative), identifying local need, matching business strengths to community needs to help companies take action, and suggesting how to measure impact.

A framework for measuring the impact on companies

The trend of measuring the impact of community programmes on businesses is a new development. There is very little out there to help companies measure the impact on things like brand and reputation, but an important recent study and the resulting report, *Volunteering – The Business Case* (sponsored by the City of London and based on the LBG model), demonstrates the business case for volunteering, and also gives some useful tools to help measure the impact (Corporate Citizenship 2010).

It gives a thorough overview of the competencies that can be developed by different kinds of volunteering such as communication, problem-solving and leadership skills, and also provides some useful template questionnaires for companies and their charity partners to use.

Measuring the impact on the charity partner

The LBG model gives helpful guidance on measuring the impact on the charity. There are no specific template questionnaires available, but it gives some impact indicators (such as ability to provide more services) that can guide your thinking when measuring the overall impact of a corporate–charity partnership.

69

FIGURE 7.1 BUSINESS IN THE COMMUNITY'S COMMUNITY FOOTPRINT

Business in the **Community**

stands for responsible business

Community Footprint: the impact you have by being there and how you choose to run your business

Business in the Community offers an easy-to-use series of practical tools allowing managers to understand the Community Footprint their business has on the local people, economies and places they work in. It assesses what they do, matches business strengths to community needs to help companies take action, and suggests how to measure impact. By collecting information locally and taking site-specific actions businesses can better assess the social and economic contribution they make regionally, nationally and internationally and the role they play in making a community thrive.

To find out more go to www.bitc.org.uk

What is out there to help companies *and* their charity partners to measure impact?

All the models outlined in this chapter help companies to understand where they can have a positive or negative impact on the community, and what to include in a report on the difference that they are making. However, how might they work directly with their charity partners to assess their actual impact?

On measuring community impact there is a plethora of models, techniques and support available. The basis for many of the current measurement techniques is a planning triangle, developed by the Charities Evaluation Service, which helps organisations to understand their aims and objectives and communicate these clearly to funders.

Big Lottery Fund guidance

The Big Lottery Fund (BIG) has good guidance on measuring outcomes (based on the Charities Evaluation Service planning triangle) and relates specifically to the projects that it funds. It could, however, also be used by any corporate–community partnership to assess its impact.

BIG defines outcomes as the changes that will happen as a result of the project. It assesses how outcomes are meeting an identified need, what difference the project will make and for whom it will make a difference. It asks applicants to describe their SMART – that is, specific, measurable, achievable, realistic and time-based – objectives for each project. This means that BIG looks for dates and numbers as well as who the project plans to support and what the planned activity is.

BIG gives examples of SMART outcomes:

By the end of the project, 300 young people demonstrate improved social skills, self-confidence and motivation as a result of their involvement in the organisation of arts events.

The involvement of 100 residents in regular recycling and environmental activities will result in refurbished green spaces and stronger community links by the end of the project's first year.

25 local families with autistic children report reduced stress as a result of respite opportunities by the end of the second year.

Big Lottery Fund n.d., p. 1

The Social Return on Investment model

The Social Return on Investment (SROI) model builds on this approach by enabling monetary values to be assigned to the outcomes of specific projects or activities.

The SROI Network defines SROI as an approach to understanding and managing the value of the social, economic and environmental outcomes created by an activity or an organisation. It is based on seven principles that are applied within a framework. These principles are as follows:

1. Involve stakeholders
   Understand the way in which the organisation creates change through a dialogue with stakeholders

2. Understand what changes
   Acknowledge and articulate all the values, objectives and stakeholders of the organisation before agreeing which aspects of the organisation are to be included in the scope; and determine what must be included in the account in order that stakeholders can make reasonable decisions

3. Value the things that matter
   Use financial proxies for indicators in order to include the values of those excluded from markets on the same terms as used in markets

4. Only include what is material
   Articulate clearly how activities create change and evaluate this through the evidence gathered

5. Do not over-claim
   Make comparisons of performance and impact using appropriate benchmarks, targets and external standards

6. Be transparent
   Demonstrate the basis on which the findings may be considered accurate and honest; and show that they will be reported to and discussed with stakeholders

7. Verify the result
   Ensure appropriate independent verification of the account
   The SROI Network n.d.

The model is very closely aligned with the LBG model in the sense that it looks at inputs, outputs and impact. Although the technique is implicit in the LBG model, the SROI model is specific about stripping out which impacts are attributable to the project.

There are also some excellent web-based tools such as CRedit 360 (www.credit360.com) and LeapCR (leapcr.com) that help companies and community partners track impact, donations and employee engagement.

Summary

This chapter aimed to give the reader an overview of the context in which companies are operating, how their social impact programmes are feeding into the overall reporting of their community strategies, the tools that companies can use to assess their impact, and a small selection of the tools that are out there to help charities and companies to measure their impact.

Notes

1   This report was released on 29 March 2011 (Oxfam America, Coca-Cola Company and SABMiller 2011). *Exploring the Links Between International Business and Poverty Reduction: The Coca-Cola/SABMiller Value Chain Impacts in Zambia and El Salvador.*

2   'LBG started life as the London Benchmarking Group as it was formed by six London-based companies. Now it represents the international standard for corporate community investment and is known simply as LBG' (LBG 2011, p. 2).

References

Big Lottery Fund (n.d.), *Outcomes Factsheet* [online document], www.biglotteryfund. org.uk, accessed 8 November 2011

Business in the Community (2011), 'Boots UK' [web page], bitc.org.uk, accessed 8 November 2011

Corporate Citizenship (2010), *Volunteering – The Business Case: The Benefits of Corporate Volunteering Programmes in Education*, London

DJSI (2011), 'Dow Jones Sustainability Indexes' [web page], www.sustainability-index.com, Dow Jones Sustainability Indexes in collaboration with SAM, accessed 8 February 2012

FTSE (2008), *Factsheet: Ftse4good Index Series*, London, FTSE International Limited

GRI (2008), *Reporting on Community Impacts: A Survey Conducted by the Global Reporting Initiative, the University of Hong Kong and CSR Asia*, Amsterdam, Global Reporting Initiative

GRI (2011), *Sustainability Reporting Guidelines: Version 3.1*, Amsterdam, Global Reporting Initiative

LBG (2011), *LBG: Measuring Corporate Community Investment, 2011 Annual Review*, London, Corporate Citizenship

Oxfam America, Coca-Cola Company and SABMiller (2011), *Exploring the Links Between International Business and Poverty Reduction: the Coca-Cola/SABMiller Value Chain Impacts in Zambia and El Salvador.*

SABMiller (2010), *SABMiller plc Sustainable Development Report 2010*, London

SROI (n.d.), 'What is Social Return on Investment (SROI)'? [web page], www.the sroinetwork.org, accessed 8 February 2012

CHAPTER EIGHT

The role of research and generating new business

Rachel Billsberry-Grass and Mathew Iredale

Introduction

Corporate research is valuable at three stages of the corporate fundraising process:

1. The strategic planning process

Every strategy requires a research phase, which includes a SWOT (strength, weakness, opportunity and threats) and PEST (political, economic, social and technological) analysis and competitor analysis. Both academic research and market research reports can be beneficial at this stage (see Appendix 5 for potential sources).

2. Identifying leads for new business

Successful corporate fundraising relies upon a constant supply of new leads. As the corporate environment changes so rapidly, research is vital to identifying leads which are appropriate for a specific charity.

3. Corporate prospect research

Once a lead has been identified some research will be undertaken to enable the fundraiser to understand the company and its objectives before making an approach. If the relationship moves to the stage of a pitch or proposal research can support their production.

This chapter explains the research process for new business through identifying leads and prospect research.

Generating leads

Prospects which have some connection, however small, with the charity should be identified first, as they will have a higher chance than cold prospects of reaping rewards. These may include past supporters, suppliers, companies where there is a personal connection with charity stakeholders (such as staff or trustees) and companies whose staff have supported the charity in some way. Research at this stage may include techniques ranging from sending emails to staff inviting them to forward leads to rifling through filing cabinets or databases for contacts which could result in useful leads. Any charity which aspires to be successful in corporate fundraising will need to develop new business proactively. As with any business activity, it is vital to generate a pipeline of good prospects: it can be too easy for a corporate fundraiser to become consumed by a current fixed-term partnership at the cost of building new business to replace it.

There are several options for how to approach new business development, each of which is applicable to any charity, whatever its size. The segments outlined in the following sub-sections could be divided between team members or, in a smaller charity, could be timetabled across the year.

By sector

New business approaches are often segmented by industry sector. By putting concentrated resources into one industry, the charity will benefit by achieving a greater understanding of the industry's motivations, discovering the commonalities that can be used in approaches and thus saving time in developing brand new approaches. If the charity is investing heavily in a particular sector, it can gain advantages by recruiting a corporate fundraiser who has experience in this area.

There are notable cases of an industry getting behind one cause, such as Fashion Targets Breast Cancer, but it should be noted that there are many industries where a company will seek exclusivity in its relationship with the charity. The company may understandably not want to dilute its own impact by being seen alongside a competitor. Therefore segmenting by industry sector might be limiting in the short term, once a success has been achieved. For example, a major charity partner of one of the leading supermarkets may find it difficult to even begin a dialogue with another supermarket until the current partnership has ended.

By geography

For local or regional charities, or national charities with a strong regional project or presence, it makes most sense to segment approaches into companies which are in a particular geographical area. They are the ones most likely to relate to the charity or project and want to support it. Many companies will seek out local charities and projects that are providing services in areas where their staff and customers live and work.

By company size

There will be a difference in the way in which a charity approaches a prospect that is potentially worth £1 million to the charity, from one that is worth £1,000, so a charity should segment its prospects by company size. In large charities with both a national function and a regional network, it is common for the central office team to take responsibility for the FTSE 100 or 250 companies, with regional staff or volunteers focusing on any company outside this list which is in their locality. While this provides a reasonable framework, a regional company can easily become a very significant partner which requires input from the central team, so flexibility within this structure should be encouraged.

By corporate fundraising function

As corporate fundraising diversifies, so too do the skills that are needed to win particular types of business. A fundraiser with commercial marketing experience is more likely to have the relevant skills for winning cause-related marketing or sponsorship deals. A fundraiser with some human resources knowledge may be able to talk more convincingly about the benefits of staff fundraising. For this reason, some charities will segment their new business by fundraising function, focusing on bringing in particular types of partnership. The potential drawback to this arrangement is when similar industries or types of company are the best prospects for two or more areas: it can be difficult to decide which approach will have the most potential for success at the highest level and therefore which fundraiser should make the approach. By encouraging shared information and keeping good records, the charity can easily deal with any debate within the team and good research will help to indicate the best way forward.

Whichever route is chosen, it is important to avoid the trap of research for research's sake. Leads are only valuable if there is some link to or potential connection with the charity. It is easy to create a list of 100 well-researched prospects which the fundraiser would simply not have time to approach. However, some information gained through reading an appropriate publication – *PR Week*, *Marketing Week* or a local newspaper for example – or by meeting a corporate executive at a networking event could have a greater chance of leading to success. Balancing research with opportunities is the solution.

Corporate prospect research

There are a number of different reasons for carrying out research into prospective company supporters.

- To establish the company's policy on charity support.

- To determine the different ways in which the company can support you.

- To establish how supporting your charity will benefit the company.

- To enable you to plan the right route into a company.

- To ensure that you are not approaching the wrong company.

It is important for those embarking on research to appreciate that some companies are far easier to research than others. Public limited companies, for example, are required by law to file detailed accounts with Companies House – they *have* to make specific information publicly available – and many exceed this requirement, to be attractive to investors. By contrast, exemptions from filing mean that only 1 in 8 of actively trading private companies file accounts at Companies House and so the information that is available on such companies will be far more variable. It may be very good in the case of some high-profile companies, or it may be non-existent. It is important not to spend hours trying to find information on a company which the company is not required to make public and has decided not to do so.

An increasing number of companies have one or more pages of their websites devoted to charitable giving, often as one part of a larger Corporate Responsibility section, and these provide much or all of the information needed such as point of contact, how to apply, previous recipients, amount of money raised and different fundraising activities. They may also provide valuable information about their previous charity partnerships. Many charities also list the companies with which they work, so some competitor analysis is helpful.

Search engines such as Google, Yahoo and Bing are obvious but invaluable. A search for the company in question with one of the following phrases or words – charity of the year, charitable, fundraising, corporate responsibility – should produce useful information. If you want to search for an exact phrase (such as charity of the year), then many search engines require you to put the phrase in double quotes: "charity of the year". For Google, the situation is slightly more complicated, as you need to put double quote marks around each word or exact phrase that you wish Google to find (for example, "tesco" "charity of the year" rather than tesco "charity of the year"). Words that are not in double quotes may be ignored by Google, which could seriously affect your search results.

A search of local and national news archives, such as Lexis Nexis, Factiva and NewsUK can provide other information about a company's charitable activities. Local newspapers are especially likely to report a company's charitable activities as this is good publicity for the company and the charity and makes for the sort of feel-good community story that local newspapers love to publish.

An often overlooked route is carrying out a personal check on a company. For some companies this is straightforward – supermarkets, banks, DIY stores or fashion retailers, for example. A visit can give a very good idea of who they are supporting and how. Other employers without a retail presence, or head offices of retailers, can be researched by simply observing the offices (one advantage of the many coffee shops these days) or by calling in to the reception.

Finally, don't forget to use the telephone. One phone call to a company may prove more useful than several hours on the internet. Appendix 5 suggests a range of research sources for corporate fundraising.

There is some specific information that a corporate fundraiser should know about the company:

• Does it have giving criteria?

• How does it give?

• How much does it give?

• Which charities has it supported in the past?

• Does it have plans for the future?

• What does it expect of the charities it supports?

• What benefits does it require or prefer?

• How is the decision made as to which charity is supported?

• Who makes the decision and is there any personal information that can be gathered about this person?

While it may be tempting to capture every possible detail about a company, it is important to bear in mind whether the information will actually be used and therefore the cost-effectiveness of research time. A company's turnover, for example, is often unnecessary information as it rarely in itself influences decisions.

Managing the research process

A key decision that needs to be made about research is whether it is carried out by the fundraiser, a specialist in-house researcher or a prospect research agency. There are advantages and disadvantages to each option and in many cases a charity will choose a combination of the three. There are some key points to consider:

• A specialist researcher needs to understand the corporate fundraising process in order to help spot leads and to decide what information is valuable. The role is far more than simply finding out specific information.

• Fundraisers should appreciate that even if there is a research function (internal or external), it is still a key part of their role to be spotting opportunities and absorbing information throughout their working day and outside work. Fundraisers are also consumers and can often come across information in the course of their lives which would not come up readily in an internet search.

• An advantage of using an agency is that identification of prospects can be the most time-consuming aspect of a fundraiser's work. Asking an agency to provide a list of company prospects or to carry out a database screening to identify individuals with a connection to a company, will enable a fundraising campaign to advance more quickly than if the identification is carried out in-house. Another advantage is that many agencies have years of experience of working with both large and small charities and so can offer valuable advice with regard to identifying and researching companies.

• The relative costs of the range of research routes should be considered. Using an agency or appointing an internal researcher comes at a cost but it should be seen as an investment. Clear monitoring and evaluation of whichever route is selected will make sure the investment is appropriate.

Developing new business

To achieve the greatest success in corporate fundraising, new business development needs to be approached strategically but with the flexibility to respond to new opportunities that arise.

It is sensible to avoid a shotgun approach to new business development as it will be difficult to manage, monitor and draw any reasonable conclusions to inform future new business work, it creates a less than positive impression of the charity among the companies approached and it increases the risk of a company receiving several approaches from different people within the charity.

There are two aspects to developing new business. The first is about identifying prospective companies through research and then approaching those targeted companies proactively. The second involves ensuring that the charity and in particular its partnerships with companies have a high profile, so that companies seeking partners actively select the charity. This is a particularly important message for small charities where local profile can be the key to winning corporate support. Help for Heroes, which is relatively young, demonstrates this: capturing the zeitgeist, mobilising mass support and generating huge volumes of media coverage have made the charity an obvious choice for corporate partnerships.

The key is simple, easy-to-understand messaging which is compelling to the mass market. Help for Heroes is clear, unambiguous and relevant to daily news reports.

Many charities use related news articles about their cause to raise the profile of their work: advances in medical research or increases in the number of incidences will provide a platform for many charities for specific types of cancer, and the ageing population and the impact of dementia and Alzheimer's have ensured that charities working in this field are now much better known than they were a few years ago. Corporate fundraisers will have more potential for success if they can coordinate corporate approaches at a time when the charity is achieving reasonable press coverage.

Companies may also be keen to speak to charities that they perceive as able to provide them with a level of expertise which is of commercial benefit, such as advice on environmental reporting or the implementation of specific discrimination legislation.

Making the approach

Having identified prospective companies, it is vital that the charity is able to articulate a compelling case for support that addresses what the charity wants and what it can offer to the company. This should include a specific 'ask' and an outline of the benefits that a company could obtain.

The charity needs to determine any method it can possibly use to reach a company that avoids the need to resort to a cold approach. It should look for existing charity supporters who work for the target company and ask for an introduction to the relevant contacts. Current corporate supporters may also be willing to recommend the charity to their own business contacts and set up meetings or invite their contacts to the charity's special events. All approaches to companies should be bespoke. It is very rare for any company to respond to mass-marketing appeals or letters which are clearly mail merged.

There are mixed views about whether a charity should invest in corporate hospitality to engage prospects. Invitations to special or exclusive events are often hard for an individual to ignore, but could be counter-productive if the company perceives that the charity is spending too much money. It is worthwhile using contacts to access free experiences that are not usually available on the open market, such as lunch at the House of Lords. These do need to be targeted well: a front-row seat at London Fashion Week will be more attractive to some than lunch at the House of

Lords. The charity could also invite prospects to a project visit but should accept that not all corporate personnel feel comfortable in that setting.

Cold invitations to bigger events at which companies can network and listen to an interesting host or speaker will generate much lower response rates but, if a low-cost invitation is possible, may produce a handful of useful contacts that can be developed.

There is certainly no 'one-size-fits-all' in corporate fundraising and different approaches will be appropriate for a particular charity or company. Whichever approach is chosen, it is important that the decision about who will lead or front it is taken pragmatically. New business is about results and the person from the charity who leads the approach needs to be the one who the company will most relate to or be impressed by.

Case study

Dreams Come True is a national charity which aims to bring joy to children with terminal and serious illnesses by fulfilling their most precious dreams. The cause has wide appeal and much of the charity's corporate support comes through employee fundraising, where individuals can be really motivated by the human interest stories behind Dreams Come True's work.

Although the charity invests in well-prepared and targeted approaches to potential corporate partners, it also believes that it is important to respond to opportunities as they are presented. For example, a relationship with healthcare provider Simplyhealth began with a substantial donation in 2006. Since then the charity has enjoyed significant support from the company.

So while this initial donation was unexpected, the charity developed the relationship with Simplyhealth to get a better understanding of what motivated the company to donate. Dreams Come True also undertook thorough desk and informal research, finding out about the other charities the company supported, the average and maximum donations it made and the projects that it had funded.

As a result, the charity recognised that the company's interest in Dreams Come True stemmed from the fact that as a healthcare company it is highly motivated to make a difference to people. Simplyhealth's particular interest in Dreams Come True was very much about the stories of the individual children they were able to help: stories that the company could publish, with photos, in its staff magazine to enable its workforce to engage with the charity and support the donation.

The charity also identified that in the past Simplyhealth had given substantial donations to charities for specific projects. Dreams Come True used this information in subsequent years and was successful in its applications to the company to donate significantly larger sums to support a major annual project involving a dozen or so children.

Summary

In summary, it is important to integrate corporate research into the stages of your corporate fundraising process. Do not be overly devoted to current partnerships at the expense of generating leads and developing new business proactively. Make sure that you organise the different approaches to new business development and divide them between team members or across the year. To develop new business, do the appropriate research and ensure that your charity's profile is high enough for a company to actively choose it. Finally, ensure that the most appropriate person and angle are chosen when making the approach.

CHAPTER NINE

The road to yes: successful pitching and negotiation

Alice Jackson

Introduction

This chapter explores the art of pitching to a company including: what it expects to see; what to consider before, during and after the pitch; and how to negotiate with a company in those final, closing stages.

Pitching: today's context

With increased competition in the charity sector and companies becoming more aware of what they are looking for in a charity partner, pitching to secure a partnership is becoming increasingly important. A company wants to know that a charity will fit its criteria, that the team it will be working with is professional and that it will deliver on commitments. For a company, a pitch is a good opportunity for it to get a sense of how a charity does business and how the cause will motivate staff (and customers); it is also a chance for the members of the pitch panel to see the people they will be working with. As with most sales interactions, the people in the pitch team can be as important as the presentation content, and in some cases more so.

Many companies have well-established Charity of the Year partnerships and they are often very process-led, one stage of which can be a pitch or formal opportunity to present. At this point, successful charities are likely to have been shortlisted and should have a solid understanding from the company about what areas to cover. Increasingly, however, companies are working with charities in a more commercial way through activities such as sponsorship and cause-related marketing. These partnerships are not usually based on a philanthropic desire and can often have little to do with the corporate responsibility or community affairs divisions within a company. They are commercial activities and as such a fee (cash or otherwise) is given in return for benefits. Charity–corporate pitches can therefore now include sales people, marketeers or brand managers, or be solely delivered to them. Presenting the charity's cause as worthy and in need of their support might not work; in this instance their criteria and objectives are likely to be very different.

With all this in mind, today's corporate fundraiser needs to be assured and commercial in their approach, and versatile in their delivery style.

How to pitch: things to consider

Pitching to a prospective partner is often cited anecdotally as the aspect of a corporate fundraiser's role that they feel least confident about. Fear over presenting ability and the post-pitch question-and-answer session can sometimes leave fundraisers feeling nervous. A pitch provides a great opportunity for each party to demonstrate what a partnership with the other organisation could look and feel like. Much like a product demonstration in a store, a pitch can be seen as an opportunity to 'try before you buy'.

Before the pitch

The audience

It is important to know who will be in the pitch panel and this should be undertaken as early on as possible. It can make a big difference to the pitch structure, team and style. Working with other fundraising teams will determine if any members of the panel are supporters of the charity already or have been in the past. A personal link to the cause could be an advantage and it is best to know about that in advance. If the panel consists of cold contacts, researching the panel members' roles can help provide a guide to what information and criteria they will be looking for in the pitch.

Know what the panel is looking for

Understanding what a pitch panel is expecting sounds obvious, but it is crucial. It is best to commit time to this before starting to create the presentation itself. Even the most visually beautiful presentation and the most confident of presenters will be wasted if the prospective corporate partner's criteria are not being addressed.

In order to be well-briefed, any assumptions will need to be clarified and, if necessary, discarded. Making assumptions without checking with the panel can be risky. Without this qualification, time and effort can end up being spent in the wrong places and on the wrong criteria. In today's climate, companies set out increasingly clear criteria and over the years have got better at articulating what it is they are looking for from a charity. More often than not, there will have been a proposal or application stage prior to the invitation to pitch; it is essential to gather as much feedback on this as possible.

There are simple questions that can provide very useful pieces of information. For example: what elements did they like or have concerns over? In which areas are they likely to probe further?

Previous and current charity partners can also hold a wealth of information, and many corporate fundraisers are happy to share their experiences with their peers. Keeping questions targeted is likely to prove more successful at understanding what clinched it for them, rather than asking for an overview.

The pitch team

Be careful to plan who goes into the room and how different people and styles will complement each other, or not. Having built up knowledge of the pitch panel and its criteria should make it easier to select the winning combination of pitch team. Try to think beyond the (corporate) fundraising team. If a specific funding project is needed, perhaps the project owner would be best suited to bring that section to life; if a key driver for the company is recognition, think about a press officer who can demonstrate how they will deliver on this objective.

It can sometimes work to bring in a beneficiary as part of the pitch team, as it provides a more authentic delivery of the charity's cause. However, increasingly companies are looking for those charities that can create a synergy with their business and can help them deliver their objectives. In this instance the cause is therefore not as important as it perhaps once was.

Whoever is involved in the pitch, it should always be the responsibility of the project lead to brief them. Each person should be clear about what their role is and what key messages they need to talk about.

Keep it simple

Having taken the time to provide criteria, the pitch panel will most likely have clear checkboxes that they are looking for the pitch to satisfy. Much like in a job interview, members of the panel will be listening out for key elements, so try to make it as easy as possible for them.

Think about structuring the presentation around their criteria so that they do not have to search for information. Any good presentation needs to be simple and it needs to have a clear structure with good navigation; a charity–corporate pitch is no different. The classic 'tell them what you are going to tell them, tell them, and then tell them what you have just told them' works well to keep people's attention and remind them of the key parts of the pitch.

It is also important to think about what the slides look like: will they complement or detract from what the presenters are saying? Images can work well; particularly as they can often convey a key point well, resulting in fewer words being needed. If there is too much text on show, the panel will read that rather than listen to the presenter.

The competition

Knowing which other charities have been shortlisted can make a big difference to the pitch structure, style and team. If another charity has a bigger claim to some criteria, do not worry.

For example, if its cause affects more of the company's staff already or it has a bigger regional structure to support fundraising, establish the aspects where your charity can compete more evenly and at the same level as these areas of strength, and direct the panel's attention towards these. For example, at a smaller charity the money could go further and the difference the corporate partner's support would make could be bigger.

Similarly, some companies like to be seen as heroes; if a company's support would make it the charity's biggest partner, make sure the panel see that as a good thing and not something to be concerned about.

Practice makes perfect (or at least provides a better chance)

A dry run in front of colleagues is vital to practise the pitch in full; speaking to an empty room is just not the same. A good way to prepare is by providing them with questions to ask you at the end of the rehearsal, the tougher the better, to ensure that there are no surprises on the day. It is much better to flounder in front of your colleagues rather than the prospective corporate partner.

Another aspect to agree before the pitch is who will be answering which questions. It can be embarrassing and look unprofessional if the entire pitch team ends up clambering to answer or follow up each question with additional information.

During the pitch

With the right preparation the pitch itself can be something to enjoy. The focus at this stage is on delivery and there are some key things to consider.

Eye to eye

Everyone knows eye contact is important: it builds rapport and trust, and encourages a level of engagement throughout the pitch. However, it can be over- or badly done which results in an unnatural and often uncomfortable atmosphere.

It can be useful to think about who to focus on at which part of the pitch. For example, who from the panel will most want to hear about public relations? Who needs to be engaged more when the pitch turns to financial information?

Some people prefer to have notes with them, which is fine; just remember to keep eyes up when talking. Think 'load, aim, deliver' – read the notes for a prompt (load), look at who this point is for (aim), then speak (deliver).

Presence

When presenting, in any form, knowing how you come across is very important. It could be good to consider more formal training or practising techniques such as videoing rehearsals. This can feel a little uncomfortable but it is one of the best ways to learn about your presentation style.

Depending on the culture of the company, delivery style is something that may need to be adapted or enhanced. The pitch could be in a very formal environment, so it can be useful to think about what areas, if any, are delivered with more warmth or even a splash of humour. Some pitches are more informal, so it may be appropriate to think about inviting more interaction from the panel.

It is also good to explore how to match body language with that of the panel, although in order to emphasise a point and to keep their attention it can also be useful to think about using appropriate movement and gestures. This can also be achieved through tone, volume and speed of voice, particularly if members of the pitch team have different styles of delivery.

In their shoes

There is no reason why a charity pitch should not be as professional as one that those on the corporate panel would deliver to their clients. Members of the pitch panel will be looking for likeminded people who understand their agenda and objectives. Put yourself in the shoes of those on the corporate panel: how would they deliver a pitch to their clients? In other words, how can the pitch be put across in a similarly commercial way?

Increasingly companies are thinking beyond philanthropic desires and seeing charities as not only useful for staff engagement and positive public relations but also as a way to achieve business objectives. Demonstrating how the charity can do this successfully will pave the way to a longer-term strategic partnership that delivers much more than money.

Technology

Everyone has their horror stories: broken projector, memory stick not working, the video will not play. Despite the best preparation, sometimes technology can fail. It is important to remain calm and remember that this has happened to everyone at some point. It can also provide an insight for the panel into how the team reacts when under pressure.

It is advisable to move on to a back-up plan sooner rather than wasting lots of time embarrassingly fiddling with equipment. Having technical issues can sometimes work to break the ice and build rapport, although purposely creating a problem could be a risky tactic!

After the pitch and beyond

The presentation is over, the follow-up questions have been answered and the pitch is nearing its end. Much like a job interview, it can be good to prepare a couple of questions to ask the panel. It is also good to think about what to leave behind. In a more process-led opportunity, it is likely that the panel will see a shortlist of charities over one or two days, so it is worth making it easy for the panel to remember the key elements of the pitch. In a more commercial setting, the budget holders or other decision-makers may not be present, so this can help the panel to sell the proposition on your behalf.

If at first you don't succeed ... get feedback. It is important to know why a pitch was unsuccessful. Sometimes gleaning useful feedback can be hard. One approach is to ask what it was that the panel liked about the successful pitch(es); this can be easier for panel members to articulate. It is also worth noting that some of the larger Charity of the Year opportunities can take a number of attempts to get right. Again, be sure to ask clear, specific questions and hopefully this will result in some useful advice.

Getting feedback is still important, even in success. This is particularly the case with a Charity of the Year opportunity, as the pitch stage may not be last; there could be a staff vote or canvassing stage next.

It is also worth noting that an unsuccessful pitch is not the end of the road with that particular company. It can lay down the foundations on which to build a relationship, and it can be good to think about other opportunities to explore with the company.

Principles for negotiation

There is a perception that negotiating with companies has not historically been the strength of charities. Nowadays this may not be the reality for many charities, particularly those with higher profiles and more media coverage, which are more likely to be experienced in this area.

However, negotiating can be a complicated and daunting prospect for anyone, particularly if you are negotiating with a big corporate organisation. In cases where a charity does see itself as subservient in some way, there is a danger that it may judge that to secure the partnership it must agree to what the company wants, even if it is not what the charity needs. The following four key principles can be taken into consideration to avoid this trap.

1. Do not be shy

It is crucial to know the value that a charity brings and why it is that the company wants to be a partner; do not undersell that value. There are lots of benefits a charity can provide to a company through association, and it is key to make sure you are getting back enough benefits from them, in money or in kind. This is of particular importance in relation to a more commercial activity, but similar principles can be worth knowing for traditional fundraising initiatives too.

Be sure to enter any negotiation as an equal; a true partnership should be balanced from the start. It could also make it harder in the long run for you or colleagues by committing to something at this stage that cannot be delivered or that involves increased resources, for example.

2. Respond but do not replace

One of the trickiest things to manage when negotiating between a charity and a company can be the balance between what a company may want and what the charity actually needs. For example, a company may want to fund specific projects in key areas that are not current priorities for the charity, or it could have a large volunteering programme for which the charity has minimal opportunities.

All partnerships involve compromise and in any negotiations there will be things to which both sides need to respond. However, try not to drift too far from what the charity wants and do not replace aspects of the partnership with something that only benefits the company. Ideally you will have identified those sweet spots where both parties can benefit, so it is useful to lead with these.

3. Where is the wiggle room?

Before negotiating with anyone, it is important to understand on which aspects there is some room for movement and on which others there is not. This gap then provides wiggle room, and this is the space in which to negotiate.

Negotiating usually takes place between two people or sometimes a small group on each side; however, both parties are representing their respective organisations as a whole. It is important, therefore, to have a good understanding from colleagues about in what areas and where different teams are prepared to go, before entering into dialogue. For example, finding out what a minimum level of commitment for a sponsorship is or what level of public relations support would be available.

4. There is more than money

A company can deliver so much more than money to a charity, and often it is those things that are low- or no-cost for the company but add huge value to the charity. It is good to explore these sorts of benefits with the relevant colleagues. For example, could a company's marketing channels or buying power be used to promote an event or activity better? Are there opportunities to speak to the company's staff and customer base? Does the company have expertise in an area that could transform a project? Not only does looking for these areas provide added benefits, it is a great way of developing more sustainable partners. Those companies which are more closely involved with a charity's work are less likely to stop their support.

Case study

HEART UK, the Cholesterol Charity, punches well above its weight. This UK charity, with less than £1 million turnover, boasts some global food brands as corporate partners. One partnership with Kellogg's has been active since 2008 and is a great example of how a charity can stand firm when negotiating and not compromise on its principles. HEART UK has developed a product approval system which is administered by a working group, consisting of eminent nutritionists and health professionals, and takes its compositional criteria from the Food Standards Agency's traffic light system.

For those products that meet the criteria and can demonstrate an important role in a heart-healthy diet, HEART UK offers a licensing system which allows on-pack accreditation of the brand. This provides consumers with the reassurance that the foods they are purchasing have a valuable role to play in maintaining heart health. Unless relevant criteria, most crucially around saturated fat, are met, then HEART UK cannot provide product approval. With the example of Kellogg's and in particular their Optivita cereal brand, HEART UK examined the on-pack claims and product ingredients of the cereal to determine whether it was a heart-healthy food. Only once this was established did HEART UK develop a partnership. The charity has enjoyed several such partnerships which have provided a range of opportunities for both organisations. For HEART UK, this includes:

• greater awareness of the HEART UK brand via on-pack communications;

• income generation through licensing agreements, the money from which is unrestricted and delivers a high return on investment;

• matched funding to deliver joint projects that are mutually beneficial;

• opportunities to raise awareness through staff wellness schemes and fundraising opportunities.

For Kellogg's it provides clear commercial benefits, including:

• that all-important unique selling point in a cluttered market;

• credibility and reassurance to consumers that the product's health claims are genuine;

• a great public relations angle.

By having established robust criteria that a corporate partner must satisfy, HEART UK has been able to negotiate from a very strong position and stand firm on its principles, while also creating a clear and lucrative proposition for companies.

Conclusion

In a rocky financial climate and with companies wising up to the potential benefits that charities can bring, the corporate fundraisers of today need to operate with the same mindset as businesses. True partnerships are based on equality, and in both pitches and negotiations a charity, if it has the skills and confidence, should demonstrate this and start as it means to go on.

CHAPTER TEN

Relationship management

Beth Courtier

Introduction: Are charities from Mars?

Are charities from Mars and companies from Venus? The answer is: it probably doesn't matter as long as you have a shared vision with the partner you are working with and an agreed way of working together. Too often there is a focus on the differences rather than the areas of mutual benefit and the additional value that can be gained from a partnership. As with any relationship, communication is at its heart.

A corporate–charity partnership is no different from any other customer relationship: it is about understanding the needs of your customer, identifying opportunities, delivering solutions and building on your relationship to gain a greater understanding through ongoing dialogue. If you were to focus on the differences, probably the greatest would lie in the impact of a successful relationship. A corporate–charity partnership built on a shared vision and genuine desire to make a positive difference can make a life-changing difference to the charity's beneficiaries and positively impact on society more widely.

What can be more motivating than a partnership which has, at its heart, the aspiration to make a genuine impact on some of the neediest in society? Work simply does not get any better.

Account management and good relationships

Structures, processes and remits

While an account management structure and formalised processes do not guarantee a successful partnership, they are critical in securing an understanding of how the partners will work together in order to drive and achieve a shared vision. The size of the account team and the seniority of those members within the team are not in themselves important; what is important is having the appropriate level of support given by both parties.

The account team does not need to be static; it can and should draw in the relevant people at the appropriate time. A successful partnership is about how both parties make the best use of those resources to which they have access. Corresponding account managers from the corporate and charity sides should lead on the account, but do not have to limit the remit of the relationship to the confines of the corporate responsibility or corporate fundraising departments. Rather than leading on every activity, they can look to explore opportunities across both organisations. They can do this by encouraging the direct engagement of other parts of both organisations and by brokering and making the introductions.

While some great activities should and will be generated, developed and delivered in this way outside an account team, there will be times when these activities are in danger of not being leveraged to the greatest possible effect and may be, if not managed properly, short-term and unsustainable.

The account leads in both organisations are those who have the broader experience and greater leverage opportunities, and who genuinely seek to add real value and longevity to the partnership. Therefore, they should be consulted and involved in any activity even if they are not leading on it, as ultimately they are responsible for making sure that activities generated from other parts of the organisations are harnessed and delivered effectively.

It is always hard to say goodbye to a good account lead, but with any departure of a lead contact comes the opportunity to bring in someone new who will have different ideas and see potential for new opportunities.

A frequent cause of frustration is where an account manager leaves and there has been no proper handover or succession planning. Neither organisation will feel like a valued partner when a new account manager asks the other organisation's account lead to explain the partnership, what it has done and what the plans are. It is important, therefore, for the new account manager to be fully briefed, by having a proper handover process before meeting the other organisation's account lead.

Commitment to the partnership

Organisations want their charity partners to know that their organisation is committed and passionate about the partnership; in turn they will want the account lead to make them believe not only that they are personally committed to the partnership, but also that the organisation is committed. Commitment to a partnership and a high level of energy need to be sustained by everyone involved; partnerships are an investment by both organisations and they should not fizzle out at the end of the contract period (as too often happens).

Constructive feedback and generation of ideas

A good account manager and a sound relationship should allow both parties to give feedback on both positives and negatives. The positives are certainly easier, but the negatives are equally important. Where there is a significant partnership – in terms of longevity, funds raised, integrated working, etc. – broader issues should be raised by a partner organisation. Being a good account manager is about understanding key stakeholders and communicating well. Significant changes in organisations can have a direct impact on partners, and they would certainly rather hear about these from their contacts than through a third party or even the press.

In addition to formal meetings, ongoing dialogue and introductions to others can often result in some unexpected opportunities or ideas. Informal introductions can result in the stimulation of new ideas. Charities should look at how all parts of their organisation could benefit from their corporate partner's engagement.

Project management and good relationships

Project management processes

Account management is about people and personalities, and inevitably results in informalities. However small or large a project, there should always be good project management processes in place and an appropriate contract. Clear meeting structures, reporting procedures and review dates are important, not to demonstrate the principles of good project management, but to provide a structure and a way of reviewing progress and measuring success. This ensures focus against objectives and, critically, ensures that everyone is kept informed and has the opportunity to learn from one another.

Assessment and measurement

Measurement is essential, and partners should try to measure everything they do, as everything should have some impact. To assess best use of efforts and a return on investment, in terms of both time and money, this is clearly critical. Some things are undoubtedly more difficult to assess, but that should not stop partners trying if it is relevant (just because something has not been costed or measured before isn't a reason not to look at it). But measures need to have relevance: being asked to come up with a figure that you cannot measure and so would not be accurate or representative is of no value to anyone.

One of the developments clearly seen over the last few years is the way that charities and companies are recognising and measuring in-kind gifts in addition to their fundraising activities – volunteering and access to products, services, rooms, suppliers, etc. These opportunities for additional value are almost endless.

Learning from each other

Like any good relationship, both organisations should be able to learn from each other. Organisations will undoubtedly have different processes, and reporting and measurement procedures, but these can be reviewed and mutually modified in a way that works best. Both organisations need to recognise that they do things differently and then work through these: both the issues and the common ground.

Charities that tell partner organisations that they have to work a certain way, as this is how they have agreed they work with all their corporate partners, need to be conscious that partner organisations will not all want to be thought of as *another* corporate. The way organisations work together needs to be agreed on an individual basis.

Reciprocity in contracts

Contracts and service-level agreements are critical in formalising partnerships; however, one size doesn't fit all. Both organisations need to recognise legal obligations as well as established processes, but open dialogue remains crucial and issues must be raised at the outset.

The definition of a partnership is not one where a contract has three pages of what one partner will deliver and no reciprocal obligations. It is important to make sure that the balance is right and that each side is happy with what is expected of them. In addition, charities should not try to use a set agreement, which has been signed off by other corporate partners, with a new partner. Just as charities are different from others in the charity sector, so are companies in theirs; therefore, a new agreement should be drawn up for each separate partnership that is tailored to the specific needs and expectations of that partnership.

Review dates

While partners need to sign up to a shared vision, the flexibility of being able to review this is critical: organisations change, the environment changes and the world changes. At worst, these changes can frustrate plans and progress, but they can also present new opportunities. In any partnership, particularly longer-term ones, you need to build in expectations for change. That is not an excuse for not delivering or changing things that are difficult.

One example of where this has worked particularly well is a three-year partnership between BT and Scope. Through regular dialogue and Scope's success in influencing key decision-makers in government, they were able to secure funding for equipment provision/support for under-18s in the second year of the partnership, rather than as planned in year 3. This was achieved by having the flexibility to change, through consultation, what had been planned and by redirecting budget and resources and investing in significant time. As a result the partnership was able to extend support in year 3 to adult provision to ensure that access to communication equipment remained intact for over-18s. Without a shared vision, aspiration for real change and dialogue and flexibility, this would not have been achieved.

The following case study further elaborates on this successful partnership.

Case study: Scope and BT

This was a three-year partnership based on a shared vision that everyone should have the right to communicate. The ambition was a shared belief that by working together the two organisations could make a real difference. This was a partnership built on an existing relationship: Scope had previously worked on BT's Inclusive Design project and so the partners understood each other. They worked collaboratively from the start (and even before), from jointly writing a proposal to secure BT funding, through to delivery.

The project was unusual in that it combined two key elements: i) No Voice, No Choice – an influencing campaign to improve the provision of communication equipment to those who need it; ii) the Wheeltop Project – a technology project at Scope's Beaumont College proving that communication technology can be cheaper and better. Neither organisation had worked in this way before, so the partnership required trust between the two organisations and a commitment to deliver. And they did deliver on the partnership, through maximising the skills, expertise and resources of both organisations.

The partnership also required robust project management: a steering group was made up of BT employees, including two apprentices with cerebral palsy; representatives from the technical team at Beaumont; policy, press and public relations representatives; and the fundraising account team. The steering group set the format for a highlight report which was produced every two months and included the budget, discussion of the project plan, progress against the plan, future focus and amendments or deviation from the original budget. The group held a formal end-of-year and end-of-partnership review and a celebration. Throughout there was collaborative working and the sharing of contacts for networking.

The partnership's achievements went beyond its set objectives, which were already ambitious. They included:

• outreach work with schools and colleges to support the development needs of their pupils;

• showcasing the project to professionals;

• free resource provision for the sector;

• shared learning with other organisations in the disability arena, both in the UK and overseas.

The project influenced three government strategies on funding and policy for children's communication equipment, culminating in £1.5 million of grants for up to 40,000 disabled children who need augmentative and alternative communication. Further funding was leveraged from the Learning and Skills Improvement Service with a grant to share project findings with a further 3,500 disabled students in 70 further education colleges.

Scope advised the Welsh Assembly on augmentative and alternative communication and assistive technology provision throughout Wales. The project was recognised by the European Union as an example of e-inclusion excellence. And the project supported the development and education of young disabled people through Wheeltop (bespoke communications aids/devices using a range of different technological solutions). This has promoted increased independence, choice and control: life-enhancing changes for students and their families.

Working with competitors

Relationships are often complex, but relationships with other organisations can add another layer of complexity. Understanding the different relationships is important in order to understand opportunities and potential conflicts.

While companies will expect and want charities to work with other companies, they would not necessarily want to be on stage with a competitor or support the same activities. Similarly, sometimes charities that are competitors will need to work together; this might not be their first choice and it won't necessarily be straightforward, but a review of the value of being involved will put things in perspective: It is better to share something from the pot rather than have nothing. Being successful at working with competitors is about looking at where the shared interest lies, taking joint ownership and being very open.

Motivating employees

In looking at relationships, wider stakeholders, and employees in particular, need to be considered. Employees within organisations are the key. Corporate responsibility and charity teams are generally small by definition, and need to galvanise people across the business to deliver on objectives. There should be an opportunity to engage every member of a company, whether by using their professional skills, fundraising efforts or personal connections, etc.

Many employees will cite their engagement with charity activities as their career highlight and that they feel they have really made a positive difference and been rewarded by what they have done. This experience has prompted many to take on additional volunteering and for some a career change. But employees also need support and need their efforts to be recognised, not only by their own organisation but also by the charity they have supported.

Making relationships last

There are sometimes expectations that successful partnerships, based on this success, will continue after the contract period. And they often do. But expectations should not be based purely on success and hope. At the start of a partnership an exit strategy should be discussed to manage expectations and to help in succession planning. If an existing partner cannot extend its support, work with that organisation to see if it can help secure another partner, or support the new partner with a handover.

The best partnerships, however, are not defined by the length of time or the size of the partnership; they are about what has been jointly achieved when measured against the shared vision.

The following case study illustrates a successful long-term partnership in terms of both achievement and longevity.

Case study: ChildLine and BT

The partnership began in 1986, with BT providing the memorable 0800 1111 number and its premises, and for which the company is formally recognised as a founding partner. The partnership works, and continues to work, because of the synergy that it created.

Communications is at the heart of the work that ChildLine does and communications is BT's business. BT shares a joint vision to help ChildLine answer all the calls it receives from children, and support is embedded within the company. BT's support is far-ranging: fundraising (short-term and long-term, with a focus on sustainable fundraising), strategic and technological support, and the recruitment of volunteer counsellors.

The length of the partnership is clearly unique, but what is more significant is the uniqueness of the support: the diverse range of activities that both parties have worked on together and that BT has cemented support for the charity across the company. This has allowed the partnership to make a genuine, lasting difference.

BT's ongoing support since the 1980s includes:

• displaying ChildLine's number for free in telephone boxes, telephone directories and BT vans;

• sending out the UK's largest ever mailshot and developing ChildLine's first database;

• sending a second mailshot to recruit more donors for ChildLine;

• funding research into why children call ChildLine;

• supporting the roll-out of regional ChildLine call centres;

• funding anti-bullying packs for schools;

• helping ChildLine find new premises;

• working with ChildLine to successfully campaign to make posting prostitute calling cards in telephone boxes illegal;

• facilitating the donation of a switch to allow three-way calling;

• leveraging support from all mobile network providers to ensure that the 0800 number is free and callers remain anonymous;

• hosting ChildLine's first ever parliamentary reception;

- supporting the ChildLine Patron's Awards which recognise corporate and individual supporters;

- acting as a 'critical friend' and supporting ChildLine's merger with the NSPCC;

- lobbying the government in support of the NSPCC's Child Voice Appeal.

Conclusion

Great relationships can make the biggest difference in creating a successful partnership and bringing about long-term sustainable benefits. Successful relationships in partnerships come from having a shared vision – and a genuine commitment to achieve that vision jointly through agreed ways of working – and in ongoing, open communication. It is critical to form good relationships, and to keep these relationships strong, by using structures, processes and competent account management. Having these strong relationships will give the partnership the flexibility to create opportunities and embrace change.

Notes

1   The European Commission established the e-Inclusion awards to raise awareness of digital exclusion, encourage participation and recognise excellence and good practice in using information and communications technology and digital technology to tackle social and digital exclusion across Europe.

CHAPTER ELEVEN

Sponsorships

Richard Gillis

What does the sponsorship market look like?

Each year, HSBC receives around 10,000 unsolicited sponsorship pro-posals. Of these, no more than four are successful.[1]

Every other major brand marketer will tell a similar story. The question this statistic poses is: how can you be one of the four, rather than the 10,000?

Although figures in this area are notoriously unreliable, indicators suggest that the market for corporate sponsorship has been growing for the last decade. For example, the European Sponsorship Association (ESA) estimates the total size of the European sponsorship market in 2010 was €23.3 billion (previously estimated at €9.54 billion) (ESA 2011). Globally, after a 0.6% drop in the growth of sponsorship spending during the 2008 recession, growth rates bounced back to 3.9% in 2009, 5.2% in 2010 and 5.1% in 2011. In Europe, spending by companies grew by 4.7% in 2011 and is expected to grow by 4.4% in 2012 (IEG 2011; Chipps 2012).

Given the media profile of football, it's unsurprising that around 70% of sponsor money in Europe still goes to sport. However, the good news for the charity sector is that brand money is expected to increase in other areas 'as brands take a wider view of sponsorship' (ESA 2011).

Forget the headline deals; elite sport is an outlier

In 2010, Standard Chartered Bank bought the rights to Liverpool's football shirt for around £20 million a year; similarly, Manchester United's deal with insurance company Aon is worth £20 million a year to the club (Smith 2009; Hunter 2009). The value of these deals is based largely on the media exposure the clubs receive both in the UK and overseas, making the logo on the shirt little more than a moving billboard. The price is based therefore on its equivalent advertising value.

The London 2012 Olympic and Paralympic Games have raised around £700 million, which has flooded in from 44 domestic sponsors (Logoc 2011). Lloyds Banking Group is a tier-one sponsor and paid in the region of £80 million to be the Official Bank and Insurance Partner to the Games. Further down the food chain are the tier-three sponsors, which are the many companies that supply essential services to help make the event happen, from McCann Erickson, which creates the advertising, to the official ticket supplier, Ticketmaster. Each of this supplier category of sponsor is likely to have paid between £10 million and £20 million, in cash and value in kind.[2]

However, for the vast majority of sponsorship proposals, the reality is very different. The average asking price for a sponsorship in Europe ranges from $177,773 in the sports sector, to $48,911 in the community to $35,051 in the health sector according to industry-wide research (Sponsorium 2011).

'Rights owners are not presenting opportunities to sponsors that are giving them everything they are looking for', said Ben Treadaway, author of the *Sponsorium Report*, who points out that sponsorship's value to brands does not exist solely in branding and hospitality but in other areas such as well-developed cause-related marketing, access to defined communities and grassroots activity and, even better, more realistic lead times.[3]

This last point is much underestimated by sponsor-seekers. The marketing departments at most large companies work to plans of up to 18 months or more ahead. Any proposal that fails this basic requirement will be automatically discarded for being impractical (see 'Getting to yes: A guide to sponsorship' on page 107).

The rise of social sponsorship

Changes in consumer and brand behaviour have led to a shift in the way that some companies are using sponsorship, not only in terms of how it is used within a company's marketing strategy but also in terms of what can be sponsored. As mentioned, sport still represents around 70% of European sponsorship revenue. But below that top-line figure, there is growth in other sectors such as charity and public sector projects; for example, the Emirates Airline cable car in London and the Barclays Bike Scheme. Another factor is the increased profile of charities in the leveraging of major sponsorships.

More enlightened brands marketers recognise that they cannot say they are 'caring and committed' without providing tangible and transparent proof. Consumer pragmatism means there is no longer an expectation that companies should save the planet, but they should be accountable for the bit for which they are responsible.

The shift from corporate responsibility to social sponsorship is more than semantics; often the budget for social sponsorship comes from the brand teams rather than the corporate communications departments. Its proponents argue that social sponsorship can help build brand trust by directly engaging in social agendas determined by the needs and concerns of their customers.

One criticism of traditional corporate responsibility is that large organisations become focused on corporate ethics, reputation and responsibility based on an agenda that they have set. In social sponsorship the agenda is determined by the consumer, not the company, and the budgets that are contributing to these activities are increasingly marketing-focused.

Social sponsorship can be a stand-alone campaign or an activation strand – i.e. the way in which the sponsorship is used within the company's marketing strategy – which is then introduced into an existing sponsorship programme. In both cases it fulfils an important function for sponsors that increasingly see the need for direct and active brand engagement rather than the traditional awareness-driven sponsorship model.

This leads to the increasingly common sponsor strategy where a sponsor links the rights it has bought for an elite event and chooses to activate them by associating with a charity or cause.

Legacy, sustainability, education, well-being and community are all strands of social activation that are coming to the fore and being used inside conventional sponsorship programmes.

There are many examples of brands adding social activation to their existing sponsorship programmes. Barclays' Spaces for Sport links with its Premier League football sponsorship. E.ON's Carbon Footy campaign built an energy-saving component into its FA Cup sponsorship and NatWest sponsors the CricketForce community project in addition to its mainstream sponsorship of cricket in England and Wales.

The following case study illustrates Lloyds TSB's support of the Youth Sport Trust, following on from its sponsorship of the London 2012 Olympic and Paralympic Games.

Case study

Lloyds TSB National School Sport Week

Lloyds TSB was the first official partner of the London 2012 Olympic and Paralympic Games. In partnership with the Youth Sport Trust, Lloyds TSB National School Sport Week is a week-long sporting celebration for primary and secondary schools across Britain. Pupils are invited to pledge to achieve a personal best in an Olympic or Paralympic sport, whether individually or with their class or club, and at every level and standard.

Registered schools are offered support to generate interest and sporting activities for pupils of all ages across a whole week. This helps fulfil school objectives for physical education and sports classes, but can be used across the curriculum to create excitement around the London 2012 Olympic and Paralympic Games and help young people live the values of the Games. The 2010 event saw almost 14,000 schools and five million children taking part and enjoying sporting activities.

Example in action: West Sussex School Sport Partnership

FOCUS

The aim was to engage primary and secondary pupils from across the School Sport Partnership in a range of Olympic- and Paralympic-themed physical and sporting activity during Lloyds TSB National School Sport Week 2010.

WHO TOOK PART?

Coach for a day programme: 6,100 young people.
Arties Olympics: 436 infant school students.
100 challenges: hundreds of secondary-school students.
Dance mat world record attempt: 130 young people and 20 sports leaders.

WHAT HAPPENED?

A range of initiatives, including:

• Coach for a day programme: funded through the School Sport Coaching scheme. The programme encouraged students to try a new Olympic and Paralympic sport.

• The School Sport Partnership sourced judo, fencing and games coaches (who delivered hockey, for example). Primary schools were offered a menu of activities and requested the activity they preferred. One coach per primary school delivered sessions across the key stages and the session content was guided by the need of the school.

• Infant schools across the School Sport Partnership were encouraged to access the 'Arties Olympics' resource. This was a great way to get infant schools involved.

• 100 challenges: focused students on the fact that Bognor Regis is approximately 100 miles from the London Olympic and Paralympic stadium. Inter-school virtual competitions and school-based challenges were held around this theme. For example, secondary-school pupils were challenged to run 100 metres in the quickest time possible while primary-school students were encouraged to run in relays.

• Dance mat world record attempt: catered for pupils who do not ordinarily participate in sporting events.

To raise awareness of the Olympic and Paralympic values (respect, excellence and friendship), Leadership Academy students helped deliver assemblies on the Olympic values, the week before or during Lloyds TSB National School Sport Week. Each day focused on one of the Olympic and Paralympic values.

The headteacher at St. Richard's School said: 'It was fantastic to have the opportunity to try out a new sport. More of the same next year please.' A pupil from St. Barnham School declared that: 'It was the best session in the world, I'd never had so much fun in my life.' And a parent from East Wittering School said: 'We loved seeing all the children compete in something they would never normally do and there was something for everyone to have a go at.'

'Example in action' adapted from Lloyds TSB's case study 12 at www.schoolsportweek.org

Building social content into the sponsorship proposition adds another value channel for brand partners to leverage. Not-for-profit rights holders such as sports governing bodies are benefiting from the increase in interest in social content, but for commercial rights holders especially in sport, there are a few dilemmas. For example, some sponsors may reject the idea of a profit being made from social content, preferring to see only the recovery of costs, as is the case with most charities.

At the same time, rights holders also need to anticipate whether those sponsors committed to sustainable, community and social programmes in their day-to-day operations may also want this commitment to be extended to their sponsorships.

Can charities live with imperfect partners?

The rise of the term 'greenwash' reveals the amorality of advertising and sponsorship, leaving consumers in a no-man's-land between claim and counter-claim. For every environmentally friendly washing powder, lobbying group TerraChoice churns out matching data that undermines virtually every claim made on the part of the products sold. The latest report suggests that more than 95% of consumer products claiming to be green were found to commit at least one of its seven 'Sins of Greenwashing', while over the same period there was a 73% increase in so-called green products in 2010 compared with the previous year (TerraChoice 2010, p.6).

This extends to other alliances between corporate and social causes, to the extent that we may have reached a sort of tipping point: for companies, the fear of being caught cheating is beginning to outweigh the benefits of claiming to be green.

> Taking a lesson from the political world, we know people will accept progress over perfection as long as shortcomings are declared in full. But a cover-up? Now that they won't forgive.
>
> OgilvyEarth 2010, p. 10

'Be as good as you can' therefore is the message for companies, and then learn from the criticism that will inevitably come along. The question for charities and other not-for-profit organisations that are looking for corporate sponsorship is: can you live with imperfect partners?

Could sponsorship over-commercialise your organisation?

This is part of the broader debate, one articulated by the author Nick Hornby. He said in an interview some 20 years after the publication of *Fever Pitch*, still the definitive book on sporting obsession: 'Going to the Emirates Stadium was closer to a visit to the cinema than a football match.' The club and the players were now very distant, he said, and the whole thing was 'too corporate'.[4]

Put another way, Arsenal's most famous fan has been on a journey that is the very opposite of that anticipated by its marketing department. Over the course of 20 years, the club has moved from being an integral part of his life to occupying a place on its margins: as Arsenal became a brand, its most obsessive fan became disengaged. Hornby's concerns have an application well beyond north London and he is articulating the central sponsorship dilemma for the charity sector.

Marketers talk a great deal of return on investment. But what about the other partners? What happens to them? Is it inevitable that as sport (and music and some areas of the arts) become corporate partners, they lose their humanity: the very thing that connects us to them?

Charities and other not-for-profit organisations are particularly vulnerable to associating with the wrong sponsor. Here is a ten-step guide to help you navigate the process.

Getting to yes: A guide to sponsorship

Step 1: Define the terms

Commercial sponsorship is not philanthropy. Immediately dispose of other uses of the term; it is not a community fundraising activity which friends are asked to support. Commercial sponsorship is an activity whereby a commercial interest pays a fee to purchase a defined association with a defined project or property that represents defined positive values and provides access to defined audiences.

It is especially important to understand that the sponsorship fee has no relationship to the financial needs of the sponsored organisation or its project. The sponsor is not financing anyone to carry out a project: it is paying for an association with a project.

Step 2: All aboard

The whole team must understand and support the sponsorship initiative.

Once an organisation has decided to seek sponsorship, the entire team needs to support the sponsorship initiative. While there may be initial valid concerns such as: 'Is there a danger of the organisation becoming over-commercialised?', if your organisation judges the benefits to outweigh the risks and decides to go ahead with the initiative, everyone needs to arrive at a point where the whole team is committed to giving value to the sponsor. Outlining clearly the benefits and the risks to the whole team and involving team members in the decision-making process will help ensure that you get everyone to buy in to the initiative, or indeed reject it if it is the wrong thing for the organisation.

Step 3: Audit, audit, audit

It is essential to carry out a thorough audit of all you have to offer. What do the sponsors get for the money?

In order to sell your sponsorship property you need to: a) clearly understand the full range of benefits on offer; and b) know all of your various audiences. Sports, for example, generally have good relations with the media alongside well-defined membership and supporters' groups. Charities are the guardians of communities of like-minded people united by a common cause. This is a big responsibility, but also offers potential benefits to a would-be sponsor if handled sensitively. Sponsors are increasingly looking beyond using charities as a branding opportunity and more into accessing a new audience. Charities, therefore, potentially have a lot more to offer than is immediately obvious.

Step 4: Making contact

The worst possible form of approach is also the most frequently used: a cold call or letter where no previous relationship exists. Before making any approach you need to know that the potential sponsor is positively aware of your organisation. Ideally you need some form of personal relationship with the decision-maker; consider using a close contact within the company or other relevant third party to achieve this.

Step 5: The proposal

The proposal needs to be created from the sponsor's perspective and must show your understanding of the sponsor's strategy and needs. It should contain:

• a description of the fit between the property and the brand;

• an analysis of the audience and opportunities to see, etc., with as much substantiated detail on the demographic as available;

• a package of benefits drawn from step 3 and carefully tailored to the particular brand or sponsor.

Step 6: Pricing

Remember, the sponsorship fee should have no direct relationship to the cost of the project. Secondly, if you are serious about sponsorship, hold out for a serious sponsor. Here are a few considerations:

• What would it cost the sponsor to reach the same audience if they were to use conventional advertising media?

• If the extra equivalent advertising values from the sponsorship are actually measurable, then the fee can be measured against this.

• At what level are similar rival sponsorships being pegged?

Step 7: Negotiating: what to expect

Decisions within a large organisation always take some time to mature, and a successful deal will probably have a lead time of between four and six months. When the answer is 'no', try to establish what kind of 'no' it is. No, not ever . . .? No, not now . . .? No, not at this price . . .?

Step 8: Under-promise and over-deliver

Some of the key concerns on the part of the people working in the sponsor's marketing department are: can we trust them to meet our requirements, and do they have the people in sufficient numbers and with the right skills and experience to service this contract? Try to involve all elements of the sponsor's organisation (staff, different departments and senior management), especially any parties not directly involved in the original negotiation, within the celebratory and fun aspects of the sponsorship.

Sponsors are busy people, so make the delivery easy, not burdensome, for them; one member of the charity's staff should be the nominated point of contact to ensure smooth communication. This will help to show the extra buttons that can be pushed to convert the sponsorship into real business benefits.

Step 9: Renewal and referral

Nothing succeeds like success, and the final report is the trigger to test the water for renewal, assuming the property – the project that has been sponsored – may be regarded as repeatable. A continued partnership based on an existing relationship is an easier proposition than starting from scratch looking for a new sponsor. If the sponsor is happy with the project, but renewal, for whatever reason, is not on the cards, ask for its help in securing new corporate friends.

Step 10: Key points and final checklist

Key points

- Clarify the rights the sponsor is buying.
- Check that the sponsorship works with the brand.
- Ensure that budgets are available.
- Never cold call.
- Provide dedicated support.
- Establish the sponsorship fee. Is it is negotiable?
- Confirm the demographic fit. Is it global, countrywide or regional?

Final checklist

- Write your strategy.
- Define your audience.

- Under-promise and over-deliver.

- Include evaluation.

- Renew the contract.

Notes

1   Figures noted by HSBC speakers at the European Sponsorship Association's Future Sponsorship conference, as reported in Sportcal's press release (2009).
2   As stated by Paul Deighton in the Select Committee on Culture, Media and Sport Minutes of Evidence, Examination of Witnesses (Questions 81–99), Tuesday 4 December 2007 in response to Q96.
3   As stated in a personal communication dated June 2011.
4   Quoted from the Melvyn Bragg interview with Nick Hornby on *The South Bank Show*; broadcast on ITV 1 on 25 October 2009.

References

Chipps, William (2012), *Economic Uncertainty to Slow Sponsorship Growth in 2012* [press release], Chicago, IEG, 11 January

ESA (2011), *New ESA Figures Double Size of European Sponsorship Industry* [press release], Surbiton, European Sponsorship Association, 22 November

Hunter, Andy (2009) 'Manchester United name Aon Corp as new £80m shirt sponsors' *The Guardian*, London, News and Media Limited, 3 June

IEG (2011), 'Sponsorship Spending: 2010 Proves Better Than Expected; Bigger Gains Set for 2011', IEG Sponsorship Report, Chicago

Logoc (2011), *London 2012 Snaps up Westfield as Latest Sponsor and Hits £700m Mark* [press release], London, London 2012, 7 September

OgilvyEarth (2010), *From Greenwash to Great: A Practical Guide to Great Green Marketing*, London, Ogilvy & Mather

Smith, Rory (2009), 'Rafael Benitez to benefit from £80m Liverpool sponsorship deal in transfer market', *The Telegraph*, London, Telegraph Media Group, 15 September

Sponsorium (2011), *Sponsorium Report: Measuring Global Sponsorship Performance*, London, Sponsorium International, April

Sportcal (2009), *Future Sponsorship Split over Impact of Recession as Biggest Shake Up for the Industry for 25 Years Predicted* [press release], London, 27 November

TerraChoice (2010), *The Sins of Greenwashing: Home and Family Edition*, UL Global Network

CHAPTER TWELVE

Promotional partnerships and the potential benefits to charities

Edwin Mutton and Martin Croft

Introduction

This chapter explores how charities can benefit from partnering with brands for promotional marketing activities. These activities can take a number of forms, from the classic donation for each pack sold through events to experiential marketing, competitions, sponsorship and online activities. Such promotions have in the past tended to be short-term and tactical, but increasingly charity partnerships are long-term and strategic. Charities can gain much, but must ensure that any partnerships are relevant and that they do not damage the charity brand.

A revolution in marketing

There has been a revolution in marketing in the last decade or so that has been driven by new technologies, most notably the Internet and mobile phones. Old-style twentieth-century mass marketing paradigms no longer work. That is to say, consumers are no longer a captive audience. They have been empowered by online and mobile developments and are no longer passive recipients of marketing communications. They are active participants in a two-way communications process, and expect to have considerable control over the information they receive, as well as when and how they get it.

This has changed the relationship between consumers and brands and has also changed the whole marketing communications industry. In particular, it has driven the evolution of the promotional marketing discipline away from a focus on traditional sales promotions (with their emphasis on offering an incentive with real value for the consumer in order to drive product sales in store over a short timescale) to today's promotional marketing, with its emphasis on changing behaviour and maintaining that change on a longer-term and more strategic level.

The Institute of Promotional Marketing, the trade body for the industry, defines promotional marketing as:

Any marketing initiative, the purpose of which is to create a call to action that has a direct and positive impact on the behaviour of a targeted audience by offering a demonstrable, though not necessarily tangible, benefit.

Getting someone to buy something is persuading someone to change their behaviour, so classic sales promotion is still a part of the wider promotional marketing industry. But promotional marketing can also be used to get people to do more than just buy something; it can be to get them to sign a petition, make a donation or take some other kind of action. It is also not just about getting people to do something; it can be about getting them to *stop* doing something, whether it is smoking, drinking, eating meat or consuming too much energy.

Furthermore, promotional marketers now use a range of mechanisms which go beyond classic sales promotion techniques and which aim at gaining consumer engagement in order to promote behaviour change. Finally, promotional marketing now also encompasses employee motivation, reward and recognition schemes, because positive behaviour change within organisations directly contributes to greater customer satisfaction, which in turn delivers greater profits.

There has also been a change in where promotional marketing fits within brand-owning companies. It used to be almost exclusively controlled by the sales or commercial departments, and sales promotion activity was often run without any reference to the consumer marketing director or to overall brand objectives and strategies. Increasingly, however, promotional marketing activities are being developed as an integral part of the brand's marketing activities, and also with reference to any corporate responsibility guidelines that the company may have.

Why should charities consider linking with brands?

The most obvious benefit for a charity from being involved with a brand for a promotional marketing activity is the immediate financial one. For example, a brand owner may agree to donate a set amount to a charity for every pack sold, as was the case in late 2011, when Breast Cancer Campaign worked closely with Debenhams and Kit-Kat. Debenhams made a donation for every bra it sold during October 2011, while Kit-Kat donated 10p per pack sold via an on-pack promotion on one million of its Kit-Kat Senseo confectionery bars.

However, charity–brand promotional partnerships are likely to work better for all parties if there is more to them than just an automatic donation of a set amount for each pack sold. This ties in with current marketing practices which are aimed at building brand engagement, effectively by creating as many links, both tangible and intangible, between a brand and the target consumer as possible.

While promotions where companies or brands make a donation for every sale are very common, other promotional elements that will benefit the charity will almost certainly be worked into the activity as well. For example, the Kit-Kat Senseo–Breast Cancer Campaign partnership also organised a special concert featuring the pop group, The Saturdays, which generated useful publicity for both parties.

The following case study demonstrates the further benefits that a promotional partnership can bring.

Case study: Radio Marsden and Times Square Shopping Centre

Radio Marsden is a voluntary organisation and registered charity which operates a radio station primarily serving cancer patients at the world-famous Royal Marsden Hospital in Chelsea, London and Sutton, Surrey.

The station wanted to secure a licence to transmit radio programmes online 24 hours a day, seven days a week, in order to achieve two main objectives: to allow friends and relatives of patients to access the station even though they might not be at the hospital in person; and to turn the station into a truly local one for Sutton and surrounding boroughs.

Times Square Shopping Centre had already linked with Radio Marsden for the station's 40th anniversary celebrations in 2009. It was impressed with listener feedback and wanted to further underline its commitment to community initiatives, so it agreed to become the station's bidding partner for the licence.

Having Times Square on board meant that the station could demonstrate to the authorities that it had the financial support needed to bring its online broadcast technology up to the required standards. Times Square also provided marketing support to publicise the new service.

In return, Times Square got a new media opportunity which it has been exploiting to the full, both promoting itself and also its tenants. The shopping centre has its own Join In initiative, comprising a community information unit and website link, and is co-developing a community programme for the Sutton area that will build on this.

Times Sq. 2010

Developing longer-term relationships

It is a good idea for charities to try to develop longer-term relationships with commercial partners which can encompass a range of different techniques, rather than focusing on short-term one-off promotions. It takes time, effort and resources to make contacts, agree the terms of a promotion and then get the activity up and running. It makes far more sense, and should provide a better return on investment, to build on an existing relationship than to start afresh every time.

It is worth considering the three-year model, which works like this:

Year 1: A steep learning curve, as both or all partners endeavour to forge a working relationship and achieve objectives. Often obstacles or unforeseen circumstances will present themselves and need resolving.

Year 2: A much smoother ride, with relationships already forged and the first year's difficulties resolved. By the end of year 2, a near-perfect partnership has been achieved.

Year 3: The maximum return is obtained from day one.

This model is also extremely cost-effective. To change partnerships annually is wasteful in terms of, for example, producing promotional materials and building new relationships.

After three years, most partnerships – charitable or commercial – will need reviewing. Both the charity and the commercial partner may have changed their objectives or budgets. If they have not changed either, then the partnership may run successfully for another year or two. Some endure for 20 years or more, but five years is a more realistic maximum life-cycle.

Why should brands consider linking with charities?

It is also a good idea for charities to think through why brands are interested in charity-linked promotions. Some of the factors behind brands getting involved are:

• the immediate sales uplift that can occur;

• the opportunity to build loyalty with existing users and also recruit new users;

• charity promotions should contribute to brand and corporate responsibility targets;

• the general public relations benefit;

• a brand-owner's employees may become more engaged with corporate objectives and more motivated because of a charity partnership.

There is another reason why some brands and companies may commit to a charity partnership: the people running the company may just want to, either for personal reasons or because of general corporate altruism.

Not all corporate charitable giving is driven by public relations and corporate responsibility goals: while it is easy to regard all corporate activity as being driven by cynical self-interest, the truth is that there are still many companies and business people that simply believe it is the right thing to do.

This last point is worth emphasising: Breast Cancer Campaign has a promotional link with Reckitt Benckiser's stain removal brand Vanish (which committed to raising £250,000 during Breast Cancer Awareness Month in October 2010). Liz Monks, director of fundraising at the BCC, was quoted in *Promotional Marketing* magazine as saying that 'while we know Vanish sales have increased' as a result of the partnership, 'we also know that Reckitt Benckiser is committed to getting the message about breast cancer to their staff, a lot of whom are young women. Partners come to us wearing their commercial hats and also wanting to do good' (Croft 2011, p. 8).

Case study: Breast Cancer Campaign and Vanish

For the second year running, Breast Cancer Campaign's flagship fundraising event **wear it pink** and Reckitt Benckiser's stain removal brand Vanish partnered for Breast Cancer Awareness Month in October 2011.

Vanish became the first title sponsor of Breast Cancer Campaign's **wear it pink** fundraising event in 2010. **wear it pink** is the charity's biggest national fundraising initiative, where people are asked to wear pink for a day, and donate £2 in support of the charity.

Vanish understands who its consumers are and aims to grow closer to them through campaigns that speak clearly to their concerns and needs. In addition to this, there is also the fact that Vanish has pink as its brand colour and uses the slogan 'Trust pink – forget stains!'

The campaign was promoted across five of its pink-packaged products, and in addition to this, Vanish created the world's biggest bra to mark **wear it pink** day, the largest day of fundraising in Breast Cancer Awareness Month.

The bra was rigged up on the ITV South Bank building, where it was officially revealed on *This Morning*, providing an eye-popping sight on both sides of the Thames. Guinness officials granted record-breaking status for the giant pink bra, which measured 31 metres around the bust and used a staggering 375 sq. m of fabric. The bra, scaled up from an original 34B, will now take its place in the *Guinness Book of Records*.

Vanish committed to raising £250,000 for the charity in 2011, taking the total raised to date from the partnership with Breast Cancer Campaign to over £half-a-million. The giant bra was modelled on a Gorgeous T-shirt design supplied by Debenhams, the official **wear it pink** t-shirt retailer.

Who responds to charity-linked promotions?

Figures from market research company Mintel show that companies and brands can definitely benefit from a 'halo effect', meaning that by linking up with charities for a promotion of some kind they can boost public perception of the company or brand.

More than two-thirds of UK consumers (68%) said they 'think positively' of brands which make a donation to charity based on purchases made, while more than half (58%) said they would choose a brand that makes charitable donations in preference to one that does not, and 28% said they were prepared to pay more for a brand that donates to charity (Mintel 2010).

It is also significant to note that the people who are influenced by charity–brand promotional partnerships tend to be younger and more affluent than the norm. This is in stark contrast to the usual received wisdom that people who donate to charity tend to be older and not high earners.

Research commissioned by *Promotional Marketing* magazine and carried out by online polling company fast.MAP shows that younger consumers are more likely to change their purchasing behaviour because of a charity–brand promotion.

One in five 18-to-34-year-olds say they have bought more of a product they usually buy because there was a charity-linked promotion, compared with the UK national average of 11%. The same percentage (20%) of 18-to-24-year-olds actually went to a supermarket they don't usually shop at specifically because of a charity promotion, compared with the average of 6% (Croft 2011, p. 9).

However, it is probably worth pointing out that the majority of UK consumers are only going to respond to a charity link if:

- the charity is relevant to them;
- the brand is relevant to them;
- there are obvious connections between the charity and the brand.

116

Beware: some partnerships seem to be made in heaven, but can actually ruin a brand. As an example, fundraising for cot death syndrome research seems to have an immediate connection to a disposable nappy brand. But would any self-respecting brand manager realistically want 'cot death syndrome' featured prominently on packs of nappies? By contrast, a campaign to raise money for premature baby research might well succeed.

Partnerships are often stronger and will have more consumer appeal if the objective is specific. Raising money for children's hospitals or hospices is an admirable objective: but if a campaign can be targeted at a consumer's local hospital or hospice, it is likely to have far more appeal to individual consumers because it is relevant to them. Similarly, raising money for a specific project, such as a CAT scanner, is more powerful than merely raising money for a local hospital.

What are the laws and regulations governing charity–brand promotions?

Before setting up any kind of joint promotion with a commercial partner, charities must understand the various laws, rules and regulations that come into play (see Appendix 1 for information on the legal framework for charity promotions).

Furthermore, all promotional marketing, charity-linked or not, comes under the UK's self-regulatory system covering advertising and marketing, which means activity must adhere to the UK Code of Non-broadcast Advertising, Sales Promotion and Direct Marketing, more commonly know as the CAP Code.

What follows is a brief introduction to some of the issues involved in charity-linked promotions, but should not be taken as a replacement for professional advice.

Legally, in any promotion which claims that charitable contributions will be made, certain things must be clearly stated. These include:

• the name or names of the institution or institutions concerned;

• if more than one institution is involved, then what percentage of donations goes to each institution;

• how the split will be made;

• the proportion of the sales price of products or services belonging to the commercial partner, or of the proceeds from a promotional venture undertaken by the commercial partner, which the institution or institutions will get;

• any other sums the commercial partner will give to the charity or charities involved.

The 1995 Regulations also say that there must be a comprehensive written agreement between the charity and the commercial partner, covering all aspects of the promotion, including how the charity benefits and what the obligations of the promoter are. Failure to uphold these commitments could lead to prosecution and a heavy fine.

Furthermore, there may be tax and VAT implications related to promotional activity. Tax laws and regulations are extremely complicated and subject to frequent changes. While some charitable promotions may not involve a direct tax or VAT liability, others definitely will. It should also be noted that the status of a promotion may change, depending on what 'benefits' – which may include the use of a charity's name or logos – a commercial enterprise receives. Expert advice should be sought before any activities are undertaken.

Complaints about charity-linked promotional marketing activity will almost certainly be handled by the Advertising Standards Authority (ASA), which looks into whether advertising or marketing activity follows the CAP Code and also whether it is legal.

Two examples of ASA adjudications highlight where problems can arise:

Case study: ASA adjudications

In August 2010, the ASA upheld a complaint against Stairlift manufacturer Minivator. Minivator ran a promotion where it promised to donate 50% of profits to Help the Aged. Unfortunately, the text of the promotion failed to make it clear that the donation would be based on sales generated by the promotion. A competitor complained that the advert was misleading. The ASA investigated and ruled that, although the promotion had raised substantial amounts for charity, the promotion was misleading (ASA 2010).

In January 2009, the ASA upheld a complaint against an on-pack charity-linked promotion for Food Brands Group's Percol Fairtrade and Organic African ground coffee. A sticker on the pack said 'Every pack raises money for Children in Africa'. The text on the packaging explained that Children in Africa is the umbrella name for Percol's own initiative to raise funds for various African charities, but then added: 'for more details on the project we are currently funding visit www.percol.co.uk'.

The ASA ruled that:

The presence of a charity-linked promotion could influence consumers' decision-making about whether or not to buy Percol

> products and therefore concluded that the packaging itself should have made clear the basis upon which any contribution would be calculated and that it was not sufficient for this information to have been mentioned only on the website
>
> ASA 2009

In both these cases, the ASA ruled that the brand involved must not run the promotions again without making sure that they conform to the CAP Code and the regulations governing charity-linked promotions.

What steps should charities take when considering linking with companies and brands for promotions?

Partnership marketing activity will, by definition, involve two (or potentially more) brands working together. There must be something that the brands have in common – some reason for them to work together – which will result in a benefit to every brand involved. How well matched two or more brands are to be partners is often referred to as 'brand fit'.

When the brands in question belong to commercial entities, then each will have a solid understanding of their brand values, their overarching strategic objectives and their audience, and will scrutinise any proposed partnership activity carefully to highlight potential threats and benefits, and the overall return on investment.

While the biggest charities are likely to have a thorough understanding of their brands, how they need to be developed and who their core audiences are, many medium and smaller charities may not have looked at this aspect of their marketing in detail. But it is absolutely necessary to do so if any partnership marketing activity is to be conducted successfully.

If you do not have a clear idea of what your brand is, then how can you get the most out of any negotiations you have with a commercial entity which wishes to link with you, and how can you establish whether there is true brand fit?

This may involve extensive 'due diligence' research. The charity must look into the potential brand partner's past and current activities and those of its owner and of any larger group of which its owner is a part. It is highly likely, for example, that a charity which links to a brand owned by Nestlé will attract criticism from those groups which are campaigning against Nestlé's marketing of baby and infant formula in less-developed countries.

Some brand partnerships will still be short-term and tactical, and there is nothing necessarily wrong with a charity getting involved with such activity.

However, given the complexities involved in many charity–brand promotions, it is likely that even a short-term promotion will need significant resources. If a charity is to maximise the return on its investment, then it should be looking at creating an infrastructure that can support a number of such promotions during the course of a year, while developing an ongoing relationship either with a single partner or with multiple partners.

A charity may also need to invest in market research, in order to understand its own audience of supporters and potential supporters. As we have already pointed out, the type of person who responds to charity–brand promotional activity may be very different from the type of person who donates to a charity on a regular basis. Existing research may only cover traditional donors.

Similarly, charities may need to expand on their traditional fundraising skills to grow their partnerships with brands. This could be by training existing staff, recruiting new staff or bringing in a relevant agency.

It should be noted that some agencies may be prepared to work for charities pro bono. Charities, however, need to be sure that they are still in control of any activity proposed or run by agencies on their behalf, even when they are not paying for it. Sometimes, marketing agencies regard pro bono campaigns as an opportunity to run work which a commercial client may baulk at, which can result in highly creative and even award-winning campaigns; but they can also be highly contentious. Charities need to remember that they will be held responsible by the ASA for promotional campaigns run on their behalf.

Case Study: Teenage Cancer Trust and Coffee Republic

In December 2010, high-street coffee chain, Coffee Republic, launched a competition called 'Who the Froth Is It?' to boost funds for its chosen charity, Teenage Cancer Trust.

Entrants had to correctly identify the name of a celebrity depicted in the froth on top of a cup of coffee to be in with a chance of winning a pair of tickets to Teenage Cancer Trust's comedy night at the Royal Albert Hall in 2011. A range of coffee-related items were also available as prizes.

Entry was by text, with each competition entry text costing £1.50, from which Teenage Cancer Trust received a minimum of 90 pence per text.

Earlier in 2010, the coffee retailer and Teenage Cancer Trust announced a three-year nationwide fundraising partnership, which kicked off with the launch of a signature cupcake. Proceeds from sales of the Teenage Cancer Trust cupcake, sold in Coffee Republic bars across the UK, went towards supporting Teenage Cancer Trust's 17 existing specialist teenage cancer units in NHS hospitals and building new ones.

Wright 2010

Conclusion

Promotions which involve both a charity and a brand now go far beyond just a set amount being donated per pack of a product sold. Charities can significantly increase their revenue through linking with commercial partners for such promotions, but they must understand the implications, and that such promotions are subject to a range of laws, regulations and rules.

Charities should always carefully examine any proposed partnership marketing or promotional activity with a commercial organisation to ensure that the benefits (which may be non-financial) justify the investment of time and resources. Charities must be sure that they clearly understand the value of their own brand and any potential threats to it from different promotional activities.

References

ASA (2009), 'ASA Adjudication on Food Brands Group Ltd' [web page], www.asa. org.uk, Advertising Standards Authority Limited, 7 January, accessed 5 December 2011

ASA (2010) 'ASA Adjudication on Minivator Ltd' [web page] www.asa.org.uk, Advertising Standards Authority Limited, 25 August, accessed 5 December 2011

Croft, Martin (2011), 'The Good Give Young', *Promotional Marketing*, London, Sales Promotion Publishing, January issue

Mintel (2010), *Season of Goodwill Extends into 2011 for Charitable Brits* [press release], www.mintel.com, Mintel Group, accessed 1 December 2011

Times Sq. (2010), 'Radio Marsden Online', *News and Events* [web page], www.times squareshopping.co.uk, accessed 5 January 2012

Wright, Maggie (2010), *Who the Froth Is It? Coffee Republic Steps up Fundraising Drive for Teenage Cancer Trust* [press release], Coffee Republic, 9 December

CHAPTER THIRTEEN

From year to eternity: managing successful Charity of the Year partnerships

Amy Franklin

Introduction

Competition for Charity of the Year partnerships has never been fiercer, and many companies are introducing more stages in the application process to unearth a charitable organisation that is exactly right for their workforce.

When a charity is fortunate enough to be successful in a Charity of the Year bid, there is one opportunity to maximise the benefits of that relationship: to turn what could be just a fundraising partnership into one that is multi-faceted and boasts mutually beneficial outcomes. This chapter provides direction on how to be a forward-thinking account manager and ensure that the charity is best equipped to attain the full spectrum of partnership benefits.

Taking a structured approach: developing a client plan

As the name suggests, with a typical Charity of the Year partner, the charity has a limited window of opportunity to maximise the relationship. Good planning in the early stages, ideally before the partnership has been formally launched, will ensure a clear plan of what the charity hopes to achieve from the partnership and what it aims to deliver for the partner, and an outline plan of how to go about it.

Developing a client plan for each partner is an excellent starting point. The purpose of this document is to focus the charity's activity and provide a reference from which it can measure progress at regular intervals. The following points should be captured within the client plan.

Objectives for the company

Research on the corporate partner should be completed to get an indication of what its objectives are likely to be, and these should be confirmed with the company at the first appropriate opportunity. Consideration should be given not only to the fundraising target but also to, for example, employee engagement, employee development or recognition in the media, which could be crucial for the company.

Objectives for the charity

Charity of the Year partnerships can be resource-heavy and time-consuming. Time should be taken at the beginning to consider everything that the charity hopes to achieve. Aside from the financial target, the corporate partner could provide volunteers, mentoring, training, gifts in kind, use of equipment or facilities, use of employees' expertise, leverage opportunities, awareness-raising opportunities or introductions to other organisations. For those partners that look as though they could bring the charity significant benefit, consulting the charity's senior management team to ensure that organisation-wide benefits have been considered and prioritised would be wise.

Key performance indicators (KPIs)

Discipline is required to make sure that KPIs are specific, measurable, achievable and realistic and have a timescale (SMART). These should be reviewed at least at the six-month stage and again towards the end of the partnership.

Income and expenditure

Consideration should be given to the key fundraising activities and how much the charity hopes to raise from them. Thought should also be given to what needs to be invested in the partnership to make it a success. Armed with these details the charity should assess the predicted return on investment (ROI), aiming for a healthy ROI of at least 3:1 and ideally nearer 4:1.

In some charities, corporate fundraisers are able to count money saved from having a corporate partner deliver the work pro bono, on in-budget development work, against their fundraising target. However, in most charities it is only the fundraised income that counts towards the ROI. With an opportunity where the financial ROI looks weak but the value-added benefits to the charity could be significant, a discussion with the management team should provide guidance on how much time to invest in the partnership or whether to go ahead at all.

Roles and responsibilities

Most Charity of the Year partnerships will need the support of colleagues beyond corporate fundraising – such as a press officer, a senior manager or, in larger charities, regional fundraisers – to deliver on the partnership objectives. The account manager should draft the roles and responsibilities and discuss these to ensure agreement. It is advisable that this project group meet on a monthly basis throughout the partnership to share successes, discuss issues and check status against KPIs.

The support structure

Having one main day-to-day contact person for the corporate partner is usually important, but developing other relationships between organisations will help to truly embed the partnership. Introductions should be set up between equivalents at senior and middle management levels. Where there are regional fundraising networks it could be beneficial for introductions to be made to regional offices, as their shared knowledge of the local area can be hugely beneficial.

Account growth activities

This section is about recording those activities that take the partnership beyond a basic fundraising relationship to one with multi-faceted and mutually beneficial outcomes. At the start of a partnership the charity may not know exactly what it hopes to achieve in each area. For example, a corporate partner may have a pro bono programme of support whereby it offers a contribution of its employees' expert skills towards a piece of work that the charity would otherwise have to pay for, but the charity might not yet be sure where such support would be best utilised.

Such a programme presents development opportunities for the corporate partner's workforce and obvious benefits for the charity. The initial client plan should capture the opportunity presented and an action plan for identifying a suitable piece of work that would qualify should be drawn up. If the charity does have a clear picture of what it hopes to gain beyond fundraising, KPIs should be set to measure these activities.

Changes in the client plan

The client plan is not intended to be a fixed document, but rather a live document which is flexible enough to adapt as the charity gets to know the partner and new opportunities arise. The onus should be on the account manager to be the expert on the client and to facilitate actions in the client plan. It is the account manager's responsibility to ensure that KPIs are met, even if they are not directly responsible for their delivery.

Knowing the partner

Once the charity has a clear perception of what it hopes to achieve and what it needs to deliver, getting to know the partner organisation is the next step. If the partner organisation is open to the idea, the account manager could ask to spend some of their working time based at the company's offices; perhaps one day a week to begin with. There is no better way to truly understand the organisation's culture, and some companies that are experienced in working with charity partners now insist that the account manager spend some – or even all – of their time based at the client organisation.

Any understanding or knowledge that can be gained from previous charity partners will be hugely valuable. A significant advantage would be to know how the corporate partner prefers to be managed and what works for the workforce. The previous charity partner may also be happy to share reporting templates to avoid the reinvention of something that already works, and specific details about the results of their partnership, such as what was raised by regional offices, which is critical for setting realistic targets.

The account manager should give some thought to the different motivations of the corporate partner's employees. If there are people with a personal connection to the charity's cause, they could obviously be good allies and spokespeople to motivate colleagues. The main contact, often in the corporate responsibility team, may have several motivations, including personal promotion or recognition within specific areas of their business. Pitching ideas in such a way as to address individual motivations as well as business objectives should make the charity's suggestions hard to dismiss.

Good communications

Developing and delivering a good communications strategy is crucial to the success of a year's partnership. At the start of the relationship the charity should get an overview of all available communications channels and plot these against key fundraising events or awareness-raising activities to ensure that all opportunities are maximised.

As the charity gets to know the partner it will begin to understand the culture at the company, and it should use that understanding to target future communications better. Perhaps some sections of the workforce lack access to the intranet, for example, so the charity could consider a printed newsletter (which could be produced in-house to save costs), posters or a wall calendar to promote events to this section of employees.

It is important to have good internal communications about the partnership. Regular meetings with colleagues within the charity who are also crucial to the partnership's success are recommended, as this presents the opportunity to share successes, scope out new ideas and troubleshoot issues.

Networking and engaging the workforce

In the first quarter the charity should use every opportunity to meet and present to employees across the partner company. Thoroughly engage them in the cause, and a significant degree of the fundraising will follow. If there is an appropriate opportunity, use video or real case studies to bring the cause to life. Large charities with appropriate resources could consider a regional roadshow to deliver induction presentations or information sessions to regional offices.

If there are existing opportunities to engage employees at a very senior level, use senior managers to reflect the importance placed on the partnership. If such opportunities are not apparent, the account manager should look to create some, perhaps combining a meeting between directors with a seeing-is-believing visit to one of the charity's services or beneficiary projects.

Providing the partner company with varied fundraising ideas is one part of engaging the workforce. Thought should also be given to the beneficiary projects that will appeal or, if funds are to be kept unrestricted, to using varied examples of the charity's work to engage supporters who are driven by different interests.

The charity should set up regular meetings with the corporate partner to report on progress and discuss future plans or ideas. At the first of these meetings the charity should establish exactly what the partner would like to see by way of reports and how often.

Potential pitfalls and strategic issues

Fundraising fatigue

Regardless of how experienced a corporate team may be in managing Charity of the Year partnerships, it is inevitable that some charities will face fundraising fatigue from the partner organisation at some point. There are a number of measures that should militate against this:

• Utilise varied fundraising ideas to ensure that there is something on the agenda for everyone.

• Celebrate the success of fundraising events throughout the year to ensure that participants feel valued for their hard work.

• Update fundraisers regularly on how much has been raised and the resulting impact on the beneficiary projects. Case studies and quotes should be used in these communications wherever possible to remind people of the charity's cause.

• Vary communications to help engage audiences: thank-you cards, posters or certificates may be appropriate for regional offices, while the use of new media, presentations or charity ambassadors might be appropriate for bigger events.

Misunderstanding of objectives or responsibilities

If a charity does not clearly understand the company's objectives it runs the risk of under-delivering on expectations at the end of the partnership or damaging the relationship, or both. This is something that the charity should take very seriously. Senior managers should challenge account managers on their client plan to be confident that the objectives have been thoroughly researched, discussed with the client and captured appropriately. Senior management should also consider asking for six-monthly progress updates against the agreed objectives to be convinced of progress.

This approach should also ensure that opportunities beyond fundraising are not missed, which is all too easy to do when the account manager is busy with the day-to-day management. Account managers should be disciplined in trying to consider all account growth activities for themselves, and capture these in their client plan, but senior managers should bring the added value of greater experience and a detached perspective to ensure that a thorough approach is taken.

Presenting problems, not solutions

At some point during the partnership, the charity is bound to encounter challenges or barriers. Presenting a positive and solution-focused approach towards the client – which is not the same as always saying 'yes' – is always recommended. The corporate partner should be looking to the charity to be the fundraising experts, and the company's employees will appreciate those times when account managers have made their jobs easier.

Senior managers should look to inspire this approach in their corporate fundraising teams, while account managers should always ask themselves 'If the client's suggestion will not work, what alternative would, and how do I support them in delivering that?'

Considering resources

Senior managers will have an eye on the investment made to deliver a Charity of the Year. Thorough planning by the account manager should provide colleagues with clear guidance on the expected ROI, which is a good starting point. But the charity will also want to consider the value – or potential value – of the added benefits, which can be more difficult to quantify.

To avoid the uncomfortable situation of having to back out, the charity should make an assessment of the ROI of a partnership (in the strictest sense and considering the added value) before pitching for an opportunity. If conversations with a potential partner have been more fluid – i.e. not following a strict application process – the charity should not be afraid to discuss financial targets at an early meeting to get a clear picture of the opportunity. This should also help to reassure the charity about the partner's commitment to working together.

Some charities ask for a minimum financial commitment before they proceed with a corporate partner. With established Charity of the Year partnerships this should not be an issue, as results of previous partners will be published and, if the opportunity is not big enough for any given charity, it will be clear that the charity should not go for it. However, those charities that are in the position of being the first partner should consider whether to ask for a minimum financial commitment.

Senior managers should be wary of false cost savings. For example, investment in a full-time member of staff to manage a Charity of the Year may seem expensive, but could mean the difference between a small opportunity and a thoroughly engaged corporate partner that feels supported throughout and smashes its fundraising target.

Celebrating success and leaving a lasting legacy

If the charity plans well, embeds the charity partnership throughout the partner organisation, maintains good communications throughout the year and monitors progress against agreed objectives, it should have not only a successful Charity of the Year partnership, but also a strong relationship with a company which will continue to assist wherever it can.

This may not be in terms of future fundraising, but may well be in some of those other areas outlined in the account growth section of the client plan, such as volunteering, expert support, introductions, awareness, gifts in kind . . . the list goes on. Hopefully, the charity will find that the partner of one year becomes a friend for many more.

Case study: The Place2Be and Credit Suisse UK partnership

Credit Suisse UK is primarily based in one large office in Canary Wharf. In 2008, The Place2Be was successful in its bid to become Credit Suisse's Charity of the Year. The Place2Be is a charity working inside schools to improve the emotional well-being of children, their families and the whole school community. Each year the charity's fundraising team of just eight people raises a total of around £7 million, with £2.5 million from voluntary sources. With the Credit Suisse UK partnership, The Place2Be raised a phenomenal £915,000 during the two years they worked together. They also explored a range of significant non-financial benefits:

• Credit Suisse opened up its Canary Wharf offices for children from The Place2Be beneficiary projects to make on-site visits. The children were invited to act as traders, buying and selling units in chocolate production. Such activities were fantastic for engaging Credit Suisse employees with the work of The Place2Be and presented an unusual perk for the children.

• Credit Suisse donated around £100,000 in gifts in kind including design and production of printed materials, digital media production, donations of raffle and auction prizes, events services and catering.

• Ten bilingual Credit Suisse employees worked as pro bono translators to support The Place2Be on a project to produce their information leaflets in a range of languages for parents who did not have English as their first language.

• The Place2Be was able to gain funding from new sources by showcasing its successful partnership with Credit Suisse.

• As key sponsors of the National Gallery, Credit Suisse introduced The Place2Be to the National Gallery's education team to discuss ways they could work together. The result was that Place2Be children from various schools attended gallery-based art workshops and this in turn provided a great volunteering opportunity for Credit Suisse employees.

In managing the partnership, Credit Suisse asked for the account manager to be based within the corporate citizen team, enabling them to fully embed within the organisation. Investment in a full-time member of staff to do this may seem like a big commitment, but it enabled the account manager to explore and develop the full range of benefits.

Summary

This partnership's success was down to several factors. It was the right opportunity to go for because the beneficiary project was relevant to Credit Suisse employees, the potential ROI was very healthy and a single account manager was able to easily engage the target workforce based in one location. Once successful in the bid, the charity displayed excellent management and was able to maximise communications, networking opportunities and therefore the financial and non-financial benefits: the key factors in any partnership's success.

CHAPTER FOURTEEN

Payroll giving: an opportunity not to be missed

Ruth Freeman

Introduction

Payroll giving is an easy, tax-efficient way for employees or those receiving a pension to support any charity directly from their pay, as long as they pay tax through PAYE (pay as you earn) and their employers have a payroll giving scheme in place. It is also known as GAYE (give as you earn).

It is the only form of tax-effective giving where the donor receives all of the tax back automatically. This is unlike Gift Aid where the repayment of tax is only calculated at the basic rate, meaning that those paying the 40% and 50% rates have to complete a self-assessment tax return to achieve further repayment. It should be noted, however, that as it is the donor who receives the tax benefits, charities will only profit if they can influence donors to pass on these benefits by encouraging them to sign up to higher levels of giving.

When applied effectively, payroll giving can assist companies with the delivery of their corporate responsibility programmes and engender a good-to-work-for culture, which is central to the success of many businesses. Most importantly, it is an excellent mechanism for providing a regular, predictable and sustainable income for a range of charities and good causes.

How it works

Product

Payroll giving donations are taken from gross pay before tax has been deducted, so the charity receives the pledged amount each month but it costs the donor less in net terms (see table 14.1). Once a donor has signed up to payroll giving, the donations continue until the donor cancels the instruction or terminates their employment. The lifetime value of a payroll giver is between five and eight years (Potter & Scales 2008, p. 42). Currently, payroll giving mandates[1] are not transferable between employers, and it is

TABLE 14.1 WHAT PAYROLL GIVING COSTS THE DONOR*			
Individual's monthly pledge/ amount received by charity (minus any admin. fee)	Cost to 20% rate tax payer	Cost to 40% rate tax payer	Cost to 50% rate tax payer
£5.00	£4.00	£3.00	£2.50
£10.00	£8.00	£6.00	£5.00
£20.00	£16.00	£12.00	£10.00
£60.00	£48.00	£36.00	£30.00

* at 2012 rates

estimated that £71 million was lost to charities between 1999 and 2007 as a result (HM Government 2011, p. 38). The charity sector is campaigning to bring about changes to address this issue.

Administration

When a company decides to set up a payroll giving scheme there is a requirement to sign up with an HM Revenue and Customs (HMRC) approved payroll giving agency which will administer and monitor the scheme; these are listed on the HMRC website (www.hmrc.gov.uk).

The agency will do most of the administrative work; all the company has to do is provide lists of donors and charities that are to be supported (via payroll giving mandates) and make one payment to the agency each month. The agency then disburses the money to the charities.

Most agencies make a small charge to the charity for this service: typically 0–4% (HMRC n.d.). Sometimes companies will agree to pay the agency costs and, if they do, these costs can be offset against their profits for tax purposes. Any additional costs incurred by the company, such as the time preparing documentation for the agencies, can also be offset in this way.

Promotion

Charities can market payroll giving in a variety of ways but, as is often the case with fundraising campaigns, the most successful method is face to face. Promoting payroll giving face to face is quite specialised and can be labour-intensive because results are unpredictable; this is why an increasing number of charities are deciding to work with professional fundraising organisations (PFOs).

PFOs are commercial organisations that promote payroll giving on behalf of a range of charities (this range is often called a basket). Typically, while there is no cost to the company, the charity pays the PFO for each payroll giver recruited (costs vary and average about £45 for a donor giving £4 per month).[2]

According to HMRC, most PFOs belong to the Association of Payroll Giving Organisations (APGO). The Association has its own code of conduct to which all its members must adhere. All members of APGO are also members of the Institute of Fundraising and therefore commit to abide by the Institute of Fundraising's codes of fundraising practice.

Adhering to APGO's code means that, while PFOs are paid by the charities that they actively promote, they are required to give employees within companies they approach an unrestricted choice:

> Members of the Association will ensure that their staff when promoting Payroll Giving and including any sub contracted employees allow donors to select ANY charity, even if this charity is not represented by that PFO.
>
> APGO 2010

IOF's code, *Committed Giving in the Workplace*, also states:

> Employees MUST be permitted to support any fundraising organisation through their employer's Payroll Giving scheme.
>
> IOF 2008, p. 6

In an IOF code of fundraising practice, 'MUST' implies that this is a legal requirement. Therefore, this statement applies to all PFOs, whether or not they are members of APGO or IOF.

This means that PFOs are obliged to take instruction for any registered charities whether or not they are in their basket, and when this happens they cannot charge that charity for the donor.

Note that PFOs sell their services directly to companies and will often try to negotiate an exclusive deal with individual companies so that these companies will not work with other PFOs. However, any exclusivity deal should only be between the PFO and the company; in other words, it should not preclude charities from independently approaching any company for support.

Choosing a PFO

PFOs, like other commercial concerns, operate in a very competitive market, so it is wise to shop around. Here are some considerations:

• What are the recruitment costs per donor?

• What is their refund policy for lapsed or non-paying donors?

• Which other charities do they work with: will the competition be too great?

• What donor information is provided?

• How flexible is the PFO? Will it allow your charity to be included in the basket on a company-by-company basis?

• What sort of accreditation do they have? Looking at testimonials is always a good idea.

Market information

Market penetration

Since its introduction in 2001 payroll giving has failed to reach anything like its potential. Of the 29.5 million people in the UK who gave to charity in 2010/11 (CAF & NCVO 2011, p. 5), only 3% chose payroll giving as a preferred option (see fig. 14.1). And while collectively they generated £114 million (Turner 2011), this accounted for just 1% of £11 billion raised (fig. 14.2; CAF & NCVO 2011, p. 8).

With just 720,000 of the UK workforce signed up to payroll giving in 2010/11 (down from 724,000 in 2009/10: Turner 2011) and with 32% of donors still preferring direct debit as their regular giving option (see fig 14.1), the challenge for charities is to understand why payroll giving take-up rates are comparatively low and consequently whether there is merit in adding this form of giving to the product portfolio.

Market potential

Given that 97% of UK donors are not payroll givers, the untapped potential appears extensive. The question is: why has payroll giving as a philanthropic mechanism thus far failed to inspire a significant level of donor support? Is there something about the promotion of payroll giving being more about the method than the cause, and that the marketing tends to centre on the tax benefits to the donor rather than the altruistic act itself? What is clear is that what should be a simple and attractive scheme has not seen the desired levels of success, except perhaps via the PFOs.

In terms, therefore, of establishing potential and making consequent decisions about investment, it is important for charities to realise that, as a stand-alone tool, payroll giving is unlikely to achieve high levels of new (cold) donor acquisition at either employer or employee level. This is unless the charity has a link to a bigger campaign, ideally where the charitable goals and outcomes are well-defined.

It is probably more pertinent to assess existing supporters. What are the current and past levels of workplace or corporate support? How many employees have already signed a payroll giving contract? With which

FIGURE 14.1 METHODS OF GIVING: PROPORTION OF DONORS, 2010/11 (CAF & NCVO 2011, P. 10)

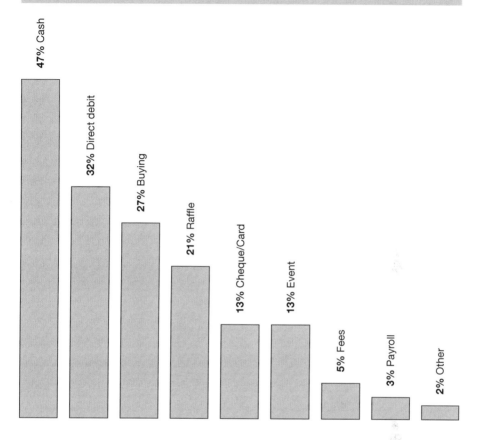

employees is your relationship at the development stage and could be developed further?

Strategy

Position

In terms of deciding a strategy for payroll giving, it's important for charities to consider how their position, in terms of support, perception and cause, could impact on their success. Charities most likely to succeed with payroll giving are those with a strong and instantly recognisable brand, those with high levels of public backing or those with a niche or dedicated supporter base.

For charities that don't enjoy high levels of public awareness, or those that fund more controversial projects, achieving results with payroll giving

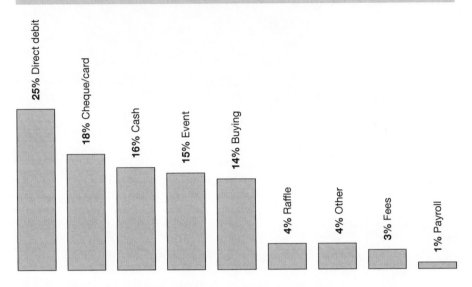

FIGURE 14.2 METHODS OF GIVING: SHARE OF TOTAL DONATIONS BY METHOD (2010/11: CAF & NCVO 2011, P. 10)

will be more challenging, and choosing a PFO as the preferred method of promotion, while offering a low-risk option in terms of investment, will most likely achieve little success.

Objectives

Some charities' goal will be to offer a new proposition to existing supporters; for others it will be a chance to reach out to a different, regular-giving demographic. Any charities that fall into one of these categories could judiciously decide to promote payroll giving themselves and expect results. For those likely to be in the front of people's minds in a competitive environment, opting to be in a PFO basket would also be a reasonable decision.

Where the goal is to maximise reach across all market sectors but where the staff resource is limited, introducing payroll giving to the portfolio and working with a PFO could provide suitable opportunities. The extent of these opportunities will, as mentioned, depend on the type and reputation of the charity. Where a charity's objective is to increase market share significantly, grow the donor database and cultivate corporate relationships, then investing in staff resources and spending time on developing bespoke payroll giving campaigns and engaging with the donors (at both employer and employee levels) should achieve the greatest levels of success.

For many charities payroll giving is undoubtedly an effective way to generate regular and sustainable income, but it can also help to deliver other strategic goals, such as increasing the longevity of Charity of the Year partnerships and increasing the matched giving opportunities offered by some of the bigger employers such as Barclays or the Royal Bank of Scotland.

Investment

Determining whether to invest in payroll giving is complex. It is not as straightforward as looking at market penetration or how to increase market share, primarily because of difficulties around assessing the activity of other charities and PFOs working within the target area. It could be argued that entering a PFO basket is a low-risk option to test the market, but how conclusive the results of such a test will be is debateable because of the number of contributory factors affecting success. These include the reach and relationships of the chosen PFO and the nature and breadth of the competition within its proposition list. What this means is that a test could fail because of a given set of circumstances rather than because payroll giving is unworkable.

In considering the options, charities would be wise to assess the potential within their existing database because if this is of a reasonable level then there is every likelihood that, with the right approach, payroll giving can be introduced to a number of them. In these cases charities may prefer to do the ask themselves rather than employing the services of a PFO. This will afford them the opportunity to develop the existing relationship and ensure that payroll giving is part of the ongoing support package. To do this will require staff trained in the technicalities of payroll giving, some robust and creative marketing and an experienced canvassing resource.

Case study: Making Payday Count appeal

The beauty of payroll giving, as with any other form of regular giving, is that it gives charities the opportunity to invite donors to become stakeholders in the long-term future of the cause that they are being asked to support. For the Myton Hospices, having just built a new hospice in Coventry, there was the potential to invite employees to play a part in securing its future, so they launched their Making Payday Count appeal.

One company that took part was a small engineering company in the heart of Coventry with 42 employees. The Myton fundraisers spent a lot of time with the company's Financial Director and the Managing Director talking about the work of the hospice and the need for support from the people of Coventry. They were invited to look round the new building and were strongly encouraged to commit to the scheme. A date was set for the promotion and, a week before, posters and flyers were circulated across every area of the company. These contained very simple statements such as 'The Myton Hospices give Coventry its own hospice' and the information that the team from Myton would be coming to talk to the company about the hospice and about how the employees could help. No mention was made at this time about payroll giving.

Four fundraisers went to do the promotion and, because of the relationship that had already been built, they were allowed to walk round and talk to employees. The response from the employees was phenomenal: they came away with 31 signed mandates (73% of the employees). The annual value of the promotion was £1,645 and the staff continue to support the hospice in other ways, making the value of their support nearly £6,000 over three years.

Charity-run promotions: a quick guide to getting started

Developing a campaign

To be really successful, charities need to decide how to position the payroll giving proposition so that it is attractive to potential corporate supporters. Ideally the ask will centre on a clear link between giving and outcomes; for example: 'If everyone at Jo Bloggs and Sons gave £1 per week via payroll giving it would provide x'. In terms of deciding the level of the ask the best model is to adopt a flexible approach based on the profile of individual workplaces.

Target lists

The best prospects will be companies that are warm to the cause or to payroll giving, and preferably to both. Lists of companies that have signed a payroll giving contract can be obtained from the agencies, although some make a small charge for the information. A second priority could be small to medium-sized companies that are unlikely to have been targeted by the PFOs.

The initial approach

Getting the initial agreement from a company to support your charity is, of course, the most important factor. When approaching a company for support, a charity is likely to see greater results if it focuses on the cause or on the desired outcome. For example, in the Myton Hospices case study the charity approached the company by asking it to help play a part in securing the future of a newly built hospice.

Once the initial agreement to support the cause has been attained and a relationship has been built, payroll giving can be introduced as the best mechanism to achieve it.

Materials

Some payroll giving agencies will only accept their own mandates or ones that have previously been agreed with them; so, when designing bespoke materials, charities should always check that they meet all of the company and agency requirements

Teaser campaigns

It is always a good idea to run some kind of teaser campaign prior to the promotion. Some charities choose something that will trigger interest in the promotion itself, such as a buffet or a competition, while others focus on publicising the work of the charity. Trying to get people's interest is the important thing, so it is worth taking time to understand the workforce dynamics and preferences; this allows the approach to be tailored. Ways of running a teaser campaign can include poster or email communications, flyers, desktop promotions and DVDs.

The promotion

Hopefully, some form of a face-to-face campaign will be agreed, which will usually be in a canteen or a communal area, or a group presentation. The important thing is to have the right people running the promotion, and the right materials. Visuals such as DVDs or PowerPoint can be very effective, and posters, table-top talkers (freestanding display material) and flyers are also promotion essentials. Mandates will be provided by the payroll giving agency. If a charity wants to use a bespoke mandate, it is advisable to get it checked by the agency. It can be a good idea to have some kind of incentive to encourage people to sign up (such as pens, key rings or little teddy bears).

Data management

Data management of payroll givers is slightly more complex than management of other types of donor, because there is a third party (the payroll giving agency) involved. The payments are received by the agency and reported to the charities as a list, so allocation to individuals can be more difficult and time-consuming. This may mean that charities prefer to work with a data management company that has the appropriate software to process the data directly from the agency.

The important thing for the charity is having the capability to track individual donations, because this means that lapsed support can be dealt with quickly. It is also prudent to ensure that all donations can be tracked back to the donor's employer.

Donor care

Payroll givers should be treated in the same way as other regular givers, which is why it is important to be able to track and monitor their giving. On receipt of a signed payroll giving mandate it is important that the Donor Care team contact the donor to thank them, and then have a plan in place to communicate regularly with them. This is easier perhaps for charities with a smaller database of payroll givers, but it is critical, whatever the size of the charity, that this happens.

If donors are recruited via a PFO, it is important that their reporting processes give the charities the right level of donor information to enable them to liaise directly with the donors.

A word about post-tax schemes

The forerunner to today's payroll giving scheme was a post-tax scheme introduced by Barnardo's in the early 1900s. Very few charities use this form of giving now, but it is worth keeping it in the portfolio because, with the introduction of Gift Aid, the value of donations given in this way is increased. Many people who give small amounts through payroll giving are not concerned with the tax benefits to themselves and are happy for the charity to gain the benefit through Gift Aid.

Post-tax payroll giving works best in cases where a charity has developed a close relationship with one company. No payroll giving agencies are involved in distributing the donations, so the company has to do this internally. Therefore, if a company is supporting one charity it only has to send one cheque, as opposed to numerous cheques to various charities.

Not having to go via an agency adds the benefit of there not being any administrative costs to pay, except for the internal cost of the time that it takes the finance department to distribute the donation(s), hence why supporting one or a few charities is helpful. Post-tax payroll giving can also be useful if donors want to give a smaller amount, because there is not a minimum donation (with pre-tax payroll giving the minimum donation is £1 a month per charity).

Conclusion

Despite the lack of popularity of this form of giving, as revealed in the low take-up figures, the untapped potential is still undoubtedly vast. Charities with a high profile or dedicated support base have good prospects for increasing employees' take-up and therefore should consider investing time and resources in campaigns and engaging with potential (or existing) donors. In doing so, these charities will have the chance to create a steadier, more dependable form of income for themselves.

Notes

1   A payroll giving mandate is the form that authorises the employer to make deductions from the employee's pay. Employees must complete the form, stating the name of the charity or charities they wish to support and the amount that they would like to give.
2   Author-calculated average using figures from PFO websites.

References

APGO (2010), *Association of Payroll Giving Organisations Code of Conduct*, London, Association of Payroll Giving Organisations, revised August 2010
CAF and NCVO (2011), *UK Giving: An Overview of Charitable Giving in the UK, 2010/11*, London/West Malling, National Council for Voluntary Organisations and Charities Aid Foundation
HM Government (2011), *Giving White Paper*, London, The Stationery Office
HMRC (n.d.), 'Payroll Giving: Introduction for Employers and Pension Providers' [web page], www.hmrc.gov.uk, accessed 1 February 2012
IOF (2008), *Committed Giving in the Workplace*, London, Institute of Fundraising
Potter, Vanessa and Jonathan Scales (2008) *Review of Payroll Giving*, Strategy Complete Ltd, commissioned by the Institute of Fundraising
Turner, Howard (2011), *Table 10.8 – Payroll Giving*, London, HM Revenue & Customs

CHAPTER FIFTEEN
Oxfam corporate partnerships

Chris Ashworth

Win-win? How innovation drives Oxfam's corporate partnerships

'Give a man a fish': so began the Chinese proverb that became the hallmark of Oxfam GB's early television advertising campaigns in the 1990s. It distilled the essence of Oxfam's work – helping people to work their own way out of poverty – into a strapline that gets quoted 20 years on and has become synonymous with the charity's work. It also catapulted one of the most successful fundraising innovations into the public consciousness: the £2-a-month direct debit scheme. That scheme, alongside the 700-strong shop network spanning the length and breadth of the UK, reveals how innovation has been a central thread through much of the charity's fundraising efforts.

While Oxfam is not as old as the Chinese proverb, it celebrates its 70th anniversary in 2012. Corporate fundraising is a relatively new discipline for Oxfam, having only been a stand-alone function since 2003. In that short space of time it has built great partnerships with other household names and benefited from being a late entrant into what is undoubtedly one of the most demanding but most rewarding of fundraising disciplines.

The particular focus of the corporate partnerships team over the last three years has been our concept of the win-win partnership model. Oxfam's flagship Clothes Exchange partnership with Marks and Spencer (M&S), its longstanding credit card scheme with Co-operative Financial Services, and more recently its 100% Giving campaign with PayPal and the PizzaExpress integrated campaign, demonstrate the results of operating with a win-win formula and bringing innovation into partnerships from the outset.

This chapter looks at the reasons for those successes, the organisational history, and the approaches Oxfam has taken to structure, ethics and, in particular, innovation.

Background to Oxfam

Oxfam was established in 1942 in response to the plight of the Greek people who were cut off from supplies due to World War II. The Oxford Committee for Famine Relief, as it was known then, continued with a mandate to help the poorest and most marginalised people on the planet. Over time its scale and purpose grew. Now in 2012 Oxfam is part of an international confederation of Oxfams that concentrates on three inter-linked areas of work: development programmes in 98 countries; campaigning for change to challenge inequality; and humanitarian response. In short, it is a global movement of people working with others to overcome poverty and suffering.

Operating in 98 countries on a vast range of programmes and initiatives requires considerable resources. In 2009/10 Oxfam's net income was £242 million, the majority of which came from individuals either as donations, through fundraising events, or through the charity's shop network (Oxfam 2010, p. 2). It is a staggering amount of income that has risen steadily since the Ethiopia famine in 1984 and is based on a wide portfolio of complementary fundraising activities.

Like many of its peers in the fundraising sector, Oxfam's income from corporate engagement is a relatively small but important contributor to its income: just 2% of overall income (£4.5 million). For the first five years, however, the income was barely 1% of fundraising efforts[1] and it has been the considerable remodelling and refining of the corporate partnerships team's approach that has seen a step change that is taking the charity into the future with confidence and intent.

Corporate engagement and corporate fundraising

Mission, credibility and integrity

While corporate fundraising is less than a decade old within Oxfam, corporate engagement within the organisation has a much longer history. It has a long association with the private sector, particularly through campaigning work. The charity's relevance and stature with the multinationals has been built over decades and is directly associated to its mission to overcome poverty and suffering.

Part of how Oxfam is working towards fulfilling this mission is by empowering the poor and marginalised. It has done so by helping establish the Fair Trade movement, campaigning publicly and privately on labour rights and working for sustainable livelihoods for the most marginalised workers in less-developed countries. And it has done this in many ways, from supporting the establishment of alliances such as the Ethical Trade

Initiative, to offering insights into and thought leadership[2] about the social impact of global supply chains and investments and helping businesses understand the true measures for corporate responsibility. Gaining credibility within the business of multinationals has never been, and never will be, a purpose for Oxfam's corporate partnerships team, but has been a consequence of our proximity to and depth of relationships in this area.

For any rights-based and campaigning organisation such as Oxfam, integrity and independence are paramount. It is important that at all times the corporate fundraising is in harmony with the charity's ethical stance. Navigating this path using a strong governance structure and ethics board is one of the key ways to have a measured approach to corporate fundraising.

Effecting positive change for beneficiaries

Equally, as corporate responsibility has developed rapidly as a discipline, the realisation both by some of the leading proponents in the private sector and by Oxfam is that a multi-layered relationship can be crucial, supportive and profitable in equal measure.

To this end, corporate fundraising within Oxfam is complementary to a wider private-sector strategy. The objective of this strategy is to work with companies to adapt business models, change policies and improve practice. From working on joint initiatives with multinationals to sharing learning across sectors and within value chains such as retail, fast-moving consumer goods and finance, Oxfam's private-sector strategy takes precedence over fundraising as a core component of its mission and purpose. It means, most fundamentally, that the charity's measures of success are effecting positive change for its beneficiaries; income generation is only one route to that.

However, this type of immersive, mature dialogue with large organisations means that creating the space for a corporate partnership is in fact more efficient. In the corporate partnerships team we have recognised that one of the key aspects to win-win (fundraising) partnerships is the ability to understand and appreciate the strategies and challenges of our partners. Through Oxfam's proximity to and engagement in private-sector work, we are able to access this first-hand.

From acorns

The corporate fundraising team's early forays into corporate fundraising began by reacting to opportunities with existing ethical partners. Oxfam's trading network was beginning to source and support small enterprises that were providing fairly traded goods for the shop network. Furthermore, its relationship with ethical leaders such as The Co-operative Group, Café

Direct and the organisers of the Glastonbury music festival meant that the corporate fundraising team could establish strong associations quickly.

Oxfam's programme work was concerned with the development and support of small enterprises in less-developed countries, and concepts such as market access were areas where help was sought from the private sector. This coincided with the decision to develop a corporate fundraising policy in 2003. This policy, much of which remains in place today, established the boundaries, benchmarks and principles upon which the charity would operate.

One of Oxfam's first initiatives was the Oxfam–Co-operative Bank credit card. Now a mainstay in charity fundraising, the charity credit-card scheme provides Oxfam with a significant and sustainable source of income, with tens of thousands of customers remaining loyal to the scheme and its impact for significantly longer than many credit-card rivals. There are now a great many affinity schemes for charities across a wide range of products and services, all of which find their roots in innovative schemes such as this one led by The Co-operative Group. This scheme was one of the first to demonstrate the advantages that charities uniquely bring to a product or service.

Overcoming barriers

Establishing those early corporate engagement principles afforded Oxfam the opportunity to look internally across all its workstreams and consider the cultural and structural barriers and opportunities created.

An organisation that for 60 years had always represented the poorest and most marginalised people and that was used to challenging those creating inequality, meant that there was a natural resistance to embracing corporate fundraising. There was a legitimate fear of being thought to be involved in greenwashing or of the charity's values being undermined by becoming dependent on organisations that pursue and prioritise profit over their social impact. Therefore Oxfam's underpinning principle is not to work with organisations that substantially or wilfully undermine its cause.

This resistance and fear also meant that the creation of the policy had to be a consultative process that was looked at from not only a fundraising perspective, but also one that understood and respected the views from the campaigning and advocacy functions as well as the development and humanitarian divisions.

The ethical checking process

Examining the potential partner

It is essential to have a robust process that supports your organisation's principles. No relationship or partnership with Oxfam can happen without first being subject to internal scrutiny. The corporate partnerships team's due diligence process examines four key areas before additional expertise and external input are brought in.

The 'four Ps' looks at the potential partner-organisation's products, principles, processes and policies. We examine two areas:

• The direction of travel of the organisation on issues of concern.

• The standards the organisation does and should subscribe to within its sector: environmental, social and those related to governance.

This enables us to make a judgement to ensure that the partner organisation will not substantially or wilfully undermine the charity's cause. This concern with the charity's mission takes precedence over the next stage, which is to examine the commercial logic of the opportunity, the cost-benefit analysis and the impact on brand.

Balancing the partnership

This approach does have benefits for the partnership that aren't immediately obvious. It improves the private sector's understanding of the charity sector and creates a firmer footing for each organisation to engage. It can be difficult in corporate–charity relationships for the charity to avoid simply supporting a company's predefined business goals and effectively becoming a supplier. It is important, therefore, to be clear about your organisation's own goals. In these situations, the balance of power can be heavily weighted in favour of the company's initiative. But by demonstrating insight, confidence and the importance of your own operating principles you will be able to add a dimension of credibility that can run through the partnership.

Our award-winning PizzaExpress partnership in 2010 was a great example of this approach whereby all the promotional materials for the campaign, such as the t-shirts and wristbands, had to be sourced ethically. We were able to build those requirements into the project plan from a very early stage. It did the relationship no harm to ensure that those areas were agreed and their importance highlighted from the outset. It wasn't done to protect the charity's image but because doing otherwise would run counter to its overall purpose.

Embarking on innovation

Oxfam's relationship with Marks and Spencer goes back all the way to 1996, but the partnerships team and M&S increased dialogue during the Clothes Code campaign in 2003. Of the retailers referenced, M&S was the most responsive; the company developed a code of conduct and became an early member of the Ethical Trading Initiative. During the long association between Oxfam and M&S, information has been shared and each organisation has supported the other on a wide range of issues, from fair trade to Plan A (M&S's plan of commitments to change the way the company works by 2012).

Most importantly, both organisations have shared values. Like Oxfam, M&S has placed ethical considerations at the centre of its business practices and continues to lead the way on a comprehensive and long-term approach to corporate responsibility.

In 2008, Oxfam launched the Clothes Exchange which saw the UK's biggest clothing retailer team up with the biggest charity-shop network. Consumers bringing back M&S clothing to Oxfam shops through the exchange receive a £5 M&S voucher redeemable against a £35 spend on clothing, home or beauty products at M&S. It is the first initiative on the high street to reward shoppers for recycling clothing. It allows consumers to keep supporting charity even while times are tight. The Clothes Exchange creates a triple win: it is good for the environment because it reduces landfill, good for both sets of customers and good for beneficiaries. Since its launch, it has raised over £6.7 million for Oxfam, and has saved over 4,500 tonnes of clothing from going into landfill (Oxfam 2011).

At the core of the Clothes Exchange is innovation. The long and fruitful relationship with M&S has meant that both organisations have a better understanding of each other's strategies and challenges. The win-win formula that has made the scheme so successful is because it does not subscribe to a prescriptive formula of corporate–charity engagement.

Both organisations have unique strengths and capabilities that complement each other. That combination and the ability to explore the shared space are fundamental to the operating principles that now underpin Oxfam's approach to corporate partnerships.

The present day: operating principles for win-win partnerships

The Clothes Exchange does not involve a financial transaction between the two organisations. Unlike a grant, sponsorship or an on-pack promotion, it creates a different type of value. Within Oxfam this has been a really important learning curve that has taught the organisation about the nature, scope and strategic intent of the charity's efforts.

Oxfam does not have a corporate fundraising team. Such a team would limit the impact it can have on behalf of the organisation. Rather, by creating a corporate partnerships team, the charity seeks to create wider value. The team has a wider scope than the income that the charity generates. While the bottom line remains of key importance, too many opportunities are missed from developing a corporate engagement team around that single direct financial dimension. By looking at the integrated nature of a partnership, the team can broaden Oxfam's and its corporate partners' horizons and find some really innovative offerings.

The award-winning PizzaExpress campaign in 2010 was shaped on this premise. The integrated appeal involved not only the corporate partnerships team, but also the shop network and the Oxfam Unwrapped Gifts team. At the heart of the initiative was the ability for Oxfam shop customers to receive a £5 voucher for PizzaExpress when they spent £5 or more in an Oxfam shop. In addition to this there were promotions on the menu, in the restaurants and through the PizzaExpress email database.

Through the scheme Oxfam was able to offer both its customers and supporters a great deal on the high street, promote its Christmas gift range and reach a wider audience with its cause.

The uniqueness of the scheme meant that the public relations coverage it received was far greater than that of a standard charity fundraiser. The wider benefits of increasing footfall into stores, promoting the gift range and generating significant column inches at Christmas would not have been realised had the charity not facilitated a wider, integrated approach to its work. It also means that Oxfam's long-term credibility to craft and create win-win partnerships is heard across the corporate landscape.

The future

A decade of learning and the recent high-profile successes of corporate partnerships for Oxfam have allowed us in the corporate partnerships team to reflect heavily on the key attributes that create value and lead to greater impact on Oxfam's beneficiaries.

The team's overall strategy is built on the principles found more often in marketing and business development than in traditional transactional fundraising techniques. We base it on understanding the market, sectors, emerging trends and the variety of stakeholders that differ from philanthropy in trusts, foundations and major donor fundraising. This overall strategy allows us to research and respond to the challenges that businesses face, track emerging brands in the UK and look for parallels in digital and new-media routes to market. We understand the charity's strengths and apply those strengths to the external opportunities.

The structure of the corporate partnerships team within Oxfam might not be particularly telling or different from that of many other charities.

Our team of seven is broadly structured around sector and account management (for instance 'technology' as a sector and 'Nokia' as a key account). However, the aspects we consider to be equally important are innovation and diversity. Each member of the team has responsibility for leading on a small portfolio of new, untried or emergent initiatives. This ensures that each of us takes ownership of innovation and most importantly understands our individual role within that area.

This approach also builds in the flexibility for us to adapt to an initiative with the right balance across the project team. A win-win partnership will not be fully realised if you only have people creating great ideas. You need team members who can optimise the general concept and those who are strong implementers. These distinct capabilities are rarely found in one person and so you need to develop a diverse, complementary team around the opportunity.

The team's role within the wider organisation also has a significant bearing on the charity's overall success. As outlined earlier, developing a strategy and structure that look at corporate partnerships rather than corporate fundraising in a vibrant and busy organisation, makes considerable sense; but the opposite is also true. For example, our corporate partnerships team is now emerging as a centre of excellence for corporate engagement within the organisation by encouraging and supporting others from all disciplines and fundraising areas within Oxfam to develop their understanding of how to succeed in this area.

By guiding teams on key requirements for sponsorship proposals, scrutinising business cases and supporting pitches, we have been able to increase the capabilities of the wider organisation and increase the overall footprint of its engagement considerably. Indeed, within Oxfam's Trading Division (which manages the charity's shops, donated stock and volunteering network), such is the level of activity that there is a newly formed team entirely focused on these areas of corporate activity. Over time it is hoped that this approach will continue to be a key driver of growth and sustainable value.

Conclusion

While Oxfam will continue to resource the portfolio of initiatives that exist in the corporate–charity space, whether that be Charity of the Year or philanthropic grants, it will also use these opportunities as springboards into innovation and collaboration for long-term partnership development. Above all, the corporate partnerships team will continue to develop relationships that go beyond fundraising and benefit Oxfam and the beneficiaries that the charity represents.

Notes

1   Income from companies is part of the donations and legacies income (£101.2 million) which is listed on page 5 of the *Oxfam Annual Report & Accounts 2010/11*. The proportions quoted here are taken from internal figures.

2   Thought leaders in this context are experts who research and develop insights on macro-level phenomena and are often those who produce policy papers or publications on new areas that get picked up in the mainstream. For example, 'Lord Stern is a thought leader on climate change' or 'Michael Porter is a thought leader in marketing strategy'.

References

Oxfam (2010), *Oxfam Annual Report & Accounts 2009/10*, Oxford, Oxfam GB

Oxfam (2011), *Twiggy Encourages M&S Customers to Recycle 400,000 Clothes in One Day for Oxfam* [press release], 5 September , Oxford, Oxfam GB

CHAPTER SIXTEEN

Alzheimer's Society: building success from the ground up

Alix Wooding

Introduction

Do you recognise any of the following thoughts?

• My charity will never win a staff vote.

• My cause is 'unsexy': no brands will want to be associated with us.

• My colleagues think life would be easier if we didn't have to work with 'evil' companies.

Most corporate fundraisers, in their darkest moments, will have felt one or all of these things. At Alzheimer's Society, there was a time when we certainly felt this way about our own chances of success. However, a focus on the Society's strengths has brought about a change in the corporate fundraising team's attitudes, and our fortunes. The team has grown corporate fundraising income tenfold in five years, from £250,000 to around £2.5 million, and we now work with several companies whose support is worth more than £1 million as well as delivering significant added value to the charity.

This chapter looks at the foundations that we in the corporate fundraising team have put in place that have enabled us to build those successful partnerships. From developing a clear vision, to analysing the resources, tools and skills of the team, to putting in place the right team structure, our approach is rigorous rather than revolutionary, with lessons that will apply to many who are seeking to turn around a disappointing or struggling corporate fundraising function.

About Alzheimer's Society

Alzheimer's Society is the UK's leading care and research charity for people with dementia and their families. There are an estimated 750,000 people with dementia in the UK, and that number is set to grow to 1 million by 2025 (AS 2007, p. 4). The charity provides a range of support services through a national network of local services, from providing one-to-one support for people with dementia and their families, to facilitating support groups and social groups for both people with dementia and their carers. The Society's campaigns and press team continually highlights the issue of dementia in the media, and raises it up the political agenda. In addition, its research programme funds groundbreaking research into the cause, cure, care and prevention of dementia.

The past five years have been a period of considerable change and growth at Alzheimer's Society. The charity has gone from having a turnover of £37.5 million in 2006 (AS 2006, p.10) to £58.7 million in 2010 and £61.6 million in 2011, and in a time of economic uncertainty (AS 2011, p.30). During this period, the charity's fundraised income, including that raised from companies, has grown significantly.

The corporate fundraising context

In the mid-2000s, the state of play in corporate fundraising at Alzheimer's Society was mixed. While there had been notable successes, including being Tesco Charity of the Year in 2001, income had dipped following that partnership, and the success had not been repeated with other companies. There were few long-term corporate supporters, and even fewer that had potential for long-term growth. A partial view of the market meant that opportunities were often missed, or came to light close to deadline, meaning that time invested in applications was limited, and quality was sometimes wanting. In our small corporate fundraising team, as it was at the time, we found our limited resources often taken up with reactive work, leaving us with little time to build a pipeline for the future, and balancing the demands of current clients with the need to generate new business was challenging.

Unsurprisingly, morale was low: the experience of losing out on a large Charity of the Year partnership by fewer than ten votes, coming quick on the heels of a run of losses, gave rise to a general feeling in the team that staff votes were not for us, and we should concentrate either on Charity of the Year partnerships that did not include this step, or on non-Charity of the Year partnerships.

However, an ambitious growth strategy for the organisation, to ensure that it could meet the needs of the growing number of people with dementia, required a shift in the fundraising performance, and corporate fundraising was identified as a key area for growth. Investments in personnel were made and the small team was restructured. Moreover, a new approach was needed alongside the new team.

The blueprint: developing a clear vision and strategy

Developing a new approach that could help meet the ambitions of the charity started with articulating a vision for the team, and what we, the team members, wanted to achieve for the charity and for ourselves. This focused on more than the financial elements of corporate fundraising, and ensured that the motivations of the whole team were reflected.

One of the important elements was allowing ourselves to state without self-consciousness what we wanted to achieve, no matter how unlikely it felt at the time. Writing down that we wanted Alzheimer's Society to be Tesco Charity of the Year again felt both foolish and unlikely. Yet, at the time of writing, Alzheimer's Society has just begun a year-long partnership with Tesco, which generated incredible press on the day of the launch, including several national television news slots and making the front page of the broadsheets.

We set about developing a simple strategy to achieve our vision. We used many familiar tools to analyse our current situation, such as SWOT (strengths, weaknesses, opportunities, and threats) analysis and Boston and Ansoff's matrices, looked at trends in the sector, and aimed to understand the factors that we could and could not influence.

Reviewing strengths and weaknesses objectively was a turning point for the team. Only via a thorough understanding of the organisation's strengths and weaknesses could we understand which types of opportunities to focus on. It also helped us to separate the opportunities from the resources, tools and processes that we applied to them.

The team undertook a full SWOT analysis, and we looked at many factors which affected the Society's chances of success. But a single strength and a single weakness were fundamental in determining the strategy. The Society's strength was the scale of the cause, and its emotive weight, which meant that many people with personal experience of dementia were committed to supporting the charity. The weakness was that, while public awareness was growing, there was still a strong stigma associated with dementia.

Appreciating these two simple facts helped us to see that brands were unlikely to link to Alzheimer's Society until some of the public perception issues had been addressed, which was beyond the control and remit of the corporate fundraising team alone. However, the strength of the cause meant that staff votes – where personal rather than brand motivations are given precedence – were an area where the charity was more likely to succeed. The team also recognised that by leveraging success in this area through good public relations (another area of strength) we could address the weakness, and start to tackle the public perceptions and stigma that stood in the way of creating brand links. This approach of leveraging from an area of strength ensured that we developed our strategy in the direction of Charity of the Year, and away from brand-based activities such as sponsorship and cause-related marketing, at least in the short term.

While the SWOT gave the team this useful insight, it also helped us to see an uncomfortable fact: the Society was failing in areas that should have been areas of strength, namely Charity of the Year. The SWOT analysis helped us to see that not winning these opportunities was not about the opportunities themselves, but about the way in which the team went about approaching them: our resources, processes and tools.

Solid foundations: processes, tools and skills

Understanding that the team was failing in what should have been the Society's area of strength led us to review our processes, tools and skills. This was particularly important, as Charity of the Year opportunities are often process-driven, rather than relationship-driven, opportunities.

The first step was to ensure that we had as much information as possible about the opportunities in advance. This was to stop the reactive behaviour of the past, and to help us to spend our limited resources where we had most chance of success.

The team invested significant time in researching the market place, with the modest ambition of knowing about all Charity of the Year opportunities in the UK. Knowing about them, however, is not the same thing as applying for them all. Our approach is to start from an informed position in order to target the right opportunities. By ensuring that team members know the facts of every opportunity, we can measure them against key criteria, which we have developed around the strengths and weaknesses of the team and the charity, and qualify them. The team's aim is to be able to rank opportunities so that we can prioritise those where there is a good fit, which deliver a specific benefit, and where we believe there is a good chance of success.

The new processes have enabled the team to take a proactive approach even to process-led Charity of the Year opportunities, and we have further strengthened our suit by ensuring we have both the tools and the skills to succeed at every step of the process. We have done this by looking at each stage of the Charity of the Year process from application through to evaluation, and looked at both the tools and skills required. This has resulted in our developing various toolkits for use at various stages. For example, staff vote toolkits ensure that the charity explores every route for securing a staff vote, and a template client plan ensures that the team's account managers think through each client opportunity in the round at the beginning of a partnership.

Our strategy has been to develop the skills of the team, using the resources available. Where necessary, members of the team have been sent on external training courses, but more often than not we have made use of other routes. One area that has been very successful is identifying where Alzheimer's Society's clients have skills in areas that the team is keen to develop, and then facilitating more information skills-sharing with their help. This has resulted in receiving a masterclass from a client who had successfully pitched an Olympic bid, and working with an account manager in private banking to develop the team's account management skills. Identifying these areas of transferable skills has helped us to build the skill base of the team, while simultaneously strengthening relationships with our clients.

The team has also been bolstered by a shift in attitude. We decided that we would focus on quality rather than quantity and that the team would be fully committed to each approach that we made to a company. From a management point of view this meant modelling a commitment to quality and a dedication to reach the highest standards in our own work, thereby creating an atmosphere where 'settling' was not accepted. We are rigorous in our approaches, and we try to leave as little as possible to chance.

Structuring for success

Focusing on resources was another important area in which we made a change. Since the strategy was to focus on developing a pipeline of new business and winning new partnerships, rather than on developing existing partners, it made sense to ensure that we dedicated resources and skills in this area. It followed that the best way to do this was through creating a dedicated resource for new business, as the team knew from experience that new business time was often compromised by the pressures of delivering to current partners. Because of this, it was decided to split the small team into new business and account management roles. The benefits and challenges of this approach are discussed more fully in Chapter 4, but from our experience there are a few pros and cons which are worth noting.

The benefit of having a dedicated new business resource is that you remove the need to make uncomfortable decisions between delivering for your current clients and building future business: ensuring you never have to decide between perfecting an important pitch and providing a report to your major partner's chief executive, for example. In addition, our experience is that the skills required for new business and account management are different and it is rare to find people who are equally skilled at both.

However, it is worth noting that there are downsides to the structure too. Many fundraisers feel more comfortable in a dual role, and so recruiting, particularly to the new business side, can be tough. As it is the new business team that gets the 'wins', it can feel like it is those members of the team who are the ones with all the glory, and so care needs to be taken to celebrate successes on both sides of the team. In addition, and most importantly, there is a risk that the positive relationships you have built up during the new business process will be lost when the people involved in new business step away from the project.

However, there are simple steps that you can take to counteract these: for example, taking steps to recruit from outside the sector where new business skills may be more developed, ensuring client successes are celebrated in the same way as new business wins, and having good handover and 'buddying' between the two teams to ensure that strong relationships are not lost.

Taking the 'two tribes' approach has been very successful for the corporate fundraising team. The new business team members have worked hard to hone their skills. Team members focus, rightly, on relationship building and on creating quality selling opportunities, whether that be through a face-to-face meeting, a formal pitch, or a written proposal or application. We are now at a stage where we specialise further within the new business team, developing sector experts, as well as experts in the different corporate fundraising mechanics such as sponsorship and cause-related marketing.

Resources go beyond the corporate fundraising team, too. The charity has consistently invested in corporate partnerships financially, and has invested senior time from across the organisation to help the team to develop and grow strong relationships which deliver many and varied benefits to the charity.

Clear boundaries

Developing an ethical policy was crucial in ensuring that the team had the confidence and the backing of our colleagues when we developed corporate partnerships. It has also helped our colleagues to have confidence in us: that we aren't out to sign up corporate partners at whatever cost to the charity's reputation or independence.

Without a policy in place, the team found that conversations about a company's suitability for partnership could be time-consuming and often hinged on deeply held, but ultimately personal, views. Our approach was inconsistent, and we were often risk-averse.

Developing an ethical policy has helped the team to focus those conversations away from the personal and on to the wider risks and benefits for people with dementia. We use a company's treatment of people with dementia as our moral yardstick: if the Society is representing the best interests of people with dementia, it simply cannot work with companies that do otherwise. The team has a clear decision-making matrix which maps types of companies against types of fundraising activities. This helps us to know which decisions lie with the corporate fundraising team, and which need to be taken by the senior management team. This has given the team the confidence that when we approach a company, we do so with the backing of our organisation. It has also helped the team to identify the riskier propositions, and deal with them appropriately.

Another thing that has helped improve our colleagues' understanding of and confidence in corporate fundraising, is that the team increasingly involves them in the early stage of applications and pitches, using their expertise to help the charity secure, as well as deliver, partnerships.

Our colleagues speak with a level of authority and authenticity about their work that the team cannot reproduce. Rather than to try and represent Alzheimer's Society and speak for our colleagues, our role is to give them the platform and to build the case for support from which they can best advocate their projects.

Involvement in the application, pitching and negotiation process helps colleagues to be confident that the team is neither underselling what Alzheimer's Society has to offer, nor over-promising what the charity can deliver. Meeting face to face with the potential corporate partner can also reassure them about the nature and the culture of the business that the Society will be working with. Perhaps more importantly, being involved in the process allows them to get excited about the benefits that working with a given company can bring. Their enthusiasm is vital because often they are crucial for the successful delivery of a project, and they can control how a project develops over time.

Challenges

The team's strategy to focus on winning and delivering Charity of the Year partnerships to the best of its ability has paid off, and we are now working with a range of companies in this way, and bringing significant income to the charity. However, all strategies necessarily have their downsides and a focus on Charity of the Year has brought challenges too: Charity of the Year partnerships are largely short-term, and they take a lot of resources to win and to manage.

When we started to focus on Charity of the Year the team was very small and had a limited capacity and little room for flexibility. This meant that with almost every new partnership we needed to recruit a new member of the team. This was easy to justify when the partnership was large, but harder when a smaller partnership took us over the edge of our capacity. However, part of our success in Charity of the Year is our commitment to providing each partnership with the resources it requires, and with the continued support and investment of the Director of Fundraising and the senior management team, we have been able to grow the team in response to our growing success.

As the team has grown, taking on new partnerships has become easier to manage, as we have more room for manoeuvre within the team. Although we try not to move partners between one account manager and another, we are able to give more support to an account manager if they are in a busy time, so that, while they remain the 'face' of a partnership, another may be doing a lot of the work behind the scenes. We have also improved our preparation for big partnerships, and ensured that we get agreement internally on how a large partnership will be resourced before we apply. This removes the need for internal negotiations which eat into valuable fundraising time.

A major issue has been that Charity of the Year relationships have built-in obsolescence, so the team's challenge is to build longer-term partnerships alongside the annual ones. We have focused our limited resources on growing a small number of multi-faceted partnerships. For example, a partnership with Bupa now spans a traditional 'charity of choice' relationship. This involves being charity of choice for the Bupa Great Runs, working with the Bupa Foundation to fund innovative dementia research, sharing Alzheimer's Society's expertise to train Bupa staff in dementia care, and joint marketing activity. The team is currently planning the next stage of the partnership, which will be more public-facing.

By focusing on a few partnerships with a lot of potential, we have been able to build our experience in the corporate fundraising team and gain some case studies that will help us to widen this work in the future. In fact, developing other corporate fundraising income streams is our priority, and we hope that by doing this we will continue the exponential growth in corporate fundraising income that the Society has seen over the past five years.

Conclusion

By taking some simple steps, the team and Alzheimer's Society have been able to turn an inconsistent performance in corporate fundraising into a successful and growing income stream.

Alzheimer's Society's success in corporate partnerships hasn't happened by accident, but has been planned and built over time. By taking simple steps, the team developed the right strategy and created the right environment to deliver it. Strategic planning tools, including a simple SWOT analysis, helped to reveal the strengths that we needed to leverage and the weaknesses that we needed to mitigate in our strategy. Once the strategy was in place, giving our fundraising a clear focus, we were able to address the resources, processes and skills that we needed to deliver it.

This approach has allowed Alzheimer's Society to grow its corporate fundraising income significantly: almost ten-fold in five years. The team is currently working with a range of partners from professional services to those dreamed-of high street stores, and we are not only building on the Society's strengths with regard to corporate fundraising, but also addressing its weaknesses so that it is in a stronger position in the future.

The team still has places that it wants to explore, and we are now working on the next evolution of our strategy, helping to develop new areas and income streams and to take Alzheimer's Society's corporate fundraising to the next level. Time invested in strong foundations means that we now have the confidence, the skills and the experience to get there.

References

AS (2006), *Alzheimer's Society Annual Review 2005/2006*, London, Alzheimer's Society

AS (2007), *Dementia UK: A report into the prevalence and cost of dementia*, London, Personal Social Services Research Unit (PSSRU) at the London School of Economics and the Institute of Psychiatry at King's College London, for the Alzheimer's Society

AS (2011), *Dementia: What We're Fighting For: Annual report 2010/11*, London, Alzheimer's Society

Keeping Communities Thriving: The Co-operative Group's approach to charity partnerships

Michael Fairclough

Introduction

The Co-operative Group (referred to as either The Co-operative or the Group throughout this chapter) comprises a family of businesses with core interests in food, financial services, travel, pharmacy, funerals and farms. In the last five years, The Co-operative has seen a dramatic level of growth, with the business seeing a doubling in profits and turnover (Co-op 2010a, p. 1). Mergers with United Co-operatives, Somerfield and Britannia have seen the family of businesses grow to some 5,000 outlets, with a store in every postal area of the UK, served by almost 110,000 colleagues. The Group is now one of the largest consumer co-operatives in the world (Co-op 2010a).

The Co-operative's membership base has tripled to six million; all members are eligible to share in profits and have a say in how the business is run. 2010 saw the largest ever membership payout: £70.5 million (Co-op 2011a).

Throughout this period of rapid expansion, The Co-operative has remained true to its heritage and continues to lead the way in social responsibility. Support for communities continues to grow, with £12.4 million invested in 2010 alone, benefiting hundreds of thousands of people, both in the UK and less-developed countries (Co-op 2011b, p. 17).

Back in 2008, the Group undertook the largest consultation of its kind, inviting members to give their views on what community issues The Co-operative should focus on. The results helped to concentrate energy and funding on three key areas:

- Inspiring young people

- Tackling global poverty

- Combating climate change

These three themes now form an integral part of a broader Group-wide Ethical Plan. The vast majority of the Group's charity partnerships fit within one of these three themes.

The Co-operative works with charities in a number of ways, including partnerships on specific projects, campaigning, colleague volunteering, sponsorship and in-store promotions. A member of the Social Goals department is given key responsibility for managing the majority of the key charity relationships. Depending on the nature of the relationship, a contract is drawn up with the charity and a series of key performance indicators agreed. These cover areas such as what funding is to be spent on, key aims of the programme that is being supported, the number of people who are to benefit, use of brand and logos and any restrictions on other corporate relationships.

This chapter discusses how the Group selects partners, what makes a good account manager (these are known as Community Advisers within the Group), the Group's funds and foundations, Charity of the Year and other partnerships, campaigns and overseas work, stakeholder engagement, and future plans.

Selecting partners

The Co-operative receives thousands of letters, cold calls and cold emails each year requesting support. As the Group's approach to community investment has matured, it has moved from reactively responding to requests to proactively seeking out charity partners.

The Co-operative selects partners that have expertise and can deliver on the ground in ways that the Group cannot. The Group identifies them by developing a strong knowledge of the sectors in which it is interested. In the Social Goals department we do this by reading the sector press, attending conferences, reading and commissioning research, and building contacts with non-governmental organisations and government departments. It is through these networks that we identify the key activists and delivery organisations, which team members then approach for informal conversations to find out more about their priorities and commitments.

Community Advisers

From our department's experience of working with charities we appreciate Community Advisers who:

• are flexible to business requirements and priorities;

• understand the business activities and see our staff's perspective;

161

• are able to quickly develop excellent communications (through images, case studies and text, for example) which can be used to communicate through the business channels;

• respond quickly to resolve issues raised;

• work openly and collaboratively on joint communications, branding and public relations;

• achieve an appropriate level of buy-in for the partnership from all relevant areas of their organisation, from volunteers on the ground to the chief executive and the main board;

• are sensitive to The Co-operative brand; for example by not engaging with competitors, not using the brand without sign-off, sharing in advance issues likely to hit the press;

• are honest and realistic.

Funds and foundations

The Co-operative offers a range of its own funds and foundations that support community initiatives. The following sections outline two of these funds and foundations.

The Co-operative Membership Community Fund[1]

The Group's members can choose to donate some, or all, of their membership payout to the Membership Community Fund, a registered charity that distributes grants of up to £2,000 to local voluntary groups, community groups, self-help organisations and charities. In 2010, £1.7 million was distributed to 1,691 groups (Co-op 2011b, p. 20). In 2011, the Community Fund was able to give away even more grants, as members were generous enough to donate £3.2 million of the money they earned in 2010 (ibid. p. 94).

To be eligible for a grant, a group must carry out positive work in the community, and the project that requires funding must:

• address a community issue;

• provide a good long-term benefit to the community;

• support co-operative values and principles.

Groups apply online and their application is then checked by the Social Goals department. If it meets all our criteria, it is sent to one of 48 area committees. The Area Committee then decides which projects to support, based on the local community's needs.

The Co-operative Foundation[2]

The Co-operative Foundation is an independent charitable trust set up in 2000. Its current grant-making programme, Truth About Youth, supports seven charities across the UK to challenge and change negative perceptions of young people by:

• supporting young people to deal positively with negative perceptions of youth;

• increasing the interaction between young people and adults;

• encouraging young people to set up their own co-operative projects;

• communicating the outputs and outcomes of the projects.

The charities are each benefiting from £280,000 over a two-year period, and additional opportunities such as workshops with the young people and media support.

Charities are invited to apply for the scheme and, if selected, are asked to devise a project that could deliver the above aims of Truth About Youth. A shortlist of charities for each of the Group's seven trading regions is then invited to present their projects to The Co-operative Foundation Board. The chosen charities have been selected based on a number of factors, including past performance and the Group board's view as to the charity's ability to deliver. The projects vary widely, from theatrical plays to young people being supported to deliver their own community initiatives (Co-op 2011b, p. 19).

Charity of the Year

Every two years, The Co-operative enters into a Charity of the Year partnership, which includes in-store collections, and sees thousands of colleagues take part in fundraising activities ranging from coffee mornings to parachute jumps.

The process for choosing a Charity of the Year is complex. In the Social Goals department, we identify an initial cause to support that fits into the Group's broader community strategy. For the 2011 Charity of the Year, we decided that this would be 'Inspiring Young People'. A long list of potential charities that operate in this field is then drawn up. To qualify, a charity needs to operate across the UK and have the means to support an extensive partnership across all of the Group's stores and branches.

The charity needs to have a proven track record in prudent financial management and excellent delivery of services to beneficiaries. We invite the charities on the long list to respond, in writing, to a set of questions. As part of the application, they must devise a new project, on which the fundraising money will be spent, and commit to an initial outlay. For example, the successful charity will need to supply items of fundraising collateral for the Group's stores and branches, including collecting tins, buckets and t-shirts. It will need to commit to monthly project board meetings in Manchester and extensive business-wide presentations. The charity must also be prepared to devise and deliver a suitable media strategy in partnership with the Group's press team.

Once applications are received, the Charity of the Year Steering Group draws up a shortlist and charities are invited to present their case in person. Numerous follow-up meetings are often required and basic checks are carried out on accounts. Those charities considered most likely to deliver the most successful partnership are then put forward to a colleague and member vote.

Charity of the Year 2009 and 2011

Two charities were selected for the colleague and member vote in 2010: Dyslexia Action and Mencap. Colleagues were able to place their vote through the intranet and various specific business channels, while members were able to vote through the Membership website. In total there were 42,000 votes cast, with Mencap and its sister charity, ENABLE Scotland, receiving 58% of the votes, and therefore being chosen as the 2011 Charity of the Year (Co-op 2010b, p.10).

A series of key performance indicators are set at the start of a partnership, including an overall fundraising target. The Co-operative Food has some 20 million customers through its doors each week and, partly as a result of this high footfall, raises the majority of the money for the Charity of the Year. Food stores are set individual targets that area managers are then responsible for delivering.

The Group raised £3.7 million for the 2009 Charity of the Year, RNID (Co-op 2011b, p. 20), and over £7 million for Mencap and ENABLE Scotland in 2011 (Mencap 2012). Along with extensive fundraising, the charity also benefits from significant awareness-raising communications, including the press, in-store collateral (such as till screens and radio), and coverage across member and colleague magazines, on the website and intranet and through social media channels.

Internal research carried out at the beginning and end of the partnership with RNID found that 42% of customers felt that they knew more about the work of the charity as a result of the promotion, and 42% were more likely to seek advice from their doctor if they were concerned about their own hearing.

Through the Group's communication channels, fundraising momentum can be maintained and colleagues are encouraged to share their fundraising ideas and successes. The Group found that, overwhelmingly, colleagues are positive about the Charity of the Year partnership and enjoy taking part in activities. The internal research found that more than 85% of colleagues participated in fundraising activities for RNID, and 92% said that they would be keen to fundraise for the charity in the future.

Depending on the partnership, additional opportunities may be identified. For example, almost 120,000 hearing checks were carried out on customers, colleagues and the public, as part of the RNID partnership (Co-op 2009, p. 18). Some volunteering opportunities were also made available for colleagues.

In a year when the Group does not have a charity partnership, stores and branches raise money for causes of their choice, supporting local, regional and national charities.

Other charity partnerships

Charity partnership: The Co-operative StreetGames Young Volunteers

The Co-operative's partnership with the national sports development charity StreetGames started in 2007. The Group initially committed £1 million to enable StreetGames to train 3,000 young people aged 16 to 25 to become Co-operative StreetGames Young Volunteers by 2012. These volunteers then coach their peers in activities such as basketball, dance, athletics and martial arts, at 100 locations across England and Wales. Along with health and social benefits, the project promotes self-belief, self-responsibility and leadership. Many of the volunteers have used the skills and experience they have gained to turn their own lives around and as a springboard into further education and training.

While StreetGames delivers the volunteering programme, the Group works closely with the charity on many aspects, especially with regard to media relations. A further £1.2 million has now been committed, which will be used to fund the programme for 2012 to 2014 and enable it to extend into Scotland and Northern Ireland (Co-op 2011b, p. 57).

The Co-operative British Youth Film Academy

The Co-operative British Youth Film Academy (BYFA) began life as a student project at South Cheshire College in 2005, with the support of United Co-operatives. In 2009, following The Co-operative Group/United merger, the Group agreed to a three-year (£500,000) partnership to provide stability and security for the initiative to make longer-term plans.

BYFA students learn the art of film-making on a real film set – by making a full-length feature film – in roles such as acting, camera operating, lighting, sound, and post-production. A further £700,000 was committed in 2011 to support the project for an additional three years, from 2012 to 2014.

Along with financial contributions, The Co-operative provides hands-on support to BYFA by managing communications and providing expertise in areas such as social media, legal and finance. BYFA is now a co-operative itself, with a membership of 18 further and higher education institutions across four regional clusters – West Midlands, North West, East Midlands and Yorkshire – and reaches more than 10,000 young people each year. It aims to become the most accessible film-making training academy in the UK, with a target of establishing two new educational regions every year until nationwide coverage is achieved (Co-op 2011b, p. 58).

Campaigning in partnership

The Co-operative has a strong heritage of working alongside charities and non-governmental organisations to campaign with its members and customers on a number of issues, from climate change to tackling Third World debt. At any one time, the Group has several campaigns under way.

Over the last few years, The Co-operative has campaigned in partnership with WWF-UK to halt the expansion of tar sands development. The extraction and production of this unconventional fossil fuel is highly energy-intensive and is destroying large areas of land in Alberta, Canada.

Together, The Co-operative and WWF-UK engaged its members and supporters to lobby the UK government and EU parliament on the issue. Also working with Greenpeace, the Group and WWF-UK created a touring street gallery, entitled Tarnished Earth, to highlight the issue of tar sands development. The Co-operative also supported the cinema release of three films on the issue of tar sands (Co-op 2011b, p. 71).

Join the Revolution

In March 2011, The Co-operative launched its Join the Revolution marketing campaign, focusing on some of the people whose revolutions the group has supported, from a community-led football club to a mobile toy library.

As part of the campaign, the Group ran a competition for people to win £5,000 to fund their own revolution. Applicants had to meet certain criteria, including being a community, self-help or voluntary group, a charity, or a local branch of a national charity, and had to support one of the following areas:

- Benefiting communities

- Inspiring young people

- Tackling global poverty

- Combating climate change

Members of the public voted for their favourite groups. These votes then determined one overall winner for each of the five regions: Scotland & Northern Ireland, Northern England, central England, southern England and Wales. Groups that did not win were invited to apply for support from some of The Co-operative's other funds, such as The Co-operative Membership Community Fund.

Work overseas

Along with its work in the UK, the Group is committed to tackling global poverty, a key area of concern for its members. The Co-operative is known as a leader in fair trade, but this is only one of the ways in which the Group is helping people in less-developed countries to lift themselves out of poverty. From providing clean water and sanitation to helping farmers to form co-operatives, the Group is providing real development solutions for communities in countries such as Kenya, Malawi and Panama. In recent years, millions of people have benefited from these initiatives.

Stakeholder engagement

At The Co-operative, we believe that corporate support should involve all the key stakeholders of a business. This includes members, customers and colleagues. Many of the community projects with which the Group is involved encourage these three groups to get involved.

Members

The Co-operative works with its members to address their communities' individual needs and aspirations. Our seven regional membership teams support 48 area committees of elected members. As well as deciding which community groups to support through The Co-operative Membership Community Fund, area committees work with the regional teams to develop a wide range of bespoke activities and initiatives for their communities, and offer support to existing projects.

Customers

The Group offers several affinity products in its stores and branches. For instance, The Co-operative has:

• a large range of charity credit cards;

• has worked with UNICEF on a handwash that supports a sanitation project in Togo;

• through its partnership with the One Foundation, has seen clean water brought to 1 million people in Africa, through sales of its own-brand bottled water (Co-op 2011b, p. 28).

Colleagues

Along with the Charity of the Year initiative, colleagues are encouraged to volunteer for a range of charitable initiatives during work time, through The Co-operative Volunteer Programme. This programme operates across all of the businesses, offering colleagues a wide range of individual and team opportunities. In 2010, more than 8,000 colleagues volunteered during work time. Placements are chosen that provide real benefits to the community and offer volunteers an enjoyable experience that develops their skills and abilities. Internal surveys show that the Group's volunteers feel a greater commitment to the business as a result of being supported to give something back to their local community.

Through The Co-operative Booster Fund, the Group offers support to causes for which employees are personally motivated to fundraise. This initiative boosts individual fundraising by £100 and team fund-raising by £400, if at least the same amount is raised by the employees who apply.

Additional support

The Co-operative's family of businesses offers additional support to charities and community groups through a variety of initiatives. For example, The Co-operative Food offers community groups 10% off most items in-store through The Co-operative Community Food Discount card.

The Co-operative Bank is a leading provider of financial services to the charity sector, offering tailored support to thousands of community organisations, including some of the largest registered charities in the UK.

The future

Launched in February 2012, The Co-operative's Ethical Plan[3] includes several key commitments to help keep communities thriving:

• We will ensure that 10% of the profits available for distribution is made available for community investment by 2013, with £5 million deployed per annum to tackle UK poverty around our stores and branches.

• Our stores and branches will act as a focus for 10,000 community initiatives per annum and we will now offer local community groups the opportunity to occupy a selection of surplus properties from our estate at nominal rent.

• Our Inspiring Young People programme will benefit one million people by 2014.

• We will progress our Co-operative Academy and create 2,000 apprenticeships.

Co-op 2011c, pp. 5 & 6

Conclusion

Our advice to charities that are seeking partnerships is, firstly, to make sure that you do your research well in order to identify – and have a thorough understanding of – potential corporate partners that are most likely to support your charity. Secondly, ensure that your account managers have the right qualities and level of understanding to be effective liaison people. Third, be clear about the specific causes and/or community investment objectives the partner is interested in and use this information to accentuate and deploy your charity's strengths and achievements when making any approach. Fourth, don't think of partnerships solely in financial terms. Take time to consider other ways that a potential corporate partner may be able to help your charity, such as supporting a campaign or offering staff time. Finally, make sure that the potential corporate partner's ethical policy fits with your charity's own ethical standpoint.

Notes

1   A trading name of Co-operative Community Investment Foundation, registered charity no. 1093028, England & Wales
2   A trading name of The Co-operative Charitable Foundation, registered charity no. 1080834, England & Wales
3   In addition to the Group's Ethical Plan, you can view a Community Map which identifies locations throughout the UK where The Co-operative is helping thousands of people. To see the Community Map visit www.co-operative.coop/communitymap

References

Co-op (2009), *Focus on Sustainability: Sustainability Report*, Manchester, Co-operative Group

Co-op (2010a), *The Co-operative Group Annual Report & Accounts 2010*, Manchester, Co-operative Group

Co-op (2010b), *Evergreen*, winter 2010 edn, Manchester, Co-operative Group Corporate Communications Department

Co-op (2011a), *Generous Co-operative Members Give £3m Profit-Share to Good Causes* [press release], Manchester, Co-operative Group, 8 June

Co-op (2011b), *Join the Revolution: Sustainability Report 2010*, Manchester, Co-operative Group

Co-op (2011c), *Setting New Sights: Our Ethical Plan 2012–14 (and Beyond . . .)*, Manchester, Co-operative Group

Mencap (2012), *The Co-operative Creates £7 Million Lasting Legacy for Young People with a Learning Disability* [press release], London, Mencap, 10 February

CHAPTER EIGHTEEN

Hilton in the Community Foundation: an example of a corporate foundation

Simon Sheehan

Introduction

In November 2000, Hilton Group (now Hilton Worldwide) established a corporate foundation, Hilton in the Community Foundation (referred to as HCF or the foundation throughout the chapter), to go beyond the ad hoc charity support of previous years. This established a transparent response to the charitable requests that the company received as well as a dedicated vehicle to support fundraising efforts. This resulted in increased charitable engagement within the company and an increased impact of support through targeted and accountable giving.

Under the banner 'Supporting Young People Worldwide', HCF supports activities in health and education that relieve suffering and equip individuals for the future. The foundation has grown to award over £1.6 million in grants annually to 573 charities in 2011,[1] engaging Hilton Worldwide employees and related partners in the process.

HCF relies on the goodwill and generosity of team members, suppliers, guests and the general public to maximise its impact. Donations are encouraged, with a guarantee to donors that 100% of the net funds raised are channelled to beneficiaries.

Grant giving is primarily focused on charities that operate within the UK and the Republic of Ireland. With the expansion of the foundation's fundraising and grant-giving activities into continental Europe in 2010, funds raised are awarded to charities and local causes working in the country where the funds were raised. These local grants in continental Europe are made in the foundation's chosen areas of focus.

HCF's grant giving

Across its grant-making processes, HCF prefers to fund projects which support disadvantaged children and young people and:

• provide and facilitate access to education;

• provide tools and opportunities through equipment, facilities and training;

• relieve suffering and improve treatment and care.

Within these broad criteria, the foundation has a number of different grant-making mechanisms which have separate processes and focus. These are: central grants; sponsored grants; and the Disaster Relief and International Development Fund.

Central grants are made from HCF's open application process, with a special focus on disabled children and young people, children in hospital, homelessness and life-limited children in hospices.

Sponsored grants go to those charities and good causes that have been nominated by hotels to receive a proportion of the funds that the hotel has raised, subject to approval by the foundation. Sponsored grants target local charities, organisations and community groups which support young people in the areas of education and health and are the broadest of the grant mechanisms to reflect different community priorities and interests of the hotels. Given the smaller size of grants and the added security from the local link between the applicant and the hotel, the application process is shorter.

The Disaster Relief and International Development Fund is a fund capped at £150,000 per annum and has a closed application process to manage demand. The fund is used to help deliver disaster relief for young people and, depending on the amount left in the fund at the end of the year, for health and education programmes in less-developed countries, with a particular focus on those in Africa and Asia.

In 2010, the overall average grant size was £3,237.92. Sponsored grants, those nominated by hotels for local causes from the funds they have raised, tend to be smaller and more numerous (£1,676 average size of 241 grants made). Central grants tend to be larger and fewer (£9,213 average size of 48 grants made). The foundation aims to award over 90% of its annual grant fund within a year (Hilton 2011a, p. 15).

The foundation has defined its public benefit as:

Raising funds from Hilton Worldwide, its team members, suppliers, guests and contacts as well as the general public, to award to charities and charitable causes working with young people in need so that they can have access to and receive the education, healthcare and support that they need. By providing this intermediary role of fundraiser and cause identifier the foundation channels funds and charitable goodwill to support programme delivery and raise the profile and understanding of vulnerable groups.

Hilton 2011b, p. 6

HCF is a corporate foundation that has to raise the funds that it awards. While recognising the difference in scale, the foundation likens its relationship and role with Hilton Worldwide to that between Children in Need and the BBC.

Relationship with the company

The foundation is linked to and supported by Hilton Worldwide. As Hilton Worldwide's nominated charity vehicle in Europe, the foundation is allowed access to fundraise within hotels and support offices, from guests, suppliers, contacts and employees.

The support provided by Hilton Worldwide to the foundation takes many forms including:

• the permanent secondment of seven employees to run the foundation;

• an annual budget for staff, administration and communication costs;

• office space;

• access to internal expertise and channels;

• the provision of hotel and conference facilities for fundraising events without charge or at discounted rates.

Formalised under a commercial participatory agreement, the foundation does not give remuneration to Hilton Worldwide or Hilton Worldwide personnel in respect of their voluntary participation in fundraising activities. Under the terms of a funding agreement, Hilton Worldwide makes an annual donation to meet the foundation's core administration costs, so that the foundation's net fundraising income can be used to make grants for charitable purposes.

The trustees or their appointed committees take all decisions concerning the foundation and its grant giving and are independent of Hilton Worldwide. Any trustee of the foundation who is an employee of Hilton Worldwide or any company associated with Hilton Worldwide withdraws from any foundation meeting where the fundamental relationship with Hilton Worldwide is discussed or reviewed, unless requested to observe by the independent trustees.

Fitting into a wider corporate responsibility strategy

Until 2011, Hilton Worldwide did not have an articulated corporate responsibility strategy. Although extremely active and effective in the areas of sustainability, employee welfare and community giving (the latter specifically through the foundation), many aspects of a traditional corporate responsibility strategy were embedded in different parts of the business (as opposed to consolidated into one area). In the future the foundation will be playing an active role in helping shape and deliver Hilton Worldwide's global corporate responsibility strategy.

The grant focus of the foundation reflects Hilton Worldwide's strategic decision to invest in future generations, and to provide children and young people with the means and aspirations to develop their own future. Although there are separate programme activity funds within Hilton Worldwide, the foundation is charged with being the vehicle for community giving in Europe as well as contributing to Hilton Worldwide's Centre of Excellence (a global forum for community action and corporate responsibility) for regions outside Europe to help support and guide their community engagement and social giving activities.

The foundation reports directly to the Area President of Europe via their additional role as Chair of Trustees. In addition, the President for Global Operations for Hilton Worldwide is also President of the foundation. This allows the foundation unprecedented access and positions HCF's work at the heart of the business.

Employee engagement

Given that it has access to nearly 25,000 employees in Europe, the foundation has a broad range of interests and local contexts. The foundation has a voluntary charity champion (called a Foundation Champion) in each hotel, who acts as liaison person for the foundation to help coordinate activities. There is no correlation between job position in the hotel and those who are chosen for this role; however, they are all highly motivated individuals and their term ranges from one year to some who have been in post for ten years.

Through handbooks, sharing best practice, workshops, training and recognition, the foundation motivates, trains and supports its charity champions and any other engaged employees. The foundation also provides financial accountability for Hilton Worldwide by ensuring that all funds raised reach the charities selected.

HCF promotes Hilton Worldwide's payroll giving scheme by match funding 10% of any donation to the foundation for the lifetime of the donation. Other charities can be supported directly, and the foundation facilitates this process.

The foundation plays an additional role in highlighting issues and causes to employees through communications about the grants that it awards. This can motivate further local support or can challenge pre-conceptions and improve understanding. With such a broad range of causes supported, HCF has the luxury of having numerous case studies to share as well as different causes to engage different interests. This humanises the grant figures, demonstrates to employees the impact of their fundraising efforts and motivates them to further support the foundation.

The foundation has been a consistent feature and charity voice to Hilton Worldwide employees. This has enabled HCF to:

• understand internal systems and structures;

• translate these for the charity sector and help charities to navigate them;

• build lasting relationships with employees;

• engage new employees (the hospitality industry has approximately 30% turnover of staff per annum).

One of the cornerstones of the foundation's mission is to give Hilton Worldwide team members the opportunity to involve themselves in charity work, be it fundraising, volunteering or facilitating in-kind giving. With nearly 25,000 team members across more than 200 hotels across Europe there is a great opportunity to make a real difference.

Every hotel has a fundraising target and works with HCF to try to maximise the money raised. This means that all of the hotels are stake-holders in the foundation.

The company provides support from the top levels to encourage employees to take part in HCF activities. This involves a range of incentives, from paid leave or time in lieu to volunteer and recognition at hotel business awards, to 'star points' (prize vouchers) in return for special efforts, all of which is decided at local hotel level.

Each hotel sets up a charity committee which may nominate local organisations that fit with the foundation's criteria to receive up to 50% of the money they raise via sponsored grants. This autonomy provides ownership and relevance for employees and allows them to see clearly the positive impact of their work locally. The other 50% of funds raised con-tributes to the foundation's central grant fund.

HCF encourages team members to visit local charities to assess appli-cations and to present awarded funds. This enables a better understanding of the charities with which they are engaged and encourages ongoing relationships. Each year several general managers and team members are invited to sit on HCF's Grants Committee and to help make guided deci-sions on some of the applications to the foundation.

Some of the best synergies in HCF's giving result from hotel team members at local level nominating particular causes for support. This means that company employees and charities have a direct connection with each other and a mutual understanding, which is one of the underlying benefits of the foundation's structure as a facilitator of local relationships. The fact that team members can nominate local children's groups to receive help provides a direct stake in the success of the foundation at local and central levels.

HCF issues a fundraising league table to hotels, which they use to give a competitive edge to their activities. Often departments will set inter-departmental targets to encourage participation and ownership. Hotel teams aim to make best use of their individual resources with charity balls and dinners, utilising volunteer hours and working at the best price available from suppliers; the hotel itself is a popular way of achieving this. Across all of the hotels HCF also runs several annual fundraising campaigns which aim to involve every employee possible.

Hilton Worldwide provides accommodation vouchers to HCF to aid charities to raise money at their events. In addition, the foundation facilitates complimentary accommodation for life-limited children through a partnership with wish-granting charity Rays of Sunshine. In 2010, 17 wish families were placed in Hilton hotels in the UK during their wishes.

HCF also works with In Kind Direct charity and with local charities to donate goods and services as they become available, such as toiletries and towels for homeless charities, and furniture and furnishings for local organisations. These initiatives mean that Hilton employees can engage first-hand with organisations.

Where possible, Hilton colleagues are encouraged to volunteer their time and expertise to projects supporting their local community. In 2010, team members gave an estimated 39,000 volunteer hours to HCF and local good causes (Hilton 2011a, p. 8). This included chefs demonstrating cooking skills and healthy eating to young people, management providing into-work mentoring, sales teams delivering training for charity fundraisers on sales techniques and maintenance workers leading on building and painting projects.

Development of grant giving

Initially HCF had a remit that focused on hospitality training which, although core to the business, did not engage employees. This was subsequently changed and the foundation added a focus on health to reflect employees' desire to support charities in this area, specifically cancer charities.

Although the foundation still supports employability training pro-grammes, these are classified under its education remit due to the training and confidence-building activities that are undertaken. This also allows the foundation to broker job opportunities by making use of its connections with the hotels.

In 2009, HCF further focused its central giving criteria by choosing to fund four particular areas of need:

1. disabled children and young people

2. children in hospital

3. homelessness

4. life-limited children in hospices

These areas were selected following a consultation with Foundation Champions in the hotels and the grants committee, and ultimately signed off by the trustees. This has had the effect of pre-filtering demand but has also enabled the growth in expertise of the grants committee around the need in each core theme. In 2011, these core areas were to be reviewed again, as 'disabled children' remains highly oversubscribed and thus over-represented at the committee meetings.

HCF has found that it can achieve the best impact with its limited resources by funding capital costs, refurbishment and equipment, which reaches a large number of disadvantaged children over a long period. As a small funder (compared with the scale of need), it makes targeted, usually small (less than £10,000) grants which may fill a gap or enable a specific piece of work to take place.

International work

HCF awards funds raised by hotels in continental Europe to charities and local causes working in the country where the funds were raised and according to the foundation's criteria. The local hotels identify potential recipients and refer them to the foundation for assessment. At times of natural disaster, hotels are requested to contribute to the Disaster Relief and International Development Fund. HCF's annual report states:

In 2010 the foundation continued the expansion of its fundraising efforts into Continental Europe. The hotels had already carried out fundraising efforts for their local communities for numerous years as well as supporting the foundation through the donation of holiday vouchers for fundraising events. This relationship was formalised and extended following legal and fiscal investigations in 23 countries across Europe, reflecting the presence of Hilton Worldwide's hotels. Following the advice received from local experts, structures for fundraising from these hotels were established in most of those countries. These varied depending on local laws and tax efficiency, and so structures include the transfer of funds:

- direct to the foundation;

- via the hotel to the foundation; or

- direct to a local charity.

Hilton 2011b, p. 7

The foundation's aim in continental Europe is to facilitate charitable giving to benefit HCF's chosen focus group of disadvantaged young people. To do this, through its European Committee the foundation has undertaken a programme of promoting its work and developed supporting materials to enlist the support of hotels. In 2011, 70 hotels in continental Europe raised £585,307, which is 317% more than funds raised in 2010.[2]

Trading

The foundation is fortunate to have access to a captive audience via the hotels. Balancing the business interests of Hilton Worldwide, the foundation engages hotel guests through a donation-on-the-bill campaign in the run-up to winter as well as via the sale of merchandise.

In 2010 the foundation established HCF Trading Limited, to raise funds for the benefit of the foundation through the sale of merchandise in hotels. Following a successful four-month trial, the trustees agreed to establish HCF Trading Limited. Profits from the trading company are donated to the foundation on a regular basis and contribute towards the foundation's grant fund. The foundation has allocated a proportion of staff time to the running of the trading arm. The two directors of HCF Trading Limited are independent trustees and hold the issued shares jointly on behalf of the foundation. Directors of the company meet regularly with monthly updates and forecasts being circulated.

Challenges

As both a grant giver and a fundraiser, the foundation has to remain relevant to the business, to local needs and to donors and supporters. Given HCF's broad remit, it also has to demonstrate impact and show a return on investment for Hilton Worldwide's support. Measuring grants awarded and the amount of public relations coverage generated, the foundation delivers 1:13 return (according to the foundation's internal budgets), which excludes any measurement of human resources value. This collective effort resulted in 605,654 young people receiving help in 2011 through the provision of equipment, training and/or support.[3]

The foundation has been able to contain the impact of the economic downturn by having the backing of Hilton Worldwide, a dispersed supporter base across the hotels, an opportunity to expand into new markets in Europe and access to markets for merchandise.

Benefits from structure

As an independent charity, the foundation has the power to make its own fundraising and grant-giving decisions and align itself with a variety of children's charities and causes. It can be sympathetic to the needs of the business, but is not governed by it. HCF seeks to support young people worldwide and this means its board of trustees can be free to envision and trial new endeavours. Other benefits of the foundation's structure include:

• a close working relationship between the charity (HCF) and the company, with internal knowledge of each other's structures and personnel;

• an independent board which keeps the best interests of the foundation at the forefront while respecting and enhancing the reputation of the corporate parent;

• local relevance and involvement;

• the involvement of employees in decision-making processes;

• employee ownership;

• inbuilt local monitors of grant support.

Lessons learned from the foundation's structure and engaging with the corporate and charity sectors

The corporate parent is your best donor

The corporate parent should be treated as a key donor to the corporate foundation: a fundamental that can sometimes be overlooked or taken for granted. We need to remember to remain relevant to employees' needs, to engage them in the work and to demonstrate impact, if we are to continue to have their support.

Like any charity, balancing the interests of supporters, beneficiaries and the independence and long-term strategy of the corporate foundation is the role of the trustees.

Clear expectations

Employees aren't professional fundraisers but they are enthusiastic. They might not have access to raising thousands of pounds (although they may raise thousands over the long term) or have the opportunity to embed practices into business processes.

From the charity's perspective, the proposed event or activity might not be the biggest event (financially or logistically) that the benefiting charity is involved with that year and so cannot support to the extent that the fundraiser wishes. To help mitigate this we believe that making efforts to understand each other's worlds, having a long-term view rather than looking for quick wins, and articulating realistic expectations are key to keeping the relationship harmonious.

Understanding each other's worlds

Each side has different business pressures and skills that they can bring to the table. Each has different expertise and experience, and recognising each other's strengths and weaknesses and being realistic helps in the long term.

A paid charity professional must show their value by bringing their expertise to the table and dedicating time to an event (especially as they are not juggling work with another day job). We take the approach that you should never ask a volunteer to do something that you are not prepared to do yourself, and this includes volunteering your own time outside office hours.

A hands-on approach

Volunteers sometimes work on different timescales, due to conflicting work priorities or just a lack of understanding of the process. This can result in delays or not delivering at the last minute. The charity has to be prepared to pick up the slack or take the first steps to get things moving. It is important not to underestimate how much support is needed to manage volunteers, and therefore it would be wise to evaluate the benefits you expect against the time investment needed.

Saying thank you

However big or small the donation, the work involved or the potential of an opportunity, every contribution should be acknowledged. We have found that many charities have forgotten this, and this has been to their detriment, as employees are left with a bitter taste, which has ultimately resulted in the hotel changing its local partner for future activities.

Ensure, therefore, that your charity has smooth-running, rigorous thanking procedures so that this doesn't get overlooked.

Things change

Even with the best relationship or results, things do change either for business reasons or just for the sake of refreshing relationships and spreading the support. As well as repeat funding, the foundation makes many one-off grants. The longest-term relationships are held at hotel level.

Your charity is not the only charity in the world

Although every charity should be passionate about its cause, we ask charities to recognise that there are other charities with equally good and emotive work. And many have the same fundraising ideas and make the same approaches.

HCF is oversubscribed 6:1 for its central grant fund and receives hundreds of enquiries and requests for help each year. Systems are designed to filter these and isolate the best matches to the funding priorities set by the trustees. No doubt other large charitable foundations face the same issue of oversubscription and deal with it in a similar way, so it is important that charities are aware of this difficulty.

Flexibility

Internal systems, such as grant application procedures or fundraising recognition processes, are there to help guide the process, not to stop efforts. They can reflect a culture or a period of time. Make sure that your systems are not set in stone but are regularly reviewed and improved. They should also be seen from the perspective of the applicant/reader; therefore be clear about what you want and what you ask for. Flexibility and an open mind can lead to some creative and productive activities and partnerships.

People give to people

Companies aren't the enemy or from another planet. They are made up of people, just as charities are, and these people all have different outlooks, interests and prejudices. We advise charities to:

• endeavour to find a good fit with a company;

• be open and transparent: this can get you far (for example, do not make unrealistic claims but do share challenges or weaknesses);

- not overuse jargon: explain your need clearly and why your solution works;

- openly address negative assumptions about your organisation;

- critically review what first impression you and your organisation make.

If you are not open and transparent at this stage, a concern – however big or small – may never be openly addressed, and the result will be that you will not get supported.

Notes

1   Figures quoted will be published during 2012 in Hilton in the Community Foundation's 2011 Annual Report.
2   See Note 1.
3   See Note 1.

References

Hilton (2011a), *Hilton in the Community Foundation Trustees' 10th Annual Report 2010*, London, Hilton in the Community Foundation
Hilton (2011b), *Annual Report and Financial Statements Year Ended 31 December 2010*, London, Hilton in the Community Foundation

Legal and Tax Issues

Anne-Marie Piper and Rebecca Fry of the Charity
& Community Team at Law firm Farrer & Co LLP

Introduction

This Appendix covers the legal and tax issues (as at October 2011) associated with corporate fundraising.

In recent years businesses have become an increasingly important source of cash and other much needed resources for charities. However, as the chapters in this book have shown, corporate fundraising today extends far beyond pure philanthropy into the realms of business development and promotion and includes:

- donations;

- companies with 'in-house' charities;

- payroll giving;

- matched giving schemes (when employers add to donations/fundraising by their staff);

- gifts in kind, including secondments;

- commercial participation;

- brand licensing;

- sponsorship.

Before examining the charity law and tax rules relating to these methods, this Appendix takes a step back to look at the legal framework charities must operate within when dealing with their corporate partners including:

- the duties of charity trustees;

- subsidiary trading companies;

- the difference between donations and other arrangements;
- different types of corporate supporters;
- negotiations (including confidentiality agreements);
- contracts and lawyers;
- using professional fundraisers;
- substantial donors.

Health warning

As this Appendix will show, the legal and fiscal consequences of arrangements between charities and their corporate supporters can vary hugely depending on the way they are structured. This Appendix should not be read as a comprehensive analysis of its subject matter; it is designed only to give its readers a very brief and general overview of the subject so that they are familiar with the general landscape, know some of the more important questions to ask and, perhaps most importantly, know when they should be seeking help.

PART I: THE LEGAL FRAMEWORK

The duties of charity trustees

The decision to accept a gift from or to enter into an arrangement with a corporate supporter is one which, in law, ultimately vests with the charity trustees of the charity.

Who are the trustees?

Under charity law the 'charity trustees' of a charity are the people who have ultimate responsibility and control over the management of the charity. With charitable trusts the trustees are likely to be called trustees (although this is not always the case); however, with charitable companies and other forms of charities the trustees may be called directors, members of the board of trustees, members of the council of management or the executive committee. The name given to them doesn't matter nor does it matter how they got to be trustees – they might have been elected, nominated, appointed, ex-officio (i.e. serve as a trustee by virtue of occupying some other post or office) – because their duties are the same.

Delegated authority/responsibility

In many charities it would be impossible for the trustees to take all the decisions involved with the running of the charity and so much decision-making will be delegated to staff and/or sub-committees.

When exercising delegated authority, staff and/or sub-committees need to have regard to the responsibilities of the trustees. The trustees and those to whom they delegate also need to be clear about the extent of the authority that is to be delegated – is the chief executive/sub-committee's brief simply to negotiate the best deal they can for the trustees to approve? Or, have they been authorised by the trustees to conclude an arrangement and, if so, are they aware of how documents need to be signed on behalf of the charity?

Trustees need to be clear about the extent of any authority they delegate (or don't delegate) not only because they will usually remain responsible for decisions taken by their delegates but also because they may be responsible for some decisions that they have not delegated, thanks to the legal doctrine of ostensible authority. Very briefly, if it is reasonable for a person to believe that someone they are dealing with has authority to enter into the arrangement they have negotiated, then, whether or not that person actually has the authority, the person in question will be treated as having it.

For example, imagine a scenario where a charity's Director of Resources looks after a charity's premises and, in that role, engages architects to draw up plans to extend one of the charity's buildings. Things don't go to plan, the project collapses, and then the architects sue the charity for unpaid fees. The trustees of the charity then deny that the Director had authority (express or implied) to engage the architects for the project. In this scenario, it would be reasonable for the architects to believe that the Director had authority to enter into the contract for the plans and, as a result, the charity would be liable to pay the architects' unpaid fees.

Trustees' duties: an overview

Charity trustees have an overriding duty to act in the best interests of their charity. This principle is easily stated but more difficult to apply in practice.

Within the duty to act in the best interests of the charity are a number of subsidiary duties which include the duty to:

• apply the assets of the charity only for charitable purposes within the charity's objects;

• maximise and protect the assets of the charity;

• exercise proper stewardship and to run the charity in accordance with its constitution and the law;

• avoid, or deal appropriately with, conflicts of interest; and

• take advice from appropriately qualified persons on areas beyond the expertise of the trustees or staff of the charity.

The duty to apply the assets of the charity only for charitable purposes within the charity's objects

The requirement that trustees apply the assets of a charity only for its charitable purposes precludes them from benefiting or subsidising commercial organisations (even the charity's wholly owned subsidiary trading companies) or indeed charities or not-for-profit organisations whose activities are outside the charity's objects.

In practice this means that it is important for trustees and their corporate fundraisers to look critically at arrangements with a corporate partner if the arrangement involves the company benefiting in some way. A benefit given as part of a corporate sponsorship deal routed through a subsidiary trading company may be fine, but a thank-you gift by a charity grateful for a donation would probably not be lawful. This subject is explored further below in the sections relating to donations, sponsorship and the use of subsidiary trading companies.

The duty to maximise and protect the assets of the charity

Many people involved with charities often overlook the fact that the charity's good name may also be its most valuable asset. Accepting a large corporate donation may not be in the best interest of the charity if, when the news gets out, it damages the reputation of the charity, causing the charity's supporters to desert them in droves.

Similarly, a sponsorship deal which requires a lot of work on the part of the charity's staff may deflect them from other work. Such a deal may not be in the best interests of the charity if the diversion could result in damage to the charity, such as losing a valuable contract.

Another aspect of this rule is that charities should seek to minimise their exposure to tax. In the case of trading activities (including sponsorship) this is often achieved by using a subsidiary trading company (see 'Trading and the use of subsidiary trading companies').

The duty to run the charity in accordance with its constitution and the law

Charities contemplating any corporate fundraising initiative need to check their constitutions to see that they have the powers they need for the proposed arrangements. Acting beyond their powers may be a breach of trust for which the trustees could be personally liable if things go wrong.

If a charity lacks the powers necessary for a particular arrangement it may be possible to amend its constitution to remedy the situation, but this is likely to delay matters and may need the prior consent of the Charity Commission.

Charities also need to look beyond charity law when fundraising to ensure that they comply with any other laws, regulations and best practice codes that may apply. It is impossible to give a comprehensive list of these – they could be anything from health and safety rules to advertising codes of practice.

The duty to avoid, or deal appropriately with, conflicts of interest

Many charities are able to forge relationships with companies connected with their trustees. There is nothing wrong with such relationships, but the trustees need to ensure that they are appropriately managed to ensure that the charity, the company and/or the trustees are not compromised in the process. Experience has shown that potential and perceived conflicts of interest can be as damaging as the real thing.

Good practice in this area is to ensure that the trustee concerned is distanced from the deal-making and approval process by following the conflicts procedure in the charity's constitution if there is one or, at the very least, by abstaining from any vote to approve the proposed arrangement.

The duty to take proper advice

Under charity law charity trustees have a duty to take advice from someone suitably qualified in relation to their plans and, unless there is a good reason to the contrary, to follow that advice.

If they are lucky enough to have staff or trustees with the necessary expertise, charities can satisfy this duty in this way. However, many types of corporate fundraising will require specialist commercial, tax and other advice and the cost of this and the time it will take to get the advice must be factored into their plans.

Charities should not lightly ignore this duty or any professional advice they receive. If things go wrong and it transpires that the charity was advised against a plan or scheme, the charity's trustees leave themselves vulnerable. If faced with unwelcome professional advice, it is always wise for charities to seek a second opinion.

Trading and the use of subsidiary trading companies

The term 'subsidiary trading company' is used, in this Appendix, to refer to a commercial trading company all of whose shares are owned by the 'parent' charity or charities.

To understand the need for a subsidiary trading company it is necessary to look briefly at the basic charity law and tax rules that apply to trading and, indeed, what activities amount to trading.

What amounts to trading?

Unfortunately there is no clear statutory definition of what constitutes 'trading'. Manufacturing goods to sell is clearly trading but, less obviously, so are many corporate sponsorship deals (because the charity is, in effect, selling the company the opportunity to advertise itself or its products).

The profit motive, whilst important, is only one of the factors that might indicate trading. A better rule of thumb is, 'are we providing goods or services on a commercial or semi-commercial basis?'

Charity law

As a matter of charity law, trading by charities is permissible only if it is either in pursuance of the primary purposes or the objects of the charity (known as 'primary purpose trading') or if it is ancillary or incidental to those purposes.

In order to ascertain whether a charity is trading in furtherance of its objects, it is essential to examine the charity's constitution. The question should then be asked, 'Does the trading activity directly further one of the charity's objects?' If it does, then it is probably primary purpose trading. Classic examples of primary purpose trading include the provision of education at independent schools in return for fees and the sale of tickets to an exhibition by an art gallery or museum.

It is common for charity constitutions to contain a prohibition against 'permanent trading activities'. In practice the term means any trading activity which is not:

- primary purpose trading;

- trading which is ancillary to the primary purposes of the charity; or

- the sale of donated goods.

Tax

The trading profits or surpluses of a charity are generally only exempt from tax (corporation tax in the case of corporate charities; income tax in the case of unincorporated charities) if all the profits of the trade are applied solely for the charitable purposes of the charity and the trade is exercised in the course of carrying out the primary purposes of the charity.

There are a limited number of exceptions to this general rule including:

Beneficiary trading

This exemption covers non-primary purpose trading which is mainly carried out by the beneficiaries of the charity (such as the sale of goods they have made).

Mixed trading

Where a trading activity is carried out partly for charitable purposes and partly for non-primary purposes (such as a gallery shop selling art-related articles and other items such as pencils and mugs), then, following changes made in 2006, HM Revenue & Customs (HMRC) will generally treat the activity as two trades and receipts and expenses will be apportioned between the two trades. Tax will be payable on the profits of the non-primary purpose trade unless it falls within an exemption such as the small trading exemption (see below).

Small trading exemption

Charities can carry out tax-free non-primary purpose trading, as long as the income from that trade is within the limits allowed by law. The limits are as follows:

Charity's total gross income from all sources	Maximum turnover from non-primary purpose trade allowed
Under £20,000	£5,000
>£20,000 – £200,000	25% of the charity's total gross income
>£200,000	£50,000

Even if turnover from non-primary purpose trading is over these limits, HMRC may not tax the profits if the charity can show that it reasonably expected turnover to fall within the limits: the charity may have traded more than anticipated, or it may have received less income from other sources than it expected.

These exemptions are not blanket exemptions. Their benefit can, for example, be reduced or eliminated if a charity incurs 'non-qualifying expenditure', and so charities planning to trade – even in a modest way – need to take care and professional advice before doing so. A good starting point for charities with only a modest budget for professional help is the HMRC website (www.hmrc.gov.uk/charities).

VAT

Charities do not enjoy a special exemption from VAT because of their charitable status. This means that if charities supply goods or services for consideration (i.e. payment in money or in-kind) they are, with a very limited number of exceptions, in the same VAT position as commercial organisations and they will need to be registered for VAT if their supplies exceed the VAT threshold.

Generally the supply of goods and services by charities will be subject to the standard rate of VAT; however, some supplies are liable to the reduced rate, the zero rate or are VAT exempt. Many charities get into difficulties by overlooking VAT (which can come back to haunt them). Again, care and professional advice are recommended and help is available on the HMRC website (www.hmrc.gov.uk/charities).

Using a subsidiary trading company

By having a subsidiary trading company a charity can avoid the charity law and tax pitfalls outlined above: non-primary purpose trading can be routed through the company to avoid breaches of charity law and although trading companies are liable to tax on their profits, the tax liability can be avoided by the company transferring its profits to its parent charity under the Gift Aid scheme.

Before setting up a subsidiary trading company, it is necessary to check the charity's constitution to ensure that it contains a power to form companies (or failing that a general 'do all other lawful things to promote the objects' type power). A charity which does not have a power to form a trading company will need to consider amending its constitution (which may require the prior consent of the Charity Commission).

The principle that charity funds may only be expended for charitable purposes prohibits charities from subsidising their wholly-owned trading companies. The relationship between charities and their trading companies must be at arm's length.[1] Practical considerations include:

The board of directors of the trading company

The board or committee of trustees of the charity and the board of directors of the trading company should not be made up of the same people; however, it is a good idea for the trustees to be represented on the board of the company (so that they are aware of what the company is doing). Trustees who are also directors of the trading company cannot usually be paid directors' fees, a salary or other benefits by the trading company (although directors who are not also trustees may receive such benefits).

Providing services to the trading company

The trading company should pay for any services provided by the charity (including the use of its name, staff and premises) and the arrangements should be recorded in a formal agreement between the two. VAT may also be chargeable on these services, so consideration should be given to forming a VAT group.

Financing the company

One of the great difficulties faced by charities wishing to use subsidiary trading companies is financing them. A charity should not invest in shares in the trading company unless the trustees are satisfied, after having taken appropriate advice, that they have the power to make the investment; that the investment is both appropriate and prudent; and that the investment will qualify for tax relief. As there are almost always better investments to be made, only rarely will charities be able to justify an investment. More usually they need to finance their trading subsidiaries by means of loans. If a charity wishes to lend money to a subsidiary it will need to do so on fully commercial terms (which should make provision for its repayment, interest and security) and then only if it is satisfied that the loan will qualify for tax reliefs (to avoid falling foul of the non-qualifying expenditure and loans rules on which guidance can be found on the HRMC website).

Conflicts of interest

Trustees of a charity who are also directors of its trading company need to be aware of the different duties attaching to, and the potential for conflicts of interest arising from, their two roles. They should abstain from voting – on both boards – on arrangements between the charity and the company.

There are no charity law restrictions on benefits being passed from a trading company to its parent charity (although there are various company law provisions which may need to be considered).

The difference between donations and other arrangements

A donation is a gift for which the donor (the person making the gift) neither asks for nor receives a benefit. It is often said that a donation must be 'pure bounty' in the hands of the charity.

A donation by a company/business to charity is generally tax-deductible (see 'Donations' in Part II).

A donation may sometimes be subject to a condition, for example, that the gift be used towards a particular project of the charity. Such a condition will not generally affect its status (or tax treatment) as a donation.

However, if a condition is one which confers a benefit on the donor or is subject to repayment in certain circumstances, the legal and tax treatment of the gift may change. For example, if a company makes a donation to a charity in connection with the publication of a research report on the condition that its logo appears prominently on the cover of the report and that its donation is mentioned in all publicity relating to the report, this may make the activity trading by the charity – the sale of advertising by the charity to the company. In such a situation the company would be advised to split the gift between an outright gift to the charity and an arrangement with the charity's trading company for the promotional element. The latter should also be tax-deductible for the company, provided that it is accepted that the cost of the promotional deal is wholly and exclusively for the purpose of the business.

As a rule of thumb, charities and companies should take care and/or advice if the donor is to receive anything much more than a simple thank you in, say, the charity's annual report.

Different types of corporate supporters

The term 'corporate' is used by fundraisers loosely to describe business donors or supporters. However, such supporters come in a variety of guises.

Companies

The vast majority of businesses will be limited liability companies – either public companies (i.e. those listed on the stock exchange) or private companies (those not so listed). In both cases the company will be run by a board of directors, owned by its shareholders and liable to pay corporation tax on its profits.

In the eyes of the law companies are separate and distinct from their shareholders and so their boards are able to make gifts and enter into commercial arrangements in the name of the company.

A company makes Gift Aid donations simply by deducting the amount of the gift from its pre-tax profits. It does not need to make a Gift Aid declaration.

Companies are required, by law, to have key facts about them (including their full name, company number and registered address) on their notepaper, etc. which makes paperwork simpler. Companies House maintains a register of companies and this can be searched on their website (www.companieshouse.gov.uk).

Partnerships

Many professional practices such as lawyers and accountants are established not as companies, but as partnerships.

In a partnership each partner is personally liable for tax on his or her share of the profits of the business (rather than the business as a whole being liable, in the case of companies). This can make donations from partnerships fiddly. First, unless the partnership specifies otherwise, the gift will be apportioned equally amongst the partners with each being treated as having made a personal gift of their share. Secondly, unless the partnership deed or some other document grants authority to one of the partners to sign a Gift Aid declaration on behalf of them it will be necessary for the charity to go through the Gift Aid procedures and paperwork for each partner.

In practice many partnerships either make no 'partnership' gifts as such (leaving partners to make their own gifts as and when they think appropriate) or do so through an in-house charity.

Commercial arrangements with partnerships will often be concluded by a managing partner or chief executive with delegated authority from the partners.

There is no central or searchable register of partnerships.

Limited liability partnerships

Limited liability partnerships (LLPs) are partnerships that benefit from limited liability status. Companies House maintains a register of LLPs, which, like the register of companies, can be searched on their website (www.companieshouse.gov.uk). However, for tax purposes, LLPs are treated in the same way as other partnerships.

Sole traders

Many people starting out in business do so, without forming a company or a partnership, by simply adopting a trading name.

When a charity is dealing with such a business it can effectively ignore the trading persona – it is dealing with the individual behind the business, who will need to make donations and/or enter into commercial arrangements in his or her own name. So, if a sole trader wants to make a Gift Aid donation, the individual behind the business will need to make a Gift Aid declaration.

There is no central register of sole traders and their trading names.

Negotiating with corporate organisations

The relationships between charities and their corporate supporters are like all relationships – some run smoothly and other less so!

For small or medium-sized charities that are desperate for funds the biggest issue in the negotiations is likely to be the actual or perceived inequality of bargaining power and resources. Some companies have sophisticated corporate responsibility departments and model charity contracts, both of which can be daunting.

This potential inequality of bargaining power can also lead to a number of problems for charities, including selling their association and/or services too cheaply and/or going further than they would like to appease a corporate partner (misguidedly adopting the attitude that 'he who pays the piper, calls the tune').

As with everything else in life, it's always a good idea for a fundraiser to do their homework when negotiating with a potential corporate partner:

• Look at their website, recent annual reports, etc. to see what they say about themselves and their CR policy.

• If possible, get in touch with charities which have been involved with them to hear about their experiences.

• If possible, look around at the deals that other charities are doing with corporate supporters.

Also:

• Do take any professional advice you need early in the negotiating process to avoid misunderstandings and/or impossible expectations later.

• Don't assume that the people you are dealing with (or those to whom they report) understand charities or the legal and tax framework within which they operate.

Contracts and lawyers

Many people are intimidated by the thought of contracts – they shouldn't be. Contracts are just a record of the agreement reached between two or more parties.

Although lawyers often use standard forms of contracts with lots of well tried and tested 'boiler-plate' provisions (legal jargon for the standard clauses such as notices and governing law), there is no magic to contracts. They can be a simple exchange of letters or a more formal (and usually much longer) document.

For complex deals sometimes 'Heads of Agreement' are used. Generally these are simply a non-binding statement setting out the main parts of the agreement that will be expanded later into a formal contract. However, sometimes they are binding and the first part of a larger multi-part arrangement. Heads of Agreement should always specify whether (and if so, which of) their provisions are to be legally binding.

If what you are doing is sensitive or innovative you may regard confidentiality and/or exclusivity as important. If this is the case, then consider entering into a preliminary but binding agreement to secure that confidentiality and/or exclusivity for the period of the negotiation.

The most important things about contracts are that:

• they record all the points agreed;

• they are clear and unambiguous;

• they anticipate things that will happen in the future which can be anticipated;

• they include a mechanism for resolving problems and disputes (for the day if and /or when things go wrong or, at least, not according to plan); and

• the parties only undertake to do things that they are actually able to do.

Many charities are unconvinced about the need for formal contracts. However, this is rarely the case if they have experienced a deal which has gone wrong and the trustees are unable to prove what was agreed, let alone finance a legal challenge against the defaulting party. The duty of proper management of the charity means that there should be a signed record or contract of all significant arrangements. However, charities can be proportionate here: if the matter is very small and following a well-established pattern, the absence of a comprehensive signed record may not be crucial. On the other hand, if the charity is investing its reputation and/or a large amount of resources (cash or staff time), then a contract is a must.

All lawyers are trained to write contracts but using a lawyer doesn't guarantee that a charity will get a good contract. There can be any number of reasons for this, including the contract may be outside the lawyer's area of expertise, the lawyer may not understand the project well enough to ensure that likely outcomes are anticipated and/or the corporate partner may refuse to budge from its standard contract.

Lawyers, even small high street firms, are expensive but there is much that a charity can do to improve the quality of a contract without necessarily paying a fortune. It always helps, both on quality and cost, if the charity puts down on paper in plain, layman's English: what the deal is about; what the parties have agreed to do and when; what might go wrong;

and what really, really matters to the charity (there is little point running up a large bill for lawyers to negotiate a point which isn't very important). A layman's analysis like this is a good way of focusing both the charity and its lawyer.

It is also worth considering seeking help on a pro bono (free) basis. When a charity has a constitutional issue (such as amending its constitution or merging with another charity) it will always be best to instruct a charity law specialist; but many contracts which fall under the title of corporate fundraising are commercial contracts of the kind that most commercial lawyers (perhaps with a little help from the charity's charity lawyers) can handle. Many large commercial law firms run pro bono schemes for just this situation. Such schemes are particularly beneficial if the corporate organisation with which the charity is dealing is a large, well-financed one with an in-house legal team (who may be wedded to their standard contracts) used to dealing with and respecting the views of the big legal hitters.

If the charity is able to secure pro bono help, make sure that the terms of the arrangement are clear. There is a world of difference between a friendly lawyer doing you a favour if and when their workload/life allows and a formal pro bono scheme which, to all intents and purposes, is just like using a paid lawyer, only without the bill.

Like so much in life, contracts benefit from careful attention to detail. Make sure that the trustee or fundraiser charged with negotiating the contract has the time, skill and attention to detail to do the job properly. It is also important that those responsible for approving the contract understand it. Many good people have signed contracts containing an obligation to use 'best endeavours' without realising that this was the highest standard of obligation, when the other party would have settled for a 'reasonable endeavours' clause (a lower standard).

Using professional fundraisers

A charity wishing to engage and pay a professional fundraiser to fundraise on its behalf should, by law, have a written contract with the professional fundraiser specifying:

• the name and address of each of the parties;

• the date on which it was signed by or on behalf of each of them;

• the period for which the agreement is to last;

• any provisions for it to be terminated early;

• any provisions relating to it being varied during the period of the agreement;

• the principal objectives of the campaign or project for which the fundraiser is engaged and the methods to be used by the fundraisers and the charity in pursuit of those objectives;

• if more than one charity is a party, how the proportion in which each charity will benefit is to be determined; and

• the remuneration and expenses the fundraiser is to receive (or the method of calculating them).

In the contract the charity should also ensure that the fundraiser is obliged to comply with fundraising law and best practice (such as the Institute of Fundraising's codes of fundraising practice) when raising funds on the charity's behalf.

Amongst the legal obligations professional fundraisers must comply with is the requirement, if they are actually approaching potential donors for funds, that they make a 'solicitation statement' in accordance with the Charities Act 1992. Paid fundraisers must specify:

• the charity or charities for which funds are being raised;

• if there is more than one charity, the proportions in which the charities will benefit;

• the method by which their remuneration is to be calculated; and

• the 'notifiable amount' of that remuneration (i.e. the actual amount the professional fundraiser will receive or, if that is not known, the most accurate estimate possible).

If the representation is made on radio or television and payments can be made by credit or debit card, the professional fundraiser must also make it clear that sums over £100 can be refunded, if the customer asks for a refund within seven days.

Employed fundraisers and others connected with the charity (such as trustees) who are paid more than £1,000 for a particular appeal (or where there is no specific appeal, more than £10 a day or £1,000 per year) will also be required to make a solicitation statement when soliciting donations from the public. Paid collectors must specify:

• the charity or charities for which the funds are being raised;

• if there is more than one charity, the proportions in which the charities will benefit;

• the collector's position within or connection to the charity; and

• the fact that the collector is being paid.

Tainted Donations

The Finance Act 2011 introduced new rules, designed to clamp down on people and companies abusing charity tax reliefs. Known as the 'Tainted Donation Rules', the new rules replace the unpopular substantial donor rules in relation to donations made on or after 1 April 2011.

Under the Tainted Donation Rules, if a donor (or a person connected with them) enters into an arrangement with a charity for the purpose of obtaining a financial advantage from the charity, the donor will lose some of its tax reliefs. The charity will not be penalised unless it has been complicit in engineering the inappropriate advantage for the donor. The rules apply to all donations, not just those above a certain threshold.

The Tainted Donation Rules will bite where three conditions (A, B and C) are met:

Condition A: The donor (or a connected person) has entered into an arrangement with a charity in circumstances where it is reasonable to assume that the donation and the arrangement would not have been entered into independently of each other.

Condition B: The main purpose (or one of the main purposes) of the arrangement is for the donor (or connected person) to receive a financial advantage. A financial advantage will be deemed to have been obtained for the purposes of Condition B where the transaction in question:

• has not been made on arm's-length terms; or

• is not of a kind that parties dealing at arm's-length might reasonably be expected to make.

Condition C: The donor is not a wholly owned subsidiary of a charity or a linked housing association.

The definition of 'connected persons' is widely drawn. In the case of companies, it includes companies that are under more or less the same control as the donor. In the case of donors who are sole traders or partnerships, it includes family members of the sole trader or individual partners.

Certain arrangements fall outside the scope of the Tainted Donation Rules, including those where the financial advantage received by the donor (or connected person) is:

• applied solely for charitable purposes;

• attributable to gifts of qualifying investments, interests in land or trading stock; or

• permitted under the Gift Aid scheme (see 'Donations' in Part II).

The explanatory note to the Finance Bill 2011 provides some examples of how the Tainted Donation Rules will operate in practice (HM Treasury 2011).

The rules, which are likely to have a major impact on fundraising charities, are both lengthy and complex and, at the time of writing, not the subject of any detailed HMRC guidance. In many cases, the types of transaction caught by the 2011 Act will be in breach of trust and it will be clear that the charity should not enter into them (see 'The duty to apply assets only for charitable purposes within the charity's objects', earlier in this Appendix). Charities should nevertheless be vigilant in order to ensure that they cannot be said to be complicit in any arrangement giving rise to an inappropriate financial benefit to a donor, and, if in doubt, should take advice. Charities with existing arrangements with substantial donors should take particular care and should seek advice on the complex transitional provisions.

PART II: TAX AND CHARITY LAW ISSUES RELATING TO DIFFERENT TYPES OF CORPORATE FUNDRAISING ARRANGEMENTS

Donations

Here, we are talking purely about gifts of money.

Gift Aid

To qualify for Gift Aid, donations must fulfil certain criteria:

• The gift must be a sum of money.

• There must not be any conditions as to repayment.

• In the case of individuals, the donor must make a Gift Aid declaration.

• The gift must not be associated with the donor or (any connected person) acquiring something.

• Any benefits received by the donor as a consequence of making the gift must not exceed the prescribed limits.

The prescribed limits are as follows:

Aggregate donations in the donor's tax year	Aggregate benefits in the donor's tax year
£0–£100	25% of value of donations
£100–£1,000	£25
>£1,000 (donations made between 6 April 2007 and 5 April 2011)	5% of value of donations, subject to maximum of £500
>£1,000 (donations made on or after 6 April 2011)	5% of value of donations, subject to maximum of £2,500

The word 'aggregate' is used in this table because, when working out the value of the donations and connected benefits, what matters is the amount of all donations and benefits the donor receives in the whole year. If the benefits or donations are restricted to a period of less than twelve months, then the figures need to be adjusted pro rata. For more information on working this out, go to HMRC's website.[2]

A charity receives no extra tax benefit from a Gift Aid donation from a company; all the benefit goes to the donor company in the form of a deduction from its profits that are liable to corporation tax.

By contrast, Gift Aid donations from individuals (including gifts from sole traders or partners in a firm) allow the charity to reclaim the basic rate of tax on donations. To claim the tax relief, the charity must make sure that individual donors make what is known as a Gift Aid declaration. This is a declaration by the donor that they want the charity to treat the gift as a Gift Aid donation. Declarations can be made in writing or over the telephone. For more detail on Gift Aid declarations, including a link to some model wording, see HMRC's website.[3]

Companies with 'in-house' charities

Some companies have established 'in-house' charities. These vary in type but often the company will retain the right to appoint some or all of the trustees. Many companies with in-house charities only make donations to 'their' charity and so they refer all requests for grants and donations to the in-house charity.

Grants made by in-house charities, like those made by other charitable funders, do not come within the Gift Aid scheme (i.e. there is no tax reclaim that can be made by the recipient charity).

Matched giving schemes

Many employers now run 'matched-giving schemes'. These are schemes under which employers agree to match (in whole or in part) whatever funds the employees pay or raise for charity, for example by matching employee donations made through payroll giving.

A company's contribution under such a scheme is treated in the same way as a donation made outside such a scheme (i.e. the company can deduct the donations from its pre-tax profits).

There are unlikely to be tax or legal issues for charities which benefit under these schemes, unless the employer intends advertising its scheme in such a way that it constitutes commercial participation. This type of arrangement is dealt with later in this Appendix.

Gifts in kind, including secondments

There are a number of tax reliefs available to companies that make gifts in kind to charities.

Gifts of land, buildings and shares

Companies can get tax relief when they make an outright gift to the charity but also when they sell property to the charity at less than its market value (i.e. at an undervalue). To qualify for the tax relief the following conditions must apply:

• Land and buildings must be freehold or leasehold properties in the UK and the company must transfer all of its interest in the property.

• As regards shares, the relief only applies to:

– shares listed on a UK stock exchange or a recognised foreign stock exchange;

– units in an authorised unit trust;

– shares in a UK open ended investment company;

– holdings in certain foreign investment schemes.

It is the company that gets the benefit of tax benefits on such gifts and the way in which those benefits are calculated is beyond the scope of this book. However, guidance is available in the charities section of the HMRC website.

Before accepting a gift of land, buildings or shares, a charity needs to be satisfied that it has the necessary powers to accept and retain the gift. A charity will only be able to accept the property if it either has a suitable power of investment or, in the case of land, can use it to further its charitable purposes. Unincorporated charities will generally be able to accept land and shares, as they benefit from the wide investment powers in the Trustee Act 2000. Charitable companies will need to make sure they have suitable powers in their Memorandum and Articles of Association.

If the charity has an appropriate power of investment to accept a gift of shares, it will still only be able to keep the shares if it considers that this would be an appropriate use of that power. There will be no tax or VAT implications if the charity decides to sell the shares.

The charity may be able to keep property, despite not having a power to invest in land, if the charity can use the land for its charitable purposes. If it cannot, then it will need to sell the land. In doing this, the charity must comply with the procedures the law requires it to undergo when selling charity land (these are in sections 117 to 129 of the Charities Act 2011).

If the charity cannot accept shares or land, it may ask the corporate donor to sell the asset and then give it the proceeds instead. The corporate donor will be able to give the proceeds under Gift Aid, as long as it meets the Gift Aid requirements (see 'Donations' at the start of Part II).

Gifts of equipment and trading stock

Where a business gives a charity:

- items that it makes or uses in the course of its business; or

- plant or machinery that it uses in the course of its business;

It will get tax relief on the gift, in that it does not need to (as it would normally on giving away this type of property) treat the market value of the item as a trading receipt in its accounts.

From the charity's point of view, similar issues arise to those with gifts of shares and land.

Secondment of staff by the company to the charity

The expenses incurred in lending or temporarily transferring staff to work for a charity (including salary costs) are tax-deductible by the company.

If the company is dealing with payment of the employee, then tax and National Insurance issues should not arise for the charity. The charity will need to comply with the legislation relevant to its other staff, such as health and safety regulations.

As a general rule, the legal rights to intellectual property created by an employee belong to the employer, even if that employee is seconded to work for another body. Charities taking secondees should therefore take care to secure any intellectual property rights in secondees' work by reaching an agreement to that effect with the company.

Commercial participation

This is the term used by the Charities Act 1992 to describe certain types of relationship between businesses and charities. The rules cover situations in which a business, in an advertising or sales campaign, says that it will give money to charity in connection with the sale of its goods and services. A classic example would be an advertisement for cornflakes that says '25p of every packet of Cornflakes will go to XYZ Charity'.

If a company has already given money to charity and mentions this in a later advertising campaign, it may or not be commercial participation, depending on the wording.

The charity thinking of entering into a commercial participation arrangement needs to consider whether it has the power to do so under its constitution (because it may be trading) and, if it has, whether in doing so it will be in the charity's interests to associate itself with the company and/or promotion in question.

The law requires that there is a written contract between the charity and the commercial organisation, before the campaign begins. As a minimum, this agreement must contain the same details as an agreement with a professional fundraiser (see 'Using professional fundraisers', earlier in the Appendix), as though references to professional fundraisers were to commercial participators. In addition, the agreement must, if the proceeds are to go to more than one charity, say what proportion each charity will get. The agreement must also set out the sums to be given to the charity by the commercial participator in connection with the sale of goods or services (or the method of calculating them).

It is preferable for the contract also to include other matters which are important to the charity, such as what expenses the company can deduct from the proceeds, how it will deal with the money before paying it to the charity and how often payments will be made. Ideally the commercial participator should be obliged to hold the money in a separate bank account so that it does not get mixed up with the company's other funds.

Commercial participation may be a type of trading. If it is, and the charity expects the income from the venture to take it over the small trading limits, the venture will have to be run through a trading subsidiary. In this case, there will need to be a three-way agreement between the charity, the trading subsidiary and the commercial participator.

Many charities have developed a standard commercial participation contract which takes the form of a basic agreement with a schedule in which the details particular to each campaign are set out (which are varied in each case). This is often a sensible approach but care needs to be taken when using any model to ensure that it is fit for purpose for the particular deal.

In addition to having a written agreement with the charity, the law also obliges a commercial participator to make a statement each time it makes a representation that it will give money to charity, in connection with a commercial participation arrangement. The law requires this statement to indicate:

• the charity or charities for which funds are being raised;

• if there is more than one charity, the proportions in which the charities will benefit;

• the 'notifiable amount' of the proportion of the sale price that will be given to the charity, or the amount that will be donated to charity in connection with the promotional venture. This is either the exact amount, if known, or the most accurate estimate possible; and

• if the representation is made on radio or television and payments can be made by credit or debit card, that sums of £100 or more can be refunded, if the customer asks for a refund within seven days.

There is much confusion and concern about these statements. Some guidance is available from the Charity Commission, but this is regarded by many as too general to help in specific cases (see Charity Commission 2011 in 'References' for details of this guidance). Charities and their partners must do their best, but it is fair to say that, if they are transparent and do their best to comply with the regulations, it is probably unlikely that there will be adverse repercussions.

Brand licensing

A charity may decide (for example, as part of a commercial participation arrangement) to license its name and logo to a company.

There are several issues to consider here. As with any corporate link, the trustees of the charity will need to be satisfied that association with the company will be good for the charity.

If the trustees are happy that it will be, then the charity will need to draw up a contract between the charity and the company. This contract will set out the ways in which the company may use the charity's name and logo and the payments that the company will make in return. To protect the charity's brand, the charity should ensure that the contract obliges the company to get the charity's prior approval for uses that are not specifically listed.

Brand licensing is not a charitable purpose, so entering into this type of agreement is generally regarded as taxable trading and, if the sums involved are large enough, is usually routed through a subsidiary trading company. In some circumstances, it is possible to change the tax treatment of the payment receivable by the charity by structuring the agreement so that the company is legally obliged to make an annual payment for use of the charity's logo.

Charities contemplating a licensing arrangement should always take professional advice.

Sponsorship

The term 'sponsorship' means arrangements whereby a company provides money to charity in return for some recognition of its support. The recognition could be anything from a simple acknowledgment in related literature to a right to use the charity's logo or enjoy special privileges, such as an exclusive right to sell goods on the charity's premises.

If the sponsor decides, of its own accord, to exploit its connection with the charity, but without the charity itself having to do or give anything in return, then the sponsorship income can still be regarded as a donation and not as trading income. As a result, it will not be taxable.

Similarly, it is quite acceptable for the charity to include a small thank you in its literature, provided the charity does not give the thank you undue visibility or make large, prominent use of the sponsor's corporate colours or logo in the literature. In these circumstances, the sponsorship funding will again be seen as a donation.

If, on the other hand, the charity gives the sponsor a more prominent acknowledgement, or grants it special privileges, then the sponsorship money may be seen as payment for advertising or other services and taxable in the hands of the charity and liable to VAT. This may not matter to the corporate sponsor (as it may still be deductible from its pre-tax profits as a trading expense and mopped up in its usual VAT reclaims) but, from the charity's point of view, it may be significant.

Sometimes sponsorship can be part of a primary purpose project and treated differently for tax purposes; for instance, where a company sponsors a production by a charitable theatre company and, in return, is allowed to put up a banner in the theatre lobby during the performances of the play. If the charitable theatre company is using the sponsorship income to produce the play, the sponsorship income may be tax-exempt (but great care is needed here because HMRC's attitude to such schemes appears to be hardening).

In many cases it will be sensible to split the agreed fee for a commercial sponsorship arrangement so that that part of the payment which represents 'value' for the sponsorship is treated as such and is separated from the balance of the payment, which can then be accepted as a donation.

Notes

1   An 'arm's length' transaction means that the parties to the transaction are unrelated and independent.
2   www.hmrc.gov.uk/charities/guidance-notes/chapter3/sectiond.htm#abthe is the web link at the time of writing (accessed 17 January 2012).
3   www.hmrc.gov.uk/charities/gift_aid/declarations.htm is the web link at the time of writing, (accessed 17 January 2012).

References

HM Treasury (2011), *Finance (No. 3) Bill Explanatory Notes*, www.hm-treasury. gov.uk, accessed 14 February 2012

Charity Commission (2011), section 'G1. What is the difference between a commercial participator and a professional fundraiser?', in *Charities and Fundraising* (CC20), updated May 2011, accessed 14 February 2012

Template for a corporate fundraising strategy

Andrew Peel

This Appendix aims to condense the many observations made throughout the book about corporate fundraising strategy into an easily digestible summary that can be used as a template or reference point by any charity, regardless of its size and/or skill level.

Executive summary

The objective of the executive summary is to provide the reader with a brief synopsis of the overall plan. Think of it as an opportunity to introduce your work and the challenges and opportunities you face to someone who may be unfamiliar with them and not have enough time to read the full document.

Generally speaking, it is easier to wait until you have finished your strategy and then to transfer a few sentences from each section into your executive summary, placed under the same main headings. Whatever your approach, however, you must aim to provide a clearly written précis of the key points that follow in the main section that leaves the reader enthused by your plans and keen to read the fuller report.

Introduction

Though the content and length of this section will vary widely from one charity to another, the goal – to introduce and clearly set the scene for the charity's work and your team's role within it – should not. You should outline the context in which your corporate fundraising is taking place and underline the fact that corporate fundraising relies upon an organisational approach and cannot succeed in isolation.

Aim to provide a full description of your team's work using clear, non-technical and jargon-free language. This is particularly important if the charity is new to corporate fundraising because there is a greater chance that colleagues will not fully appreciate the nature of your or your team's work.

The broad areas you might address in the introduction include:

• Who are we? i.e. a general outline of the organisation's vision, mission, ethos, aims and operation.

• An explanation of how your corporate fundraising strategy flows out of the wider fundraising strategy and how it relates to the organisation's business plan.

• Why corporate fundraising? i.e. an explanation of why the charity needs a corporate fundraising function and its wider role and remit.

• A top-line description of your team's purpose, values, current position, recent successes, near misses, key challenges and opportunities.

Situational analysis

This section gives you the opportunity to provide more detail about your strategic approach to date, your key successes and challenges and the main internal and external factors likely to impact upon your ability to meet your objectives over the short, medium and long term.

It can be helpful to divide it into the following sections:

1. Where are we now?

Include:

• a description of the corporate fundraising 'marketplace': the economic conditions; trends such as the advent of more 'strategic' company giving and less philanthropy; increased employee involvement in charity adoptions; the performance of key competitors, etc;

• an overview of your current corporate fundraising: your team structure; where your income comes from; the nature of existing partnerships and how you plan to develop them; target companies or sectors to be approached in the future, etc;

• a description of which corporate fundraising mechanisms (for example, donations, cause-related marketing, sponsorship, employee fundraising, direct marketing, etc.) are working best for you and why, and a summary of the areas in which you are now planning to invest;

• a top-line financial analysis of your past and current performance: net and gross income, expenditure, return on investment, percentage of repeat/reliable income, benchmarks against other charities, etc;

• a fuller analysis of your fundraiser's or your team's work, performance against targets and predictions and timings for the next planning period;

• an overview of the charity's positioning and 'USPs' (unique selling points) in relation to corporate fundraising;

• the key internal and external factors impacting upon your ability to fundraise from companies, including the outputs from your SWOT and PESTLE analyses;

• a summary of the outputs from other strategic planning tools and workshops.

This would also be a sensible juncture to summarise all other critical timings, concerns and issues that you believe are likely to impact significantly upon your team's work and your colleagues' strategic plans and workload.

These may include, for example:

• the case for additional investment in the team, such as for new staff, and the return that that extra resource will realise;

• your need for greater levels of support or buy-in from senior managers, trustees and key departments;

• your need for access to appealing, corporate-friendly projects, better project information and outputs, good quality reports and case studies;

• the quality of your database – or your need for one!

2. Where do you want to be?

This part should begin with an outline of the organisation's direction, plans and funding needs over the next three to five years, and an explanation of the role you and your team will play in this period. How do you, as the person responsible for corporate fundraising within the charity, see the charity's future and your role within it? This is your opportunity to stamp your personal mark on the strategy by conveying, in a few sentences, your overarching vision for corporate fundraising.

Here's an example of a 'vision' for a larger charity:

The Corporate Fundraising Team will continue to develop into a key fundraising and marketing hub for the charity. It will be generating £2.5 million net by the end of 2014/15 – an increase of 25% on our current income level – funding which will be secured through a combination of integrated, creative fundraising and marketing and by maximising the potential of our corporate relationships at a local, regional, national and international level.

And for a smaller charity, something along these lines may be more appropriate:

The Corporate Fundraising Team will double its net income over the next three years, increasing it from £175,000 to £350,000. This will be achieved by improving our corporate 'offer' and case for support; by maximising the potential of the partnership with Acme plc; by building a sustainable supporter-base of committed local and regional companies and by identifying ways in which we can create additional value for other teams within the charity.

3. How are we going to get there?

Now try setting out four to six objectives – as 'SMART' as possible – that paint a picture of your desired future state and provide a framework upon which to hang your strategy.

The larger charity's corporate fundraising strategy could, for instance, be built around core objectives such as:

By 31st March 2015:

1. We will have increased the income we generate from community affairs and CSR budgets, Charity of the Year relationships, employee fundraising, corporate foundations, payroll giving and other 'non-commercial' sources by 20%, from £1.5 million to £1.8 million.
2. By better harnessing the power of the charity's brand, and by focusing on marketing-led partnerships such as cause-related marketing, sponsorship, affinity deals and licensing, we will have increased the level of 'trading' income generated by 20%, from £100,000 to £120,000.

3. We will have adopted a more logical, sector-focused approach to corporate fundraising and new business. We will have secured a minimum of one company partnership worth at least £75,000 in each of the following sectors: banking, airlines, pharmaceuticals and IT.

4. By working more collaboratively with community fundraising, trusts, events and the major donor team, we will have a more strategic, coordinated approach to networking and prospect cultivation that is generating more high calibre leads, income and opportunities for the charity.

Next, outline the main actions required to realise each of these objectives.

For example, by elaborating on the first objective above, the following actions, activities and outcomes could be highlighted:

By 31st March 2015, we will have increased income generated from community affairs budgets, Charity of the Year relationships, employee fundraising, corporate foundations, payroll giving and other 'non-commercial' sources by 20%, from £1.5 million to £1.8 million.

Key actions/activities in year one (2012/13)	Success criteria/outcomes/key performance indicators
1. Recruit an additional corporate fundraiser by end Qtr 2.	✓ New team member in place to increase our new business approaches and pipeline.
2. Recruit new Payroll Giving Manager by end Qtr 2. Review payroll giving strategy by the end of Qtr 3.	✓ Improved relationships with PFOs and agencies. 10% increase in income by year-end.
3. Update Charity of the Year strategy and introduce new timetable to track applications. Focus on exceeding the 2011/12 level of submissions (i.e. 50). Monitor progress at monthly team meeting.	✓ Rolling timetable of quality submissions to companies. Team submits at least 5 applications per month, and achieves a 10% hit-rate in 2012/13. At least £500,000 generated.

Key actions/activities in year one (2012/13)	Success criteria/outcomes/key performance indicators
4. Continue to professionally manage our flagship relationships with X plc and Y Ltd	✓ Targets for both partnerships (£100,000 and £300,000) respectively are exceeded.
5. Use our strong challenge events offer to attract companies and bolster our Charity of the Year pitches.	✓ New and existing events products (such as marathons and challenges) help garner support from within target companies.
6. Work closely with operations team to develop stronger funding asks for our corporate audiences.	✓ Team is targeting companies with a wider range of attractive products and 'off the shelf' proposals.
7. Research and approach corporate foundations and companies likely to support our work philanthropically.	✓ Team applies for philanthropic corporate support on a rolling basis. Income from this source growing at least 10% per year.
8. Work with the PR team to identify opportunities for local, regional and national profile-raising activity to drive brand awareness.	✓ Increased PR activity leads to a higher public profile and an improved conversion rate for Charity of the Year and other applications.
9. Develop a range of volunteering opportunities suitable for a corporate audience.	✓ Team has in place a range of skills exchange/pro bono roles for company employees.
10. Research companies able to donate suitable non-financial gifts that will support our business.	✓ Team has developed a 'bank' of companies willing to provide products, venues, prizes, etc.

A smaller charity's strategic objectives might focus on the following kinds of issues:

• The strategy for retaining, managing and developing your existing supporters, with clear outcomes and income targets given for each account.

• An overview of your new business strategy, with an explanation of your targets by industry/ sector, size, location or propensity to support your kind of cause and proposed corporate fundraising mechanism.

• The need for additional investment in your team. This may be about recruiting an extra fundraiser or a new researcher, or highlighting the need for additional training for your current staff.

• The ways in which the charity needs to prepare itself for the 'growing pains' and demands that a significant corporate partnership can place on a smaller organisation.

• The need to improve the marketing or packaging of your work, materials and funding opportunities.

• The need for internal buy-in and support of corporate fundraising, particularly at a senior level within the charity.

• Networking and how you intend to maximise the impact of senior internal contacts (your founder, directors, trustees and patrons) and other key colleagues (such as your major donor and events teams).

• The need to boost the charity's profile (via increased trade press and PR, reciprocal website links, a targeted direct mail campaign, a corporate networking event, etc.) because heightened brand awareness is likely to improve your new business conversion rate.

• Your perceived need for more challenge and networking events to engage current and potential supporters.

• Your latest 'big ideas' – for example, a 'quarterly corporate lunch with the Chair' event or the development of a new venture philanthropy scheme aimed at companies.

Financials: translating your plans into figures

The larger charity's five-year corporate fundraising budget could be presented as follows:

(x £100,000)	2011/12	2012/13	2013/14	2014/15
General funds	1350	1450	1600	1750
Restricted funds	300	400	450	500
Trading income (incl. sponsorship, CRM, etc.)	100	150	200	250
Total income	1750	2000	2250	2500
Expenditure	175	225	300	350
Net contribution	1575	1775	1950	2150
Return on investment (ROI)	10:1	8.89:1	7.5:1	7.14:1

Sample commentary to support the budget

The fundraising budget reflects the priorities and restraints highlighted in this strategy, namely:

• The need to reduce our reliance on a small number of corporate donors and develop a wider portfolio of sustainable income streams and fundraising 'products'.

• The need to deliver growth, both in general and restricted funds, with total budgeted net income increasing by 36.5% over the next three financial years (from £1,575,000 this year to £2,150,000 in 2014/15).

• The likely growth in restricted income (67% increase 2011–15) and slower growth in unrestricted income (just under a 30% increase in the same period), reflecting the shift away from 'untied' corporate support towards more project-based or earmarked contributions.

• The need to continue to build unrestricted marketing-led income (channelled via the trading company).

• The lead-in times (up to 18 months) that are often required to secure new corporate partners.

• The need for new staff to be recruited and for the new team to 'bed in'.

• The need to invest in this area of fundraising, whilst achieving acceptable ROIs.

Much of the above can obviously be amended to apply to smaller charities too. However, when budgeting and forecasting be sure to consider the following:

• Have you considered all potential income sources and expenditure? Carefully reappraise your plans and regular income streams, likely new sources, probability of success, phasing of donations and the impact of that phasing on cash-flow, etc.

• Have you made your financial targets as specific as possible rather than 'as much as possible'?

• Have you been conservative in your financial estimates? The best approach to setting fundraising income and expenditure targets is to under-promise and over-deliver.

Monitoring and evaluation

Fundraising strategies are usually written with a three- to five-year planning period in mind. They can, however, quickly lose their relevance or be blown off course, so it is recommended that they be revisited at least quarterly and amended as necessary. A lot can change in the course of a few months, particularly in a smaller charity!

It's important, too, for fundraising teams of all types and sizes to determine a set of measurements or key performance indicators that will help the managers to manage their business. From the outset of your planning period, therefore, be clear about what success will look like for you in a number of areas, and agree with your fundraisers how the various strands of your corporate fundraising activity will be measured and monitored.

Your performance indicators or success measures could include some of the following:

Financial

• Net income – monthly and annual

• Return on Investment

• Average value of corporate donations

• Minimum number of new partnerships secured per quarter with a value of at least £x each

• Portfolio of committed corporate donors increasing by x% per annum, with x giving <£y per annum

• Payroll giving income increasing by x% and number of donors by y% per annum.

Operational

• X number of additional corporate account executives recruited to support the delivery of the strategy

• No. of companies contacted and conversion ratio

• X number of new Charity of the Year adoptions secured annually

• X number of marketing-led promotions agreed

• Improved range of 'products', campaigns and projects available for corporate support

• X number of people attending y event(s)

• The number of companies 'actively engaged'[1] in supporting our work.

Qualitative

• Client satisfaction (external) – i.e. qualitative indicators regarding supporter satisfaction

• Client satisfaction (internal) – i.e. qualitative indicators regarding your team's image/service to other departments

• A clearer and more inspiring corporate case for support has been developed

• Greater focus is being placed internally on securing and resourcing partnerships with companies

• Improvements made to the website mean a better on-line experience for corporate visitors

• Staff turnover

• Industry award won by 2015

And finally . . .

There is, of course, no point in producing a strategic plan that nobody reads. So, before proudly putting your new document into a ring-binder and placing it on a shelf, have a go at condensing what you have written into a one-page version that outlines the strategy's core components and your planned direction of travel. (In fact, you may be able to take much of what you've already written for your executive summary and amend it slightly for this document, or you may choose to put it into a different format; for example, using bullet points to capture the headlines or transposing the information into table-form.)

Producing a short synopsis of your strategy will not only help you to think again about the best way to articulate the key points contained within it but, by doing so, you will be almost certainly making your plans clearer and more accessible to a wider audience of busy fundraising and non-fundraising colleagues, the very audience upon whom delivery of your strategy depends.

Note

1   Some possible definitions of 'actively engaged': a company or its staff support us in a range of ways; a company is a regular giver or has given recently (for example, in the last twelve months); company representatives play an ambassadorial/door-opening role for the charity; company representatives have attended an event in the last twelve months; company staff have volunteered for us; a company has been added to our mailing list; company representatives have visited one of our projects or offices in the last six months, etc.

Ethical framework for accepting or rejecting corporate support

Ian MacQuillin

Introduction

Ethical decision-making frameworks can only be used as a guide to take you through some of the issues and questions that are at stake. They are not algorithms into which you plug a few variables and arrive at the ethically correct decision at the other end.

An ethical decision-making framework is not the same as a professional code of best practice.

This ethical decision-making framework (and indeed any such framework you use) *must* be used in conjunction with the Institute of Fundraising's codes of practice, *Acceptance and Refusal of Donations* and *Charities Working with Business*.

1. Identify that there is – or may be – an ethical issue

For instance:

• Does the company's core business area conflict with your cause or service delivery (for instance, if your organisation is a cancer charity and the potential corporate donor or partner is a tobacco company)?

• Does the company have a history of public controversy or negative media coverage?

• Does it work in an area that you or your staff consider problematic or unethical?

• Is it in financial difficulty?

2. Identify your objections, if any, to the offer of support and list them

Have you understood the difference between consequentialist and deontological ethics ? Decide whether your objections are consequentialist (it would be detrimental for your charity to work with this company) or deontological (it would be 'wrong' for your charity to work with this company) – or a mix of the two – and list them separately (see chapter 6 for a full explanation of these terms).

For instance (C = consequentialist; D = deontological):

• The company is an arms company and I do not want to work with people that make weapons (D)

• The company is an arms company that has recently been accused in the press of supplying outlawed anti-personnel devices (D + C)

• When we last partnered a defence company, several major donors withdrew their support and it took us two years to get our major donor income back to a comparable level (C)

• Most of the fundraisers in the department have heard that the company exploits its workers in the Philippines (D)

• Although our organisation is a children's charity, this company conducts animal experiments and we can't be seen to be supporting or endorsing such practices (D)

• We are a homelessness charity and this house-building company wants to secure planning permission to build on green land and we think it is using us as part of its public relations offensive (C)

3. Test the objections

Run each objection through the 'filter' of the Institute of Fundraising code of practice on accepting or rejecting donations. Is each objection independent of:

• individual or personal opinions;

• political or commercial interests; and

• your personal moral position?

. . . which are not directly related to the charity?

If you have allowed the ethical objection to be swayed by any of these conditions, then reformulate the objection to take this into account. If you cannot, you must ditch the objection. For instance, if you do not want to accept money from an arms company because you think arms companies are wrong in principle, that is a personal choice that does not survive the acceptance/rejection filter.

For each separate objection that survives the filter, decide how – if you acted on this objection and refused the offer of support – you would be able to justify this to the Charity Commission as having acted 'in the best interests of the charity' (see chapter 6 for more information on this phrase).

This means that, for each of your listed objections, you will need to compile evidence to support your assertion that rejecting the offer of support is in the best interests of the charity.

To do this you will need to get the facts about the company; for example:

• Its business practices

• Its financial state

• Its corporate responsibility practices

• What it wants out of the corporate partnership

• A thorough understanding of problematic ethical issues

See section 3.1 of the Institute of Fundraising's code of practice (*Charities Working with Business*) for more advice on researching companies.

Does this knowledge about the company undermine any of your objections? For instance, what if most of your fundraisers believe that the company operates an unethical Third World supply chain, but an endorsement from third-party social responsibility monitoring organisations refutes this? Note that, if this is the case, even if your fundraisers still believe the *status quo ante* holds, then the objection is still undermined because the correct ethical decision is not dependent on what your staff erroneously believe to be true but on what actually is true.

You will then need to test your ethical objections. To do this you will need to do one, some or all of the following.

Ask your donors

Ask your donors how their support or giving would be affected were you to accept the offer of corporate support. If you believe that your donors will stop giving but your market research shows that they don't care at all about this company supporting you, then your (consequentialist) objection is undermined.

This research must be open, honest and scientific, based on a statistically robust sample. If it has been designed to elicit certain responses to support your prejudiced decision to reject a donation, then you would be allowing your personal view to influence the decision, in contravention of the Institute of Fundraising code of practice. In any event, it is unethical to fake scientific research.

Ask your beneficiaries

Ask your beneficiaries whether they would want you to accept the decision. As a fundraiser you have a responsibility to respect the dignity of your beneficiaries. If they do not wish you to associate with a particular company, you have strong evidence that rejecting that support is in the best interest of the charity's core stakeholder group. In fact, 'our beneficiaries don't want it' is about the strongest defence you could have and will be an important part of your evidence base. On the other side of the coin, so is: 'our beneficiaries want it'.

N.B. There is a difference in the questions you ask your donors and beneficiaries. With donors, you are assessing the possible consequences of accepting corporate support. You should not ask your existing donors whether you *should* accept that support, because their views on this are not relevant. This is a question that you should direct to your beneficiaries.

Do *not* ask your staff, either fundraisers or the whole charity. The views of staff are not relevant in determining whether an issue at hand is ethical or unethical. Ethical correctness is not derived by majority vote.

Look at previous partnerships

Look at how similar corporate partnerships (with this company, with your charity and with similar charities and companies) have played out in the past. Is there anything you can learn that might inform your course of action?

Do a public relations risk assessment

Conduct a media risk assessment to assess the likelihood, extent and consequences of negative media coverage.

4. After making the decision

1. Ensure that you can make a consistent justification. Do not switch from consequentialist to deontological justifications and back again. If you turn down a donation from a company that conducts animal experimentation because you fear negative media coverage and then pretend you did so because animal experimentation is morally 'wrong' (even though your organisation is, say, a children's charity), then you will end up tying yourself in philosophical knots as you try publicly to make a deontological defence of a consequentialist position.

2.   Monitor how it plays out. If you find that your donors do in fact desert you in droves, then you have reason, and a responsibility, to end the relationship, if it is no longer in the best interest of the charity to do so. However, the commercial participation agreement you sign with the company *must* allow you get-out clauses if certain outcomes result.

3.   The ultimate justification. If you came face to face with one of your beneficiaries or an inspector from the Charity Commission, would you be able to say to them, hand on heart, that you made the best decision for the charity?

Sample job descriptions

Macmillan

Client Services Manager

Job title: Client Services Manager
Purpose: To ensure that the Corporate Partnerships Department (CPD) has the most effective tools, processes and information in place to achieve the department's goals
Reports to: Account Management Leader
Direct reports: Client Services Administrator

Main responsibilities

To deliver relevant and concise financial information to the Account Management Team as and when required.

To monitor management accounts and investigate discrepancies.

To ensure that the Account Management Team has fit-for-purpose tools in order to monitor income, expenditure, gifts in kind and value of all partnerships.

To manage the ongoing development of Fusion systems ensuring CPD requirements are considered and implemented.

To liaise with Marketing Services and ensure collaborative and resource-effective working.

To proactively improve existing processes in order to minimise the amount of time spent on administrative duties within the department and ensure best-practice way of working is shared effectively amongst the Account Management Team, in particular with the Account Management Coordinators.

To account manage PFOs, liaise with PGMS and Valldata for payroll giving tracking and fulfilment.

To develop impact assessment and measurement tools for complex accounts.

To develop and review all payroll giving tracking systems, to include income generation and direct costs.

Maintain and improve the income tracking process from National Events, e.g. Big Picnic, WBCM.

To manage the Client Services Administrator.

To develop a volunteering request system for general administration support.

Measures of performance

Feedback from Account Managers, RCDMs, Regional Fundraisers and the New Business team re the effectiveness of Fusion systems.

Reduction of time spent within CPD on admin. due to changes in working practices.

Smooth running of centralised CPD services (e.g. hotline calls), ensuring best-practice donor care for all corporate supporters.

CPD volunteers motivated and valuable to the department.

Person specification

Pleasant and helpful, flexible in approach

Strong planning skills

Works well with others and is able to firmly champion CPD

High attention to detail and consistent follow-through

Self-motivated: able to work alone as well as in a team

Strong administrative skills

Be able to prioritise work in multi-task situations

Use of MS Office or appropriate alternatives: word processing and mail merge, spreadsheets, basic graphics and presentation packages

Competency profile

Please refer to definitions on the Macmillan website:

	Expert	Advanced	Skilled	Competent
Building and maintaining relationships				X
Communications and influencing				X
Personal effectiveness			X	
Planning and decision-making			X	
Specialist knowledge			X	
Innovation				X
Developing yourself and others			X	

Qualifications: Educated to A-Level standard or equivalent
Desirable if educated to degree level

Experience: Minimum two years experience working in not-for-profit or commercial sector
Strong written and verbal communication skills

Account Development Manager

Job title: Account Development Manager
Purpose: To lead the Account Management team in maximising income generation and duration of existing Macmillan partnerships.
Reports to: Account Management Leader
Direct reports: Account Manager(s), Account Management Coordinator

Main responsibilities

Ensure strategic approach to each CPD client with appropriate fundraising plan, proactively identifying and developing opportunities for cooperation using a multi-product portfolio approach.

Build capacity and capability within the Account Management Team via appropriate deployment of resources, effective leadership of the career development process, and day-to-day coaching.

Work with Account Management Leader to jointly develop account management targets and budget; manage income and expenditure budgets for the team, ensuring that targets are met.

Monitor performance of existing partnerships in terms of revenues and client satisfaction, working with Account Managers to identify growth opportunities.

Develop and maintain effective and professional relationships that enable long-term commitments across partner organisations.

Champion the activities of the Account Management Teams via timely communication to regions and all other relevant departments and CPD teams.

Provide expertise and counsel to other members of the Account Management Team as appropriate.

Work with Account Management Leader as required to develop and build cross-CPD capacity and capability.

Measures of performance

Consistency and quality of strategic approach to all clients and active consideration of multi-product portfolio approach with fundraising plan.

Quality of staff development and management.

Value of contribution to the development of account management target and budget. Achievement of targets and budgets.

Client feedback and achievement of individual revenue targets and identification and development of growth opportunities where appropriate.

Quality of professional relationships with partner organisations as appropriate.

Timeliness and quality of communication of activities of the Account Management Team to regions and other relevant departments and CPD.

Appropriateness and quality of expertise in counsel provision.

Value of contribution to the development of effective processes, systems and formal training programmes.

Person specification

Individual with personality, social skills and presence to deal with main Board Directors in the largest national companies.

Experienced in public speaking and able to address large meetings, small groups or individual VIPs.

Persistent but polite, with the ideas and enthusiasm necessary to encourage and support staff in their fundraising.

Self-motivated: able to work alone as well as in a team.

Competency profile

Please refer to definitions on the Macmillan website:

	Expert	Advanced	Skilled	Competent
Building and maintaining relationships			X	
Communications and influencing	X			
Personal effectiveness		X		
Planning and decision-making			X	
Specialist knowledge		X		
Innovation			X	
Developing yourself and others		X		

Websites and subscription services to support corporate fundraising research

Valerie Morton and Mathew Iredale

www.192.com/people/director-search claims to list more businesses in the UK than any other directory. Its Director Reports come directly from the Companies House records for appointed and resigned Directors and key executives. 192.com merges these records with its edited Electoral Roll listings and Directory Enquiry listings to give a complete profile of an individual.

www.boardex.com is a subscription site for information on key business people that gives you the capability to analyse current and historical linkages between companies, individuals, not-for-profit organisations and other private associations.

www.bvdep.com
Bureau van Dijk has a range of subscription-based online databases. One product is *DASH* – a comprehensive database of companies, directors and shareholders and the links between them. *FAME* provides UK and Irish financial company information and business intelligence. *MINT UK* is presented in four modules: companies, news, market research and directors. It is more expensive than *DASH* or *FAME* which reflects the greater depth of information provided.

www.carol.co.uk
CAROL is an online service offering direct links to the financial pages of listed companies in Europe and the USA. CAROL provides direct access to companies' balance sheets, profit & loss statements, financial highlights, etc. Access is free of charge.

www.chambersandpartners.com is a popular guide to law firms (and lawyers) in the UK.

www.companieshouse.gov.uk is a free service that gives basic information on all UK listed companies. A £5 per month subscription service allows you to access more detailed information including downloading director details. For some information there is an additional download fee.

www.companygiving.org.uk
Directory of Social Change's site is a database of company support created for voluntary and community organisations. Subscriptions start at around £315. Contains details on 560 companies, including how they give and what they may fund.

www.corporatecritic.org
Corporate Critic is a product of the Ethical Consumer Research Association. Corporate Critic indexes and rates the corporate responsibility records of over 25,000 companies.

www.corporateregister.com
This quarterly publication contains information on every one of the UK's 2,000 quoted companies, 14,000 senior executives and 1,800 professional advisers, including career history, remuneration, hobbies and interests. Current annual subscription cost is £249.

www.corporatewatch.org.uk
Corporate Watch is a small independent not-for-profit research and publishing group that undertakes research on the social and environmental impact of large corporations. Particularly useful when considering ethical issues.

directorholdings.com and **www.digitallook.com** provide shareholder information, including number of shares and the price of the shares when the director bought/sold them, and is searchable by both company and director.

www.dnb.com
Key British Enterprises: This database provides you with the facts about the corporate background, activities, decision-makers, finances, operations and markets of Britain's leading businesses. Search by region or industry. Also has the 'Who Owns Whom' database.

www.dowjones.com provides in-depth company information for more than 18 million private and public companies, executive profiles for more than 36 million individuals and information from more than 28,000 of the world's leading news and business sources.

www.duedil.com provides financial records, litigations, directorships, people search, stock information and more on every company in the UK. Free. 7.9 million companies, 9 million Directors

www.eiris.org
EIRIS is a leading global provider of independent research into the environmental, social, governance (ESG) and ethical performance of companies.

www.insidermedia.com produces *Business Insider* magazine for seven regions of the UK plus a *Top 500 Companies* guide.

www.kompass.co.uk
Kompass produces a database of 1.9 million companies in over 70 countries. Search by company name, sector or region. Basic searches are free.

www.lexisnexis.co.uk has a number of subscription services including a database of approximately 12,000 publications from national and local newspapers, press releases, transcripts of television broadcasts, newswires, statistical bulletins, magazines and trade journals. Useful for searching for news items about specific companies.

littlesis.org is a free database of who-knows-who in business and government (the title is the opposite of Big Brother). The site aims to track the social, financial and political ties between thousands of powerful people and organisations. The site is focused on the US, but there are plans for a UK version, littlesis.org/local/uk

www.londonstockexchange.com is a complete list of companies listed on the Stock Exchange, and contains other useful information, which can be found at: **www.londonstockexchange.com/statistics/home/statistics.htm**

www.MarketingManagersInfo.co.uk includes over 10,500 UK companies and 60,000 marketing decision-makers including marketing, PR, and sponsorship contacts. The former Hollis Sponsorship is now part of Marketing Managers Info and so you can also find sponsorship consultancies and various sponsorship services including market research in its database.

www.morningstar.co.uk/uk is a free service providing financial information on 23,500 UK and Irish Listed companies as well as those listed on the S&P 500.

opencorporates.com describes itself as 'the open database of the corporate world' and has information on almost 7 million UK companies, taken from Companies House.

Websites with information about corporate responsibility

www.accountability.org – AccountAbility

www.bitc.org.uk – Business in the Community

www.sa-intl.org – Social Accountability International

www.ftse.com/products/indices/FTSE4Good – FTSE4Good

www.globalreporting.org – Global Reporting Initiative

www.oecd.org – Organisation for Economic Co-operation and Development

www.unglobalcompact.org – United Nations Global Compact

The City Business Library based at Moorgate in London is a public reference library specialising in current business information. The link at the time of writing is: www.cityoflondon.gov.uk/business/economic-research-and-information/city-business-library/Pages/default.aspx

Index